D1593774

The Economics of
Seasonal Cycles

The Economics of
Seasonal Cycles

Jeffrey A. Miron

The MIT Press
Cambridge, Massachusetts
London, England

This book was set in Palatino by Windfall Software using ZzTEX.

Library of Congress Cataloging-in-Publication Data

Miron, Jeffrey A.
  The economics of seasonal cycles / Jeffrey A. Miron.
    p.   cm.
  Includes bibliographical references and index.
  ISBN 0-262-13323-7 (hc : alk. paper)
  1. Seasonal variations (Economics) 2. Business cycles.
I. Title.
HB3711.M49   1996
338.5′4—dc20   95-52634
                                                    CIP

To Patty, Laura, and Daniel

Contents

List of Figures

List of Tables

Acknowledgments

This book would not exist were it not for my many collaborators on the research presented in this book: Bob Barsky, Joe Beaulieu, Jeff MacKie-Mason, Greg Mankiw, David Weil, and Steve Zeldes. I am indebted to them for their ideas and efforts on our joint work, and I am grateful for their encouragement at many points in the development of the research.

My work on seasonality also owes a tremendous debt to my graduate school thesis advisors, Stan Fischer and Larry Summers. They recognized far earlier than I that seasonality was a thesis topic worth pursuing, and I would not have initiated or continued my work in this area without their advice and support. Olivier Blanchard and Julio Rotemberg, my shadow thesis committee, also provided invaluable insights and constructive criticism during many stages of this research program.

Finally, I am grateful to Terry Vaughn of the MIT Press for his patience in awaiting the completion of this book. I would have given up many times had it not been for his regular reminders. Although I cursed him often as I plodded through production of the book, I am happy now that he did not take no for an answer.

1   Introduction

Since economists first began the study of aggregate fluctuations, empirical researchers have struggled over the proper treatment of seasonal fluctuations. Initially many researchers found seasonal fluctuations to be of significant interest (e.g., Jevons 1884, Kemmerer 1910, Bursk 1931, Kuznets 1933, Woytinsky 1939), but over time this attitude changed. Beginning during the worldwide contraction of the 1920s and 1930s, interest in business cycles became preeminent, and researchers came to regard seasonal fluctuations as a kind of noise to be removed from the data before analysis of the underlying business cycle could begin. Arthur Burns, Wesley Mitchell, and Frederick Macaulay were not only pioneers in business cycle research; they also founded the practice of using seasonally adjusted data to study short-term, aggregate fluctuations (Burns and Mitchell 1946, Macaulay 1938). Their practice, of abstracting from seasonal fluctuations through use of adjusted or annual data, has continued to the present day.

The research presented in this book returns to the older tradition of examining seasonal fluctuations explicitly and treating them as economically interesting in their own right. Within this general framework, the book has two main goals. The first is to convince macroeconomists that seasonal fluctuations are an interesting object of study. Because seasonal fluctuations have been ignored for so long (and because seasonally unadjusted data are more difficult to obtain), many macroeconomists simply presume that seasonal fluctuations are uninteresting, if they have considered the issue at all. Implicitly, the reasoning must be that seasonal fluctuations are generated by an economic propagation mechanism that is both inherently uninteresting and fundamentally different from that for business cycles. The research presented here suggests instead that seasonal cycles are themselves interesting and that examination of them can reveal much about the nature of business cycles.

The second goal of the book is to summarize evidence that analyzes seasonal fluctuations explicitly and uses them to learn about aggregate fluctuations generally. The book therefore reviews a number of pieces of research where the use of seasonal fluctuations provides substantial information about particular economic phenomena, both seasonal and nonseasonal.

The analysis begins in chapter 2 by stating precisely what I mean by the term *seasonal fluctuations* and then explaining why these fluctuations are likely to be an interesting object of study. The claim is that the seasonal dummy components of economic time series hold particular interest for the study of aggregate fluctuations because identifying assumptions about these kinds of fluctuations are usually more plausible than analogous assumptions about other kinds of seasonal fluctuations or about conventional business cycle fluctuations. The value of studying these fluctuations, then, is that these identifying restrictions can be employed both to show that seasonal fluctuations themselves provide compelling examples of various macroeconomic phenomena and to analyze the behavior of business cycle fluctuations generally.

Chapter 3 demonstrates that seasonal fluctuations in aggregate variables are quantitatively important, and it presents the seasonal patterns in these variables for the United States and other countries. Examination of these patterns indicates that seasonal fluctuations provide examples of a number of interesting macroeconomic phenomena, including preference shifts, production bunching, and endogenous monetary policy. The patterns also suggest a number of identifying restrictions about seasonal fluctuations that can be employed to test particular economic hypotheses.

In chapter 4, the book compares seasonal cycles and business cycles by determining whether seasonal cycles display the key business cycle "stylized facts." Perhaps surprisingly, seasonal fluctuations in aggregate variables display the critical cross-correlations that characterize business cycle fluctuations, in most cases even more dramatically than the business cycle itself. In particular, over the seasonal cycle as well as over the business cycle, output movements are strongly correlated across sectors, production and sales covary closely, output fluctuations are highly elastic with respect to fluctuations in labor input, and real output is strongly correlated with nominal money. The similarity of seasonal cycles and business cycles suggests that both are generated by similar economic propagation mechanisms. Thus, the study of seasonal cycles can shed light on the nature of business cycles.

Chapter 5 addresses the similarity of seasonal and business cycle propagation mechanisms more directly by examining the correlation across industries and countries in the amounts of seasonal and business cycle variation. The finding is that these amounts are strongly and consistently positively correlated, across both countries and industries. The most natural explanation for this finding is that a similar economic propagation mechanism is at work in producing both types of cycle, and the chapter offers an example of such a mechanism.

The first part of the book, then, undermines the view that seasonal cycles are uninteresting and creates a presumption that study of these cycles can shed light on the nature of business cycles. The results presented also suggest a number of important conclusions about the nature of business cycles, but they are not conclusive on these issues. The second part of the book considers research that attempts to use seasonal fluctuations to shed light on more precise models and hypotheses.

Chapter 6 employs seasonal fluctuations to examine the production-smoothing model of inventories. A great deal of research on the empirical behavior of inventories examines some variant of the production-smoothing model, but most of this work uses seasonally adjusted data and omits analysis of seasonal fluctuations. This approach is problematic, however. As noted in the first part of the book, seasonal fluctuations account for a major portion of the variation in production, shipments, and inventories. Further, seasonal fluctuations are likely to be particularly useful in examining the production-smoothing model because they are anticipated. In addition, adjusted data are likely to reject models even when they are correct because such data are a two-sided moving average of the underlying unadjusted data, thereby invalidating a key orthogonality condition of the model.

This chapter posits a production-smoothing model that explicitly accounts for the seasonal fluctuations in production and sales and tests this model using seasonally unadjusted data. The key fact documented is that the seasonal patterns in production and sales are virtually identical. The model can account for this fact only if the seasonal pattern in sales is virtually identical to that in the technology. Since this condition is unlikely to hold, the model is not easily reconciled with the data.

The next two chapters examine the relation between seasonal fluctuations and the founding of the Federal Reserve. Chapter 7 considers the claim that concern about seasonality constituted a primary reason for the establishment of the Fed. After the founding of the Fed in 1914, both the frequency of financial panics and the size of the seasonal movements in nominal interest rates declined substantially. Since the Fed was established in part to "furnish an elastic currency," it is natural to hypothesize that the Fed caused these changes in the behavior of financial markets. A number of other major changes in the economy and in the financial system occurred during this period, however, including World War I, the shift from agriculture to manufacturing, and the loosening of the gold standard; thus, the role of the Federal Reserve is not immediately clear. This chapter argues, however, that the Fed caused the decrease in the frequency of panics by pursuing the open market policy that reduced nominal interest rate seasonality.

The conclusion that the Fed was responsible for the reduction in interest rate seasonality has not gone unchallenged, however. Clark (1986) notes that the disappearance of seasonal fluctuations in nominal interest rates was a worldwide phenomenon. Although the United States was certainly not a small country by 1914, neither was it so dominant that it should have been able, acting on its own, to alter greatly the stochastic processes of world prices and interest rates. Clark instead attributes the altered behavior of nominal interest rates to the dissolution of the worldwide gold standard at the start of World War I.

Chapter 8 summarizes research that evaluates the role of the destruction of the gold standard and the founding of the Federal Reserve, both of which occurred in 1914, in contributing to the seasonal and other changes in the behavior of interest rates and prices after 1914. The chapter presents a model of policy coordination in which the introduction of the Fed stabilizes interest rates, even if the gold standard remains intact. It also offers empirical evidence that the dismantling of the gold standard did not play a crucial role in precipitating the changes in interest rate behavior.

Having argued that the elimination of seasonal fluctuations was a primary motivation for establishment of the Fed, the book examines the desirability of this policy, which continues through the present day. Although the Fed policy of accommodating seasonal asset market fluctuations continued after the Great Depression, the relative absence of financial panics since that period probably reflects factors other than the accommodation of interest rate seasonals, particularly the introduction of deposit insurance in 1934. In addition, the elimination of financial panics need not be the only effect of accommodating interest rate seasonals, even if this was the original motivation for the policy. It is therefore interesting to analyze the more general effects of smoothing nominal interest rates over the seasons.

Chapter 9 appraises the seasonal monetary policy that the Fed has pursued since its founding in 1914. It does not advocate a particular alternative; rather, it raises a question that has received too little attention from monetary economists. The literature contains almost no discussion of how monetary policy should respond to seasonal fluctuations in demand; yet, as documented here, seasonal fluctuations in output and employment are at least as large as business cycle fluctuations. The analysis suggests that the welfare implications of smoothing seasonal fluctuations in interest rates are likely modest.

Chapter 10 concludes by offering further thoughts on the welfare implications of seasonal fluctuations. One possible justification for the standard practice of ignoring the seasonal fluctuations is that these fluctuations have no interesting welfare consequences and are therefore associated with no interesting policy issues. This chapter explains, however, that seasonal fluctuations *do* raise welfare and policy questions and are therefore of interest per se, even if they are unrelated to business cycle fluctuations. The analysis raises a broad range of interesting questions for the future study of seasonal fluctuations.

2   Identifying Restrictions and Seasonal Fluctuations

This chapter provides extensive information on the nature of seasonal fluctuations in aggregate time series. It does not consider all types of seasonality, but is limited to analysis of the seasonal dummy components of aggregate variables. Relatedly, the analysis compares the behavior of the seasonal dummy components of economic time series to that of everything else, lumping together both the traditional business cycle component and the so-called stochastic seasonal component.

In taking this approach, I depart from much of the literature, so I defend the particular focus adopted. The argument has two components. First, theoretical reasoning implies that seasonal dummies are likely to provide a good approximation to the statistical behavior of economic time series, and existing empirical evidence is consistent with this reasoning. Second, and more important, economists are likely to have stronger prior beliefs about the seasonal dummy component of economic time series than about other kinds of seasonal fluctuations or about conventional business cycle fluctuations. These identifying restrictions can be employed to show that seasonal fluctuations themselves provide compelling examples of various macroeconomic phenomena and to analyze the behavior of business cycle fluctuations generally.

2.1   Kinds of Seasonality

The literature on seasonality typically considers three logically distinct types of statistical processes: stationary, indeterministic seasonality; nonstationary indeterministic seasonality; and stationary, deterministic seasonality. The three types are neither mutually exclusive nor exhaustive (see, e.g., Hylleberg 1986).

Stationary, indeterministic seasonality consists of stochastic processes whose spectra have power concentrated at the seasonal frequencies. More or less equivalently, such processes have autocorrelations functions with peaks at the seasonal lags. A simple example of such a process is

$$x_t = \rho x_{t-12} + \epsilon_t, \tag{2.1}$$

where x_t is a monthly series and ϵ_t is an uncorrelated error term.

Several characteristics of stationary, indeterministic processes merit attention. First, the means of such series are constant across seasons. In any finite sample, the estimated mean will generally differ across seasons, but as the sample size increases, these estimates will converge to the overall population mean of the process. Second, the spectra of such series have power at all frequencies. The amount of power differs across frequencies and tends to be higher at the so-called seasonal frequencies, but some "nonseasonal" frequencies can have more power than some seasonal frequencies. Third, no natural method exists for allocating the variance of such series to seasonal versus nonseasonal components (just as the R^2 of a regression cannot be uniquely apportioned to individual regressors). This is essentially a restatement of the second point.

Nonstationary, indeterministic seasonality consists of processes with unit roots at seasonal frequencies. A simple example of such a process is

$$x_t = x_{t-12} + \epsilon_t. \tag{2.2}$$

This particular process has unit roots at all seasonal frequencies, but other processes have unit roots at a proper subset of these frequencies. (Engle et al. 1990 provide a more detailed discussion.)

The key characteristic of nonstationary, indeterministic seasonality is that the seasonal means are not defined. Over any given sample, an indeterministic, nonstationary process might appear to have a mean that differs by season, depending on the initial conditions and the variance of the error term. Over time, however, the value of such processes in a given season drifts without bound, just as the average value of a standard unit root process drifts without bound. Heuristically, these processes allow for Christmas to migrate to July.

A priori reasoning suggests that both kinds of purely indetetreministic models of seasonality are likely to be poor approximations of the statistical behavior of most economic time series. Stationary, indeterministic models fail to imply seasonal differences in the mean of the series in question, yet many economic series display dramatic differences in their mean values across seasons, and these differences persist over decades. Nonstationary models imply that in any given sample, the mean of a series may differ, but nothing guarantees that the mean stays the same across sample periods. Thus, at a purely statistical level, it appears unlikely that indeterministic models can provide a complete description of many economic time series. The statistical description of some series might include stationary, indeterministic seasonality, but this cannot be the whole story.

Stationary, deterministic seasonality consists of processes whose means vary by season. A simple example of such a process is

$$x_t = \sum_{i=1}^{S} \alpha_i d_t^i + \eta_t, \tag{2.3}$$

where α_i is a coefficient, d_t^i is a seasonal dummy for season i, S is the number of seasons, and η_t is any stationary stochastic process. In particular, η_t might contain stationary, stochastic seasonality.

In contrast to indeterministic models, the seasonal dummy model is likely to be a good approximation for many economic times series, since a number of significant economic phenomena are likely to produce seasonal dummy–type variation in some economic time series. For example, certain holidays are likely to produce regular increases and decreases in retail sales, production, and labor input. Calendar effects, such as the beginning and end of the school year, are likely to generate regular flows such as changes in the labor force. Similarly, the regular fluctuations in the weather are likely to produce regular responses in production, sales, and consumption of certain goods. The ups and downs created by these factors will not necessarily be identical year after year. For example, consumers might be less often liquidity constrained during Decembers that occur in booms, so the amount of Christmas shopping might be higher than average in such years. Nevertheless, a good first approximation will still be that retail sales in December are much higher than in all other months, independent of the state of the business cycle.

The reasoning I have offered suggests that the seasonal dummy model is likely to provide a good approximation to the behavior of many aggregate series, while other models are substantially less likely to be appropriate. Nevertheless, if examination of the data reveals that the seasonal dummy assumption is a poor approximation, a priori arguments become less relevant. The next section therefore presents evidence on the degree to which the seasonal component of aggregate time series can be well approximated by seasonal dummies.

2.2   Evidence

A necessary first step in determining the validity of the seasonal dummy approximation is to analyze the presence or absence of seasonal unit roots. If these unit roots are present but unaccounted for in times series, inferences based on such series are likely to be incorrect.

Beaulieu and Miron (1993) use the techniques developed by Engle et al. (1990) to examine this issue. The technique, a modification of the general Dickey-Fuller approach, consists of regressing a given series on dummies, other deterministic terms, and variables that are functions of lags of the dependent variable. The results indicate consistently that aggregate data are not generally characterized by the presence of seasonal unit roots. For most series, the data reject unit roots at most seasonal frequencies and never fail to reject unit roots for at least one of the seasonal frequencies. These conclusions apply to the entire set of aggregate data series considered in this book for the United States and OECD (Organization of Economic Cooperation and Development) countries. The results do depend in part on the treatment of residual autocorrelation, but the overall conclusions are robust to a variety of treatments for this problem (Beaulieu and Miron 1992).

Thus, although one can never say absolutely that unit roots are absent (seasonally or otherwise) and although in a minority of cases the data do not reject the presence of some seasonal unit roots, the data nevertheless fail to indicate that the seasonal unit roots model provides a good approximation to the data series considered here. Given the strong a priori implausibility of this specification, this empirical evidence is overwhelming.

The absence of seasonal unit roots, however, does not by itself demonstrate the reasonableness of the seasonal dummy approximation. A more direct check on this assumption is to consider whether the seasonal patterns in aggregate data differ across National Bureau of Economic Research (NBER) expansions and contractions. Table 2.1 presents the seasonal patterns in U.S. gross domestic product (GDP), estimated separately for NBER expansions and contractions. The two

Table 2.1
Seasonal patterns in expansions and contractions, quarterly data

	Q1	Q2	Q3	Q4	$\overline{R}^2$	χ_3^2	Sea σ
GDP, United States							
Expansion	−7.38	3.68	−.40	4.09	.879	4.78	5.32
Contraction	−8.58	3.78	.31	4.50		(.189)	6.01
Above	−7.86	3.87	−.53	4.52	.873	3.13	5.70
Below	−7.48	3.63	.06	3.79		(.372)	5.28
GDP, Japan							
Expansion	−21.28	1.70	3.25	16.34	.966	1.27	15.63
Contraction	−20.27	2.18	2.86	15.23		(.737)	14.79
Above	−21.14	1.76	2.18	17.20	.971	18.52	15.82
Below	−20.41	2.20	4.13	14.09		(.000)	14.57

Source: Calculations by J. Joseph Beaulieu.

patterns are strikingly similar and not statistically different. Table 2.2 presents similar results for industrial production and retail sales. In these cases the differences in seasonal patterns are statistically significant, but the expansion and contraction patterns are similar in their main features. Both the expansion and contraction data for industrial production show enormous July slowdowns, August and September upturns, and a winter slowdown. Both the expansion and contraction data for retail sales show an enormous December increase and a January decrease. This result, of statistically significant but economically modest differences in seasonal patterns across expansions versus contractions, is consistent across the macroeconomic time series considered in this book.

Similarly, other possible specifications fail to suggest time variation in seasonal patterns that is large compared to the magnitude of seasonal fluctuations themselves, although in many cases the interactions or changes are statistically significant and large by some relevant metrics (e.g., Cecchetti, Kashyap, and Wilcox 1995, Cecchetti and Kashyap 1995). In particular, comparisons of patterns across periods of high versus low output—as opposed to growing versus contracting output—give almost identical results to those in tables 2.1 and 2.2. Barsky and Miron (1989) show that although many patterns differ statistically across the first and second halves of the post–World War II period, the differences are small in comparison to the magnitudes of the seasonal

Table 2.2
Seasonal patterns in expansions and contractions, monthly data

	Jan.	Feb.	Mar.	Apr.	May	June	July	Aug.	Sep.	Oct.	Nov.	Dec.	$\bar{R}^2$	χ^2_3	Sea σ
Industrial production															
Expansion	.05	1.49	−.38	−1.09	−.67	1.58	−5.87	3.52	1.57	−.45	−2.23	−2.49	.761	24.37	2.43
Recession	−1.62	.64	−1.72	−2.71	−1.54	.62	−6.15	2.95	.22	−2.03	−4.42	−5.30		(.011)	2.65
Above	.54	2.53	.60	−.49	.04	2.54	−4.55	4.63	2.24	.71	−1.90	−1.92	.760	19.54	2.46
Below	.77	1.92	−.03	−.32	.24	2.21	−5.56	3.99	2.24	−.29	−1.47	−2.16		(.052)	2.48
Retail sales															
Expansion	−30.73	−3.13	13.47	.97	4.57	−.42	−1.97	1.67	−4.44	4.27	1.01	18.55	.940	31.96	11.86
Recession	−30.12	−4.15	11.52	1.45	2.72	−1.58	−.10	1.02	−5.16	3.74	−.45	15.19		(.001)	11.03
Above	−30.14	−2.53	14.14	1.49	5.29	.39	−1.60	2.35	−4.56	4.30	2.23	18.99	.943	32.08	11.87
Below	−31.21	−4.29	12.04	.46	3.22	−1.81	−1.88	.57	−4.57	4.00	−.62	16.97		(.001)	11.58

Source: Calculations by J. Joseph Beaulieu.

patterns themselves, and the cross-correlations between seasonal patterns are virtually invariant to sample period. Osborn (1989) finds that impulse response functions allowed to differ by quarter in fact differ only modestly, and Ghysels (1991) finds that in post–World War II data, NBER turning points fail to display a statistically significant seasonal pattern.[1]

The claim made here—that the seasonal dummy model is a good approximation for most series—is distinct and far weaker than the claim that seasonal dummies are time invariant or that the seasonal dummy specification is the true model. No parameter of any empirical exercise is literally constant, nor is any assumption, statistical or economic, literally true. Moreover, it is both feasible and interesting to determine whether interactions exist between factors that can be well approximated by seasonal dummies (e.g., Christmas) and factors that vary cyclically (e.g., liquidity constraints). Such an approach, however, is different from relying on mechanical statistical assumptions that merely allow seasonality to differ from the simplest, dummy variable model, and examining interactions provides evidence on economic hypotheses rather than simply tailoring statistical assumptions to fit the behavior of various time series. The assertion here is merely that the seasonal means of aggregate series change sufficiently slowly that treating them as constant for the purposes discussed in the next several chapters is a reasonable first approximation.

2.3   Identifying Restrictions

Given that the seasonal dummy model appears to provide a good approximation to the behavior of aggregate time series, why do seasonal dummies hold special interest for macroeconomists? Because in many instances, identifying restrictions about this kind of seasonal fluctuation are more believable than analogous restrictions about other kinds of seasonal fluctuations or about the conventional business cycle fluctuations. Many of the factors that produce seasonal dummy-type fluctuations in economic variables—including holidays, calendar effects, tax laws, and the weather—are readily observable. The factors contributing to stochastic seasonality and conventional business cycle fluctuations are, by contrast, often unobservable. Thus, identifying restrictions about these kinds of fluctuations are difficult to evaluate, and a potentially fruitful approach to the identification of models of aggregate fluctuations is to consider the reasons for the seasonal dummy variation in the relevant series.

In the absence of specific examples, the value of this approach is hard to determine. The remaining chapters of the book provide a number of concrete cases. The rest of this chapter discusses how these identifying restrictions can be employed, assuming they are valid.

A first approach to exploiting identifying restrictions about seasonal dummy fluctuations is to examine the behavior of these fluctuations themselves. If reasonable identifying assumptions are available, then determining the presence or absence of particular phenomena over the seasonal cycle is likely to be easier than resolving the same issue over the business cycle. One can then ask whether the conclusion derived for the seasonal cycle is informative about the presence or absence of the same phenomena over the business cycle. In some cases the answer might be no, but the analysis in this book suggests the answer is often yes. At a minimum, demonstrating the presence of a particular phenomenon over the seasonal cycle proves that such a phenomon exists and almost certainly affects the prior belief that it occurs generally.

A second approach to using seasonal fluctuations to learn about business cycle fluctuations is to use seasonal dummies as instruments. All structural estimation requires instruments, yet in practice valid instruments are few and far between. In particular contexts, however, it is plausible to exclude seasonal dummies from certain equations, yet they clearly enter other equations because the endogenous variables are highly seasonal. This approach is not always practical, but in many concrete examples it provides a far more compelling approach to identification than the standard methodology.

The remainder of this book examines and analyzes the seasonal dummy component of economic time series. For simplicity, the remainder of the analysis uses the terms *seasonal* and *seasonal dummy* synonymously, as well as the terms *nonseasonal* and *business cycle*. If my analysis is correct, this simplification is entirely appropriate.

3

Basic Facts about Seasonal Fluctuations

Seasonal fluctuations in aggregate variables are quantitatively important. This chapter documents the seasonal patterns in these variables and suggests that one can plausibly pin down the reasons for many of the seasonal fluctuations in the data using prior information. Chapter 4 uses this information to interpret many of the comovements in seasonal fluctuations across variables.

The chapter considers, respectively, quarterly data for the U.S. economy as a whole (Barsky and Miron 1989), monthly data for the U.S. manufacturing sector (Beaulieu and Miron 1990a, 1991), and both quarterly and monthly data for OECD countries (Beaulieu and Miron 1990b, 1992). Together, these data paint a consistent picture of the magnitude and nature of aggregate seasonal fluctuations.

3.1 Quarterly Data for the United States

Table 3.1 presents three summary statistics for a set of quarterly macroeconomic variables in the post–World War II period. The table contains results for log growth rates, except for the unemployment rate and the nominal interest rate, which use the change in the level; the real interest rate, which uses the level; and inventories, which use the change in the level divided by the level of final sales.

Each summary statistic is computed from a regression of the relevant variable on seasonal dummies. The first statistic is the standard deviation of the fitted values of the regression; this is an estimate of the standard deviation of the seasonal component of the dependent variable. The second statistic is the standard error of the regression; this is an estimate of the standard deviation of the business cycle component of the dependent variable. The third statistic is the R^2 of the regression,

Table 3.1
Summary statistics, United States, 1948–1985

	Standard deviation of dummies	Standard error of regression	R^2
Gross national product	5.06	1.91	.875
Consumption	6.61	1.93	.921
Durables	14.24	5.62	.865
Nondurables	11.33	2.11	.967
Services	1.09	1.05	.518
Fixed investment	8.72	3.77	.843
Nonresidential	6.54	4.04	.724
Structures	9.98	3.79	.874
Producer durables	7.07	5.87	.591
Residential	16.89	6.78	.861
Nonfarm structures	17.51	6.79	.869
Farm structures	21.46	38.92	.233
Producer durables	14.76	22.26	.305
Government	3.79	3.50	.540
Federal	5.34	6.14	.431
Defense	3.91	5.97	.300
Other	18.13	17.88	.507
State and local	4.89	2.31	.818
Exports	5.09	5.16	.493
Imports	3.08	5.14	.264
Change in inventories	1.04	1.32	.384
Final sales	6.19	1.81	.921
Unemployment rate	.65	.51	.617
Employment	1.50	.89	.739
Average hours	.87	.38	.841
Labor force	1.27	.53	.855
Price level	.17	.95	.030
Nominal interest rate	.02	.21	.007
Real interest rate	.18	.74	.055
Nominal wage	.13	.52	.059
Real wage	.20	.70	.076
Nominal money stock	1.10	1.09	.506
Nominal monetary base	.76	.82	.462
Money multiplier	.57	1.00	.243

Source: Barsky and Miron (1989), pp. 510–511.
Note: The sample period is 1948:2–1985:4 except for residential investment (1948:2–1983:4), monetary base and money multiplier (1959:2–1985:4), and hours, nominal wage, and real wage (1964:2–1985:4).

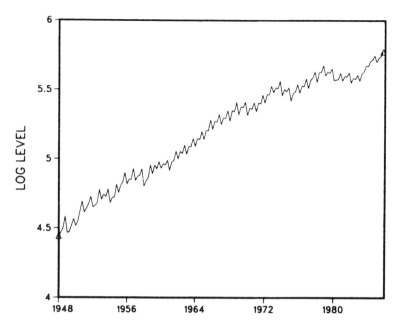

Figure 3.1
Log of real GDP, United States. Source: Barsky and Miron (1989), p. 512.

which measures the percentage of the variation in the dependent variable due to seasonality.

The standard deviation of the seasonal component in the log growth rate of real GNP is estimated to be 5.06 percent, and seasonal fluctuations account for more than 85 percent of the fluctuations in the rate of growth of real output. Business cycles represent a relatively small percentage of the fluctuations in real output. Plots of the log level of real output (figure 3.1) and the log growth rate of real output (figure 3.2) make this point even more clearly. The seasonal fluctuations are so large and regular that the timing of the peak or trough quarter for any year is rarely affected by the phase of the business cycle in which that year happens to fall.

Seasonal fluctuations are present in every major component of GNP, as well as in all other aggregate quantity variables. The standard deviation of the seasonal dummies is particularly large in consumption purchases of durables and nondurables, residential fixed investment, and nondefense government purchases, while the fraction of total variation explained by the seasonal dummies is largest for consumption

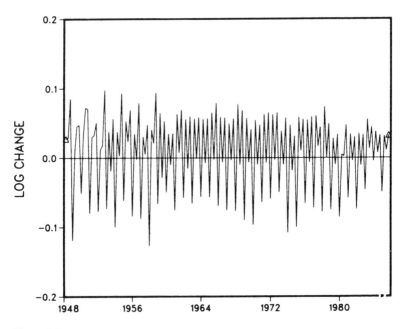

Figure 3.2
Growth rate of real GDP, United States. Source: Barsky and Miron (1989), p. 512.

purchases of durables and nondurables. Seasonal dummies also explain a quantitatively important percentage of the fluctuations in the
labor market variables, although the magnitude of the seasonal dummies is smaller than in many of the national income accounts. Seasonal
dummies account for approximately 50 percent of the variation in the
log growth rate of money.

Seasonal movements in both real and nominal price variables are
noticeably smaller than those in quantity variables. For example, the
standard deviation of the seasonals in the growth rates of prices is
0.2 percent, and seasonal dummies explain only 3.1 percent of the total
variation. The same conclusions hold qualitatively for nominal interest
rates, real interest rates, nominal wages, and real wages.

The estimated seasonal patterns in these aggregate variables are
presented in table 3.2. The entries in the tables are the ordinary least
squares (OLS) estimates of the coefficients on the seasonal dummies.
The overall mean of the dependent variable has been subtracted from
each dummy coefficient, so the entries in the tables are the difference
between the average growth rate of the variable in each quarter and

Table 3.2
Seasonal patterns, United States, 1948–1985

	Log growth rates			
	Q1	Q2	Q3	Q4
Gross national product	−8.08	3.72	−.49	4.85
Consumption	−10.34	4.27	−.94	7.02
Durables	−21.30	12.73	−4.66	13.23
Nondurables	−18.22	7.20	−.43	11.45
Services	1.80	−1.15	−.26	−.39
Fixed investment	−12.33	12.33	.35	−.35
Nonresidential	−8.56	8.09	−3.77	4.23
Structures	−16.33	10.04	5.74	.55
Producer durables	−4.02	7.29	−9.47	6.20
Residential	−21.50	22.65	8.45	−9.60
Nonfarm structures	−22.22	23.50	8.78	−10.06
Farm structures	−33.28	19.46	18.45	−4.63
Producer durables	−24.61	7.95	2.48	14.18
Government	−6.47	3.23	1.31	1.93
Federal	−7.21	.31	−.93	7.82
Defense	−2.51	3.27	−5.04	4.28
Other	−21.26	−14.59	18.63	17.23
State and local	−5.37	6.14	3.37	−4.15
Exports	−2.48	4.29	−7.08	5.27
Imports	−1.20	4.69	.24	−3.73
Change in inventories	1.14	−.39	−.10	−.66
Final sales	−9.83	5.24	−.81	5.40
Unemployment rate	1.08	−.67	−.17	−.24
Employment	−2.49	1.46	.25	.79
Average hours	−1.08	.74	.95	−.61
Labor force	−1.27	1.55	.96	−1.23
Price level	−.19	.14	.19	−.14
Nominal interest rate	−.00	−.01	−.01	.02
Real interest rate	.18	−.16	−.20	.17
Nominal wage	−.16	−.09	.13	.12
Real wage	−.05	−.27	.03	.29
Nominal money stock	−1.05	−.82	.13	1.74
Nominal monetary base	−1.25	−.00	.55	.70
Money multiplier	.04	−.37	−.52	.93

Source: Barsky and Miron (1989), pp. 514–515.
Note: The sample period is 1948:2–1985:4 except for residential investment (1948:2–1983:4), monetary base and money multiplier (1959:2–1985:4), and hours, nominal wage, and real wage (1964:2–1985:4).

the overall growth rate. For clarity, the table omits standard errors. The data reject the null hypothesis of no seasonality at the 1 percent level for all variables except the nominal interest rate.

The coefficient estimates show that the growth rate of real output is strongly positive in the second and fourth quarters, strongly negative in the first quarter, and insignificantly negative in the third quarter. The seasonal patterns in consumption purchases of durables and nondurables are similar in timing but greater in amplitude than those in output as a whole. The seasonal patterns in government purchases are also dominated by first quarter declines and fourth quarter peaks. Fixed investment behaves somewhat differently. It grows most strongly in the second quarter, grows slightly in the third quarter, declines weakly in the fourth quarter, and declines strongly in the first quarter.

Some exceptions to these overall tendencies occur. The growth rates of consumption purchases of services show a first quarter peak rather than a fourth quarter peak. Residential investment shows strong growth in both the third and second quarters. State and local government purchases reach their peak level in the third quarter. None of these exceptions, however, is sufficiently strong to overturn the overall pattern. In particular, the decline in measured output from the fourth quarter to the first quarter occurs in almost every component of economic activity.

The movements in the labor market variables are for the most part procyclical, particularly with respect to the large decrease in output from the fourth quarter to the first quarter. The unemployment rate increases markedly (1 percentage point) from the fourth quarter to the first and declines somewhat moving into each successive quarter, most notably the second. The labor force and average hours per employee increase moving into the second and again into the third quarter but (perhaps surprisingly) decrease in the fourth quarter, contrary to the behavior of output. Employment (as measured by the Bureau of Labor Statistics' Establishment Survey) falls sharply from the fourth quarter to the first and then rises in each successive quarter, peaking in the fourth.[1] Total hours (average hours times employment) increase only slightly from the third quarter to the fourth quarter. The explanation for the apparently anomalous countercyclical behavior of the labor force may be large numbers of withdrawals by workers whose productivity is low—that is, teenagers and agricultural workers.

The seasonal dummy components in the price variables are far smaller than those in the quantity variables. For example, the largest seasonal factor in the price level is only 0.2 percent. Thus, although the seasonal patterns are statistically different from zero for all price variables other than the nominal interest rate, these variables are essentially acyclical over the seasonal cycle.

The money stock and the monetary base are both generally procyclical, showing significant peaks in the fourth quarter and their largest negative growth rates in the first quarter. The amplitude of the seasonal in the base is smaller than that in the nominal money stock (M1), reflecting the procyclicality of the money multiplier. Between the base and the money multiplier, it is the base that exhibits the greater seasonal fluctuations. The amplitude of the seasonal in money is considerably smaller than that in output.

These seasonal patterns in quarterly aggregate data allow a preliminary characterization of the underlying causes of seasonal fluctuations. The results in table 3.2 suggest that Christmas and the weather are the primary determinants of the seasonality of economic activity, with Christmas playing the greater role. The large increases in consumption spending on durables and nondurables in the fourth quarter are almost certainly related to Christmas, and the increases in investment spending on structures in the second and third quarter are likely a reflection of the weather conditions in the spring and summer. The increases in purchases of producers' durables in the fourth quarter, rather than in the second or third, may reflect installation of those parts of structures put into place indoors at later stages of construction.[2] The large decreases in virtually all kinds of economic activity from the fourth quarter to the first quarter plausibly reflect both the end of the Christmas season and the comparatively poor weather in the first quarter.

3.2   Manufacturing

Although the results presented above suggest several interesting conclusions about the causes of seasonal fluctuations, the use of quarterly data potentially masks several interesting phenomena. The discussion turns next to monthly series for the manufacturing sector of the U.S. economy. The series considered include production, shipments, hours, employment, wages, and prices in twenty two-digit manufacturing

industries for the period 1967–1987. Beaulieu and Miron (1990a) describe the series in detail.

Tables 3.3 through 3.10 report summary statistics on seasonal fluctuations in the monthly manufacturing series. The results indicate that
seasonal fluctuations are a dominant source of variation in the growth
rate of quantity series in two-digit manufacturing output, with seasonal dummies typically explaining 50 to 70 percent of variation in production and shipments and 40 to 60 percent of the variation in hours
and employment. The seasonals are much less important for wages,
explaining 30 to 40 percent of the total variation and displaying standard deviations of the seasonal component of 0.4 percent as opposed
to 7 to 8 percent for production and shipments. For prices, the seasonals usually explain less than 10 percent of the total variation and
display standard deviations of only 0.2 to 0.3 percent. The result that
quantities are highly seasonal while wages and especially prices are
essentially aseasonal is consistent with the quarterly results already
presented.

Tables 3.11 through 3.18 present the seasonal patterns in these
monthly manufacturing series. These results demonstrate a high degree of comovement across two-digit industries, producing a large
aggregate seasonal cycle in manfacturing.

This seasonal cycle displays two main features: a midsummer slowdown and a late fall to early winter slowdown. Production is marked
by a pronounced increase in June, a dramatic slowdown in July, and a
strong recovery in August. Production declines rapidly in November
and December but then recovers in January or February. A notice-
able decline also occurs in April in most two-digit industries. The
timing of shipments is similar in most respects to that in production. Shipments grow strongly in June, decline dramatically in July,
and recover in August and September. Shipments decline strongly
again in November through January and recover in February and
March.

The four different measures of labor input all follow roughly the
same seasonal pattern as does production, although the amplitude of
the seasonal pattern is considerably smaller and the behavior of labor
input in January is inconsistent with that of production. Labor input
is high in the early fall but then declines in the late fall or early winter, especially in January, whereas production tends to recover in January. Consistent with the behavior of output, labor input grows in June,

Table 3.3
Summary statistics, U.S. manufacturing, output

	Summary statistics		
	Standard deviation, seasonal	Standard deviation, nonseasonal	R^2
Food	3.914	2.492	.712
Tobacco	9.456	13.472	.330
Textiles	10.254	3.881	.875
Apparel	10.478	6.007	.753
Lumber	6.487	5.625	.571
Furniture	8.906	5.070	.755
Paper	5.041	2.628	.786
Printing	3.486	3.960	.437
Chemicals	4.636	3.054	.697
Petroleum	1.583	3.268	.190
Rubber	6.906	4.470	.705
Leather	7.084	8.644	.402
Stone, clay, glass	5.416	3.564	.698
Primary metal	5.424	4.480	.594
Fabricated metal	7.394	5.262	.664
Machinery	8.473	4.095	.811
Electrical machinery	8.313	4.118	.803
Transportation equipment	9.000	6.443	.661
Instruments	7.486	6.526	.568
Other	8.413	6.407	.633
Nondurables	4.216	1.502	.887
Durables	6.901	2.764	.862
Total	5.539	1.797	.905

Source: Beaulieu and Miron (1990a), p. 18.
Notes: The sample period is 1967:5–1987:12.
Data are in log growth rates.

Table 3.4
Summary statistics, U.S. manufacturing, shipments

	Summary statistics		
	Standard deviation, seasonal	Standard deviation, nonseasonal	R^2
Food	4.14	2.30	.764
Tobacco	10.70	15.68	.318
Textiles	10.24	2.96	.923
Apparel	11.94	4.37	.882
Lumber	6.40	4.39	.680
Furniture	9.04	3.60	.864
Paper	4.62	2.21	.814
Printing	4.44	2.70	.730
Chemicals	5.32	3.14	.742
Petroleum	1.66	2.78	.263
Rubber	6.49	3.25	.800
Leather	8.64	5.56	.707
Stone, clay, glass	6.73	3.18	.818
Primary metal	5.75	4.96	.574
Fabricated metal	6.22	3.05	.807
Machinery	9.86	3.81	.870
Electrical machinery	8.06	2.75	.895
Transportation equipment	10.58	16.14	.748
Instruments	7.60	2.60	.895
Other	11.01	15.58	.796
Nondurables	4.35	1.53	.890
Durables	7.54	2.65	.890
Total	5.93	1.86	.911

Source: Beaulieu and Miron (1990a), p. 19.
Notes: The sample period is 1967:5–1987:12.
Data are in log growth rates.

Table 3.5
Summary statistics, U.S. manufacturing, total production worker hours

	Summary statistics		
	Standard deviation, seasonal	Standard deviation, nonseasonal	R^2
Food	3.657	1.127	.913
Tobacco	7.716	4.514	.745
Textiles	2.343	2.440	.480
Apparel	3.087	2.186	.666
Lumber	2.687	2.081	.625
Furniture	2.822	2.150	.633
Paper	1.429	1.040	.654
Printing	1.408	0.724	.791
Chemicals	0.847	0.754	.558
Petroleum	2.650	5.165	.208
Rubber	1.926	2.519	.369
Leather	3.343	2.259	.687
Stone, clay, glass	2.624	1.667	.713
Primary metal	1.410	2.006	.330
Fabricated metal	2.074	1.506	.655
Machinery	1.707	1.519	.558
Electrical machinery	1.653	1.620	.510
Transportation equipment	3.709	3.723	.498
Instruments	1.444	1.172	.603
Other	3.487	1.587	.828
Nondurables	1.948	1.113	.754
Durables	1.893	1.463	.626
Total	1.820	1.215	.692

Source: Beaulieu and Miron (1990a), p. 20.
Notes: The sample period is 1967:5–1987:12.
Data are in log growth rates.

Table 3.6
Summary statistics, U.S. manufacturing, average weekly hours of production workers

	Summary statistics		
	Standard deviation, seasonal	Standard deviation, nonseasonal	R^2
Food	0.89	0.65	.656
Tobacco	2.43	3.03	.392
Textiles	1.44	2.05	.331
Apparel	1.38	1.80	.370
Lumber	1.31	1.35	.485
Furniture	1.89	1.61	.581
Paper	0.81	0.69	.578
Printing	1.00	0.54	.779
Chemicals	0.60	0.44	.648
Petroleum	0.94	1.61	.253
Rubber	0.88	1.07	.403
Leather	1.19	1.43	.410
Stone, clay, glass	1.09	0.88	.602
Primary metal	0.76	0.87	.431
Fabricated metal	1.25	1.01	.605
Machinery	1.22	0.94	.627
Electrical machinery	1.14	0.91	.609
Transportation equipment	1.79	1.85	.484
Instruments	0.98	0.83	.583
Other	1.06	1.06	.499
Nondurables	0.87	0.84	.519
Durables	1.15	0.92	.610
Total	1.03	0.84	.599

Source: Beaulieu and Miron (1990a), p. 21.
Notes: The sample period is 1967:5–1987:12.
Data are in log growth rates.

Table 3.7
Summary statistics, U.S. manufacturing, total employment

	Summary statistics		
	Standard deviation, seasonal	Standard deviation, nonseasonal	R^2
Food	2.20	0.59	.932
Tobacco	5.14	2.87	.763
Textiles	1.02	0.80	.620
Apparel	2.00	0.83	.853
Lumber	1.47	1.13	.632
Furniture	1.11	0.96	.569
Paper	0.63	0.55	.568
Printing	0.33	0.29	.549
Chemicals	0.35	0.37	.466
Petroleum	1.44	3.85	.123
Rubber	1.02	1.61	.287
Leather	2.46	1.34	.772
Stone, clay, glass	1.39	0.98	.666
Primary metal	0.60	1.18	.207
Fabricated metal	0.79	0.85	.466
Machinery	0.45	0.83	.226
Electrical machinery	0.45	0.91	.199
Transportation equipment	1.49	2.14	.326
Instruments	0.37	0.55	.313
Other	2.15	0.87	.860
Nondurables	0.99	0.46	.824
Durables	0.65	0.79	.404
Total	0.73	0.60	.595

Source: Beaulieu and Miron (1990a), p. 22.
Notes: The sample period is 1967:5–1987:12.
Data are in log growth rates.

Table 3.8
Summary statistics, U.S. manufacturing, production employment

	Summary statistics		
	Standard deviation, seasonal	Standard deviation, nonseasonal	R^2
Food	3.03	0.85	.927
Tobacco	6.17	3.37	.771
Textiles	1.13	0.89	.619
Apparel	2.21	0.91	.854
Lumber	1.64	1.27	.627
Furniture	1.27	1.11	.570
Paper	0.79	0.69	.565
Printing	0.49	0.43	.567
Chemicals	0.40	0.54	.357
Petroleum	1.97	5.08	.131
Rubber	1.28	2.03	.284
Leather	2.71	1.49	.769
Stone, clay, glass	1.68	1.24	.647
Primary metal	0.77	1.43	.224
Fabricated metal	1.03	1.05	.492
Machinery	0.72	1.09	.304
Electrical machinery	0.70	1.25	.238
Transportation equipment	2.29	3.20	.339
Instruments	0.57	0.76	.362
Other	2.66	1.06	.863
Nondurables	1.30	0.58	.833
Durables	0.92	1.04	.440
Total	0.99	0.77	.620

Source: Beaulieu and Miron (1990a), p. 23.
Notes: The sample period is 1967:5–1987:12.
Data are in log growth rates.

Table 3.9
Summary statistics, U.S. manufacturing, wages

	Summary statistics		
	Standard deviation, seasonal	Standard deviation, nonseasonal	R^2
Food	.480	.441	.542
Tobacco	2.774	2.162	.622
Textiles	.332	.699	.184
Apparel	.479	.548	.433
Lumber	.550	.672	.401
Furniture	.336	.487	.323
Paper	.465	.456	.510
Printing	.320	.341	.469
Chemicals	.295	.371	.387
Petroleum	.676	.997	.315
Rubber	.412	.880	.180
Leather	.428	.523	.401
Stone, clay, glass	.324	.438	.353
Primary metal	.429	.729	.257
Fabricated metal	.423	.497	.420
Machinery	.382	.448	.421
Electrical machinery	.360	.433	.409
Transportation equipment	.649	.878	.353
Instruments	.342	.436	.381
Other	.475	.403	.581
Nondurables	.410	.392	.523
Durables	.428	.435	.493
Total	.424	.376	.560

Source: Beaulieu and Miron (1990a), p. 24.
Notes: The sample period is 1967:5–1987:12.
Data are in log growth rates.

Table 3.10
Summary statistics, U.S. manufacturing, prices

	Summary statistics		
	Standard deviation, seasonal	Standard deviation, nonseasonal	R^2
Food	.348	1.589	.046
Tobacco	.329	1.763	.034
Textiles	.094	.459	.040
Apparel	.172	.360	.187
Lumber	.718	1.775	.141
Furniture	.129	.390	.099
Paper	.250	.694	.115
Printing	—	—	—
Chemicals	.223	.937	.053
Petroleum	.241	2.034	.014
Rubber	.142	.644	.047
Leather	.372	1.130	.098
Stone, clay, glass	.378	.602	.282
Primary metal	.248	1.032	.055
Fabricated metal	.219	.824	.066
Machinery	.096	.443	.045
Electrical machinery	.102	.444	.050
Transportation equipment	.992	.795	.609
Instruments	—	—	—
Other	—	—	—
Nondurables	—	—	—
Durables	—	—	—
Total	—	—	—

Source: Beaulieu and Miron (1990a), p. 25.
Notes: The sample period is 1967:5–1987:12, except for transportation equipment, which is 1969:2–1987:12.
Data are in log growth rates.

Seasonal patterns, U.S. manufacturing, output

Seasonal coefficients

	JAN	FEB	MAR	APR	MAY	JUN	JUL	AUG	SEP	OCT	NOV	DEC
Food	-2.14	3.97	2.00	-2.40	1.01	3.08	-5.55	7.08	3.71	-1.33	-4.91	-4.53
Tobacco	2.27	5.17	5.08	-5.53	2.48	9.39	-17.08	14.57	9.49	-2.47	-11.21	-12.15
Textiles	-0.10	9.69	4.47	-6.81	1.11	3.96	-23.22	20.89	2.74	-0.04	-5.01	-7.68
Apparel	13.66	11.39	1.50	-5.62	-1.52	4.10	-9.81	15.84	-2.85	-0.15	-2.53	-24.02
Lumber	1.33	11.54	3.27	2.36	-2.69	5.33	-9.83	8.69	-0.77	-3.88	-9.90	-5.45
Furniture	5.57	7.62	-0.71	-2.17	-0.98	-0.28	-16.62	21.44	-0.88	1.41	-7.36	-7.03
Paper	5.98	4.22	1.06	-1.27	-1.85	3.03	-10.88	7.75	-0.46	1.97	-3.30	-6.26
Printing	-2.56	5.24	-0.18	1.50	-2.06	0.56	-4.58	5.06	3.32	1.38	-1.13	-6.55
Chemicals	1.58	7.44	0.89	0.29	-3.36	0.53	-10.85	5.50	4.58	-2.64	-2.87	-1.09
Petroleum	-2.50	1.02	-0.66	1.86	1.67	2.00	-0.96	0.17	0.83	-2.31	0.92	-2.05
Rubber	4.61	8.99	-0.97	-0.49	-4.50	3.98	-14.41	9.54	4.11	3.30	-7.20	-6.97
Leather	5.45	4.55	1.51	-6.55	4.06	-3.69	-11.38	15.86	-2.32	4.00	-5.18	-6.31
Stone, clay, glass	0.44	7.43	3.14	2.83	-0.68	3.12	-9.70	6.39	1.47	1.06	-5.89	-9.61
Primary metal	7.68	5.38	3.42	-0.72	-1.37	-0.27	-13.56	2.75	4.14	1.17	-3.49	-5.14
Fabricated metal	-0.05	10.95	1.89	-2.09	-0.68	2.75	-17.23	11.91	2.42	1.62	-6.13	-5.34
Machinery	-6.86	11.94	4.11	-7.35	-1.44	4.85	-19.67	5.74	11.24	-4.19	-0.87	2.50
Electrical machinery	-3.54	10.43	2.81	-5.73	0.25	3.99	-20.08	12.24	7.31	0.72	-4.12	-4.29
Transportation equipment	5.13	8.96	2.49	-3.89	0.78	0.76	-19.96	0.58	15.79	5.47	-4.74	-11.37
Instruments	-1.07	7.10	3.76	-4.93	-0.39	5.60	-18.95	9.59	7.85	-1.38	-2.75	-4.43
Other	-0.34	8.69	3.92	-3.34	1.01	4.47	-16.45	15.34	16.76	-2.46	-7.84	-9.75
Nondurables	0.49	5.43	1.35	-1.39	-0.50	2.36	-8.30	7.35	2.72	-0.77	-3.31	-5.42
Durables	0.52	9.25	2.93	-3.50	-0.43	2.62	-17.21	6.79	7.84	0.82	-4.26	-5.37
Total	0.38	7.44	2.20	-2.49	-0.45	2.55	-13.00	7.05	5.40	0.05	-3.80	-5.34

Source: Beaulieu and Miron (1990a), p. 18.
Notes: The sample period is 1967:5–1987:12.
Data are in log growth rates.

Table 3.12
Seasonal patterns, U.S. manufacturing, shipments

						Seasonal coefficients						
	JAN	FEB	MAR	APR	MAY	JUN	JUL	AUG	SEP	OCT	NOV	DEC
Food	-4.93	5.81	2.19	-4.28	1.23	3.73	-7.13	3.83	5.56	-1.86	-2.47	-1.69
Tobacco	-24.24	9.07	9.19	-7.41	6.92	7.64	-15.86	9.04	3.05	-7.88	2.94	7.52
Textiles	-5.49	10.45	7.29	-7.18	0.52	7.07	-22.56	18.44	4.86	-0.90	-6.07	-6.42
Apparel	6.24	19.88	0.73	-10.56	-4.85	10.93	-3.60	15.30	-2.20	-0.28	-4.35	-27.24
Lumber	-0.73	10.83	6.03	3.62	-0.05	4.44	-7.93	6.20	-0.97	-1.78	-11.34	-8.31
Furniture	-1.46	11.86	0.49	-3.60	-0.73	2.93	-16.83	20.61	0.94	-0.43	-6.80	-6.98
Paper	2.51	5.83	1.24	-2.59	-0.63	4.46	-10.11	7.18	0.75	-1.01	-3.43	-4.20
Printing	-8.28	6.42	0.18	1.19	-1.58	0.90	-5.25	5.85	5.65	1.22	-1.25	-5.05
Chemicals	2.37	6.78	4.45	-1.04	-2.10	0.48	-11.98	6.26	5.38	-5.47	-4.14	-0.98
Petroleum	-3.03	0.79	-1.27	1.07	0.93	3.05	-2.43	1.27	0.04	-1.53	0.48	0.63
Rubber	2.59	9.30	1.81	-0.02	-1.95	4.33	-13.52	7.73	3.08	2.39	-7.76	-7.97
Leather	14.07	7.50	-4.95	-8.68	-2.06	6.01	-0.83	14.31	-5.10	2.43	-9.71	-12.98
Stone, clay, glass	-1.72	7.30	7.57	2.61	1.08	5.02	-10.43	8.07	1.18	-0.04	-9.08	-11.56
Primary metal	4.86	7.13	4.04	-1.72	0.40	2.20	-15.01	3.24	4.31	-0.48	-4.42	-4.55
Fabricated metal	-2.43	9.51	3.77	-1.85	0.35	4.17	-13.50	8.40	3.58	-0.73	-6.08	-5.18
Machinery	-13.11	12.41	7.70	-8.07	-1.07	8.85	-20.02	2.80	11.89	-5.00	-3.33	6.94
Electrical machinery	-9.86	10.38	3.11	-6.08	-0.51	8.55	-16.99	8.34	8.95	-2.65	-1.83	-1.40
Transportation equipment	-4.24	11.53	4.02	-3.73	1.34	3.49	-26.77	0.84	18.91	3.53	-3.23	-5.70
Instruments	-11.71	7.96	5.75	-6.27	1.64	7.61	-14.64	7.36	8.45	-4.09	-1.52	-0.53
Other	-7.60	14.10	7.76	-5.44	-0.98	9.99	-19.39	16.73	8.40	-0.73	-9.68	-13.17
Nondurables	-2.08	6.58	2.18	-2.76	-0.40	3.64	-8.54	6.41	3.46	-1.68	-2.98	-3.84
Durables	-5.36	10.31	4.89	-3.86	0.29	5.51	-18.19	5.42	9.14	-0.87	-4.37	-2.89
Total	-3.79	8.50	3.60	-3.34	-0.02	4.63	-13.60	5.90	6.40	-1.24	-3.70	-3.34

Source: Beaulieu and Miron (1990a), p. 19.

Seasonal coefficients

	JAN	FEB	MAR	APR	MAY	JUN	JUL	AUG	SEP	OCT	NOV	DEC
Food	-5.54	-1.54	0.33	-0.81	2.68	4.38	3.16	6.86	0.81	-5.25	-3.05	-2.03
Tobacco	-8.21	-4.66	-4.37	-4.28	1.00	3.64	-5.58	20.98	7.78	0.22	-5.78	-0.74
Textiles	-4.45	1.62	0.85	-0.96	1.43	1.94	-4.62	3.77	0.20	-0.21	0.50	-0.08
Apparel	-4.81	3.58	1.54	-1.81	1.59	1.95	-5.91	5.24	-0.23	0.74	-0.11	-1.78
Lumber	-5.37	2.14	1.64	1.18	2.85	4.41	-2.02	1.92	-1.02	-1.49	-3.04	-1.20
Furniture	-6.22	0.72	1.10	-1.19	0.17	2.23	-4.45	5.06	0.94	0.90	-0.48	1.23
Paper	-3.14	-0.80	0.71	-0.39	0.75	2.55	-1.70	1.06	0.59	-0.98	0.43	0.92
Printing	-4.08	0.35	1.25	-0.76	0.02	0.19	-0.63	1.06	0.58	-0.37	0.77	1.63
Chemicals	-1.88	0.28	0.76	0.25	-0.32	1.17	-1.15	0.21	0.64	-0.86	0.52	0.37
Petroleum	-6.17	-0.92	2.39	3.70	2.61	2.56	1.59	1.18	0.28	-1.19	-0.91	-2.75
Rubber	-2.74	-0.28	0.55	-0.55	-1.05	2.23	-3.74	3.29	2.19	-0.08	-0.17	0.35
Leather	-3.85	0.36	0.46	0.01	3.44	3.40	-7.51	5.33	-2.51	0.35	1.29	-0.77
Stone, clay, glass	-6.34	-0.14	2.99	3.23	2.31	2.64	-1.18	1.34	-0.25	-0.68	-1.47	-2.44
Primary metal	-0.69	0.14	0.98	0.56	-0.29	1.09	-2.86	0.81	2.08	-2.25	0.79	1.26
Fabricated metal	-4.18	-0.19	1.07	-1.06	1.38	1.75	-4.06	2.30	1.89	-0.37	0.39	1.09
Machinery	-2.72	0.65	0.68	-1.70	0.25	0.83	-3.13	0.05	2.37	-0.79	1.18	2.33
Electrical machinery	-3.40	-0.06	0.58	-1.31	0.78	1.22	-2.95	1.77	2.07	0.13	0.22	0.94
Transportation equipment	-5.91	-1.14	2.42	-1.52	2.40	0.62	-5.61	2.53	7.73	-0.93	2.67	3.80
Instruments	-3.04	0.15	0.67	-1.22	0.74	1.28	-2.61	1.36	0.91	-0.25	1.20	0.82
Other	-6.34	1.77	2.45	-0.41	1.43	1.94	-5.02	6.11	1.92	1.47	-0.70	-4.61
Nondurables	-4.10	0.43	0.82	-0.73	1.14	2.31	-1.99	3.79	0.50	-1.28	-0.43	-0.46
Durables	-4.03	0.16	1.28	-0.64	1.13	1.52	-3.52	0.90	2.49	-0.62	0.20	1.13
Total	-4.10	0.24	1.14	-0.70	1.15	1.87	-2.90	2.08	1.67	-0.84	-0.09	0.47

Source: Beaulieu and Miron (1990a), p. 20.
Notes: The sample period is 1967:5–1987:12.
Data are in log growth rates.

Table 3.14
Seasonal patterns, U.S. manufacturing, average weekly hours of production workers

						Seasonal coefficients						
	JAN	FEB	MAR	APR	MAY	JUN	JUL	AUG	SEP	OCT	NOV	DEC
Food	-1.93	-0.67	0.27	-0.43	1.36	0.52	0.34	0.79	0.29	-1.35	0.18	0.63
Tobacco	-3.37	-0.47	0.76	-0.42	2.08	2.28	-5.51	3.31	2.30	0.65	-0.78	-0.83
Textiles	-3.44	1.53	0.76	-1.32	1.33	1.03	-1.94	1.37	0.02	0.03	0.43	0.21
Apparel	-3.39	2.02	1.09	-1.53	1.19	0.80	-0.64	0.73	-0.87	0.56	0.24	-0.19
Lumber	-3.03	1.65	0.85	0.21	1.00	0.99	-1.77	1.06	-0.17	-0.10	-1.20	0.49
Furniture	-5.15	1.13	1.20	-1.10	0.65	1.42	-1.79	2.10	0.04	0.51	-0.55	1.55
Paper	-2.08	-0.54	0.54	-0.45	0.53	0.68	-0.43	0.26	0.69	-0.47	0.20	1.07
Printing	-2.82	0.19	1.03	-0.84	0.33	0.10	0.06	0.75	0.33	-0.62	0.36	1.12
Chemicals	-1.37	0.05	0.29	0.16	-0.26	0.27	-0.63	-0.05	0.94	-0.54	0.64	0.50
Petroleum	-1.84	-0.06	0.77	1.11	0.06	0.22	0.97	-1.14	1.42	-0.57	-0.07	-0.85
Rubber	-1.88	-0.25	0.51	-0.77	0.51	0.68	-1.36	1.05	0.57	-0.07	0.10	0.91
Leather	-2.46	-0.02	0.29	-0.39	2.20	1.48	-1.17	-0.52	-1.08	0.37	0.64	0.66
Stone, clay, glass	-3.05	0.65	1.44	0.59	0.83	0.58	-0.74	0.57	-0.01	0.03	-0.65	-0.23
Primary metal	-0.96	0.10	0.32	0.01	-0.35	0.55	-0.93	-0.56	1.31	-1.08	0.62	0.97
Fabricated metal	-2.92	-0.02	0.91	-1.23	1.28	0.65	-1.73	0.88	0.50	0.05	0.25	1.37
Machinery	-2.70	0.29	0.54	-1.51	0.62	0.41	-1.50	0.45	0.99	-0.12	0.65	1.89
Electrical machinery	-2.63	0.03	0.64	-1.23	0.84	0.67	-1.63	0.96	0.57	-0.03	0.66	1.14
Transportation equipment	-4.19	-0.07	1.06	-1.46	1.93	0.34	-1.51	-1.24	1.98	0.57	0.14	2.46
Instruments	-2.37	0.20	0.64	-1.10	0.60	0.39	-1.24	0.59	0.80	-0.15	0.87	0.77
Other	-2.57	0.45	1.10	-1.06	0.56	0.42	-1.40	1.18	0.49	0.50	0.32	0.02
Nondurables	-2.42	0.31	0.62	-0.71	0.85	0.66	-0.53	0.66	0.15	-0.39	0.29	0.52
Durables	-2.89	0.29	0.77	-0.91	0.87	0.59	-1.50	0.40	0.83	-0.04	0.25	1.34
Total	-2.73	0.27	0.76	-0.85	0.88	0.63	-1.11	0.47	0.56	-0.13	0.24	1.01

Source: Beaulieu and Miron (1990a), p. 21.
Notes: The sample period is 1967–1987.12

Seasonal patterns, U.S. manufacturing, total employment

Seasonal coefficients

	JAN	FEB	MAR	APR	MAY	JUN	JUL	AUG	SEP	OCT	NOV	DEC
Food	-2.66	-0.64	0.07	-0.19	1.04	2.99	2.11	4.22	0.18	-2.86	-2.36	-1.88
Tobacco	-4.08	-3.36	-4.33	-3.18	-0.89	1.21	0.09	14.68	4.52	-0.38	-4.28	-0.00
Textiles	-0.91	0.11	0.07	0.32	0.09	0.84	-2.42	2.17	0.13	-0.19	0.08	-0.29
Apparel	-1.32	1.40	0.41	-0.24	0.36	1.08	-4.77	4.07	0.53	0.22	-0.32	-1.43
Lumber	-2.17	0.40	0.76	0.87	1.64	3.07	-0.19	0.75	-0.81	-1.18	-1.63	-1.51
Furniture	-0.96	-0.35	-0.10	-0.04	-0.39	0.74	-2.32	2.59	0.68	0.37	0.03	-0.28
Paper	-0.86	-0.24	0.14	0.04	0.15	1.56	-0.94	0.65	-0.21	-0.35	0.18	-0.11
Printing	-0.83	0.06	0.09	-0.06	-0.18	0.34	-0.37	0.10	-0.05	0.27	0.33	0.30
Chemicals	-0.46	0.10	0.31	0.05	0.01	0.88	-0.05	0.09	-0.49	-0.24	-0.08	-0.12
Petroleum	-3.30	-0.33	1.04	1.54	1.95	1.86	0.59	-0.12	-1.07	-0.54	-0.45	-1.18
Rubber	-0.72	-0.06	0.03	0.20	-1.22	1.34	-1.87	1.78	1.24	-0.05	-0.21	-0.45
Leather	-1.41	0.34	0.10	0.39	1.04	1.75	-5.82	5.32	-1.18	0.01	0.59	-1.12
Stone, clay, glass	-2.67	-0.64	1.27	2.15	1.25	1.78	-0.30	0.61	-0.29	-0.62	-0.72	-1.82
Primary metal	0.21	0.04	0.51	0.45	0.10	0.59	-1.47	-0.22	0.42	-0.99	0.13	0.23
Fabricated metal	-1.03	-0.15	0.14	0.10	0.08	0.94	-1.76	1.08	1.00	-0.32	0.13	-0.21
Machinery	-0.03	0.25	0.13	-0.20	-0.22	0.48	-0.98	-0.28	0.68	-0.49	0.33	0.34
Electrical machinery	-0.60	-0.11	-0.06	-0.08	-0.01	0.59	-0.77	0.49	0.86	0.11	-0.29	-0.14
Transportation equipment	-1.18	-0.80	0.91	-0.03	0.29	0.34	-2.58	-0.76	3.76	-1.06	0.27	0.84
Instruments	-0.45	-0.09	0.00	-0.06	0.06	0.85	-0.67	0.44	-0.18	-0.06	0.18	-0.03
Other	-3.07	0.96	1.10	0.42	0.70	1.27	-3.08	4.03	1.13	0.85	-0.78	-3.54
Nondurables	-1.34	0.07	0.15	-0.01	0.25	1.42	-1.03	2.31	0.12	-0.66	-0.54	-0.74
Durables	-0.87	-0.12	0.38	0.18	0.21	0.84	-1.38	0.37	1.06	-0.44	-0.07	-0.16
Total	-1.06	-0.04	0.29	0.10	0.22	1.08	-1.24	1.17	0.67	-0.53	-0.26	-0.40

Source: Beaulieu and Miron (1990a), p. 22.
Notes: The sample period is 1967:5–1987:12.
Data are in log growth rates.

Table 3.16
Seasonal patterns, U.S. manufacturing production employment

						Seasonal coefficients						
	JAN	FEB	MAR	APR	MAY	JUN	JUL	AUG	SEP	OCT	NOV	DEC
Food	-3.61	-0.88	0.07	-0.38	1.32	3.86	2.82	6.07	0.52	-3.90	-3.23	-2.66
Tobacco	-4.84	-4.19	-5.13	-3.86	-1.08	1.37	-0.07	17.67	5.48	-0.43	-5.00	0.08
Textiles	-1.00	0.10	0.09	0.36	0.10	0.92	-2.68	2.40	0.18	-0.23	0.07	-0.29
Apparel	-1.41	1.56	0.45	-0.28	0.40	1.15	-5.27	4.52	0.63	0.18	-0.35	-1.59
Lumber	-2.34	0.49	0.79	0.97	1.85	3.42	-0.25	0.86	-0.85	-1.39	-1.84	-1.69
Furniture	-1.08	-0.41	-0.11	-0.09	-0.48	0.81	-2.66	2.96	0.90	0.39	0.07	-0.32
Paper	-1.06	-0.26	0.17	0.05	0.21	1.87	-1.26	0.80	-0.10	-0.51	0.23	-0.15
Printing	-1.27	0.15	0.22	0.08	-0.31	0.10	-0.69	0.30	0.25	0.25	0.41	0.51
Chemicals	-0.50	0.23	0.47	0.09	-0.07	0.91	-0.52	0.27	-0.30	-0.32	-0.12	-0.14
Petroleum	-4.33	-0.86	1.62	2.59	2.55	2.34	0.63	-0.03	-1.14	-0.63	-0.83	-1.90
Rubber	-0.86	-0.03	0.04	0.22	-1.57	1.54	-2.38	2.24	1.62	-0.01	-0.27	-0.55
Leather	-1.39	0.38	0.16	0.40	1.25	1.92	-6.34	5.85	-1.44	-0.02	0.65	-1.43
Stone, clay, glass	-3.30	-0.79	1.55	2.65	1.48	2.07	-0.44	0.77	-0.24	-0.71	-0.82	-2.21
Primary metal	0.27	0.04	0.66	0.55	0.06	0.54	-1.93	-0.25	0.76	-1.17	0.18	0.29
Fabricated metal	-1.26	-0.17	0.16	0.17	0.10	1.11	-2.33	1.42	1.38	-0.42	0.14	-0.28
Machinery	-0.02	0.36	0.14	-0.20	-0.37	0.42	-1.62	-0.40	1.39	-0.68	0.53	0.44
Electrical machinery	-0.78	-0.09	-0.06	-0.08	-0.06	0.55	-1.32	0.81	1.49	0.16	-0.43	-0.20
Transportation equipment	-1.72	-1.07	1.36	-0.07	0.47	0.28	-4.10	-1.28	5.76	-1.50	0.53	1.34
Instruments	-0.68	-0.05	0.03	-0.12	0.15	0.89	-1.37	0.76	0.11	-0.10	0.33	0.05
Other	-3.77	1.33	1.34	0.64	0.87	1.52	-3.62	4.93	1.44	0.97	-1.02	-4.63
Nondurables	-1.68	0.11	0.20	-0.02	0.30	1.65	-1.46	3.14	0.35	-0.89	-0.73	-0.98
Durables	-1.13	-0.13	0.51	0.27	0.27	0.93	-2.02	0.50	1.66	-0.59	-0.06	-0.22
Total	-1.36	-0.03	0.38	0.15	0.28	1.23	-1.79	1.61	1.11	-0.71	-0.34	-0.54

Source: Beaulieu and Miron (1990a), p. 23.

Seasonal coefficients

	JAN	FEB	MAR	APR	MAY	JUN	JUL	AUG	SEP	OCT	NOV	DEC
Food	0.45	-0.30	-0.08	0.24	-0.10	-0.56	-0.22	-0.84	0.32	-0.35	0.84	0.61
Tobacco	1.94	1.67	1.42	1.60	0.43	1.48	-1.24	-6.95	-3.15	-1.20	4.05	-0.05
Textiles	0.03	-0.41	-0.25	-0.42	-0.17	-0.07	0.28	0.60	0.61	-0.22	-0.04	0.04
Apparel	0.73	-0.41	0.10	-0.36	-0.48	0.13	-0.68	0.35	0.95	-0.32	-0.18	0.18
Lumber	-0.07	0.01	-0.35	-0.08	0.59	1.29	-0.05	0.14	0.39	-0.86	-0.48	-0.53
Furniture	-0.26	-0.30	0.00	-0.23	0.11	0.32	-0.39	0.52	0.43	-0.41	-0.23	0.43
Paper	-0.39	-0.52	-0.26	0.05	0.02	0.56	0.91	-0.41	0.51	-0.69	0.10	0.11
Printing	-0.32	-0.10	-0.02	-0.34	0.26	-0.12	0.10	0.13	0.77	-0.44	-0.17	0.25
Chemicals	0.00	-0.39	-0.37	0.28	-0.13	0.16	0.43	-0.38	0.49	-0.21	-0.01	0.11
Petroleum	1.49	0.52	-0.18	0.65	-0.82	-0.47	0.03	-0.71	0.64	-0.70	0.07	-0.51
Rubber	-0.08	-0.60	-0.44	-0.21	-0.41	0.14	0.49	-0.17	0.83	-0.27	0.05	0.46
Leather	0.86	0.02	0.09	-0.21	-0.29	-0.25	-0.78	-0.06	0.66	-0.37	0.15	0.17
Stone, clay, glass	-0.33	-0.32	0.06	0.68	0.32	0.22	0.08	-0.16	0.32	-0.44	-0.13	-0.31
Primary metal	-0.12	0.06	-0.44	0.42	-0.22	-0.10	0.14	0.23	0.59	-1.06	0.43	0.07
Fabricated metal	-0.44	-0.24	0.11	-0.33	0.41	0.01	-0.52	-0.10	0.71	-0.45	0.07	0.77
Machinery	-0.51	-0.08	-0.02	-0.44	0.13	0.04	-0.30	-0.24	0.76	-0.07	0.01	0.72
Electrical machinery	-0.36	-0.39	-0.06	-0.41	0.04	0.05	0.18	-0.15	0.47	-0.24	-0.00	0.87
Transportation equipment	-0.82	-0.64	0.05	-0.58	0.33	0.08	-0.47	-0.51	1.01	0.13	0.00	1.41
Instruments	-0.20	-0.13	-0.21	-0.51	0.12	-0.15	0.12	-0.13	0.38	-0.29	0.15	0.85
Other	0.56	-0.39	-0.26	-0.30	0.09	-0.31	-0.31	-0.58	0.41	-0.24	0.23	1.12
Nondurables	0.31	-0.54	-0.18	0.10	-0.22	-0.11	0.57	-0.61	0.64	-0.51	0.20	0.33
Durables	-0.33	-0.32	-0.07	-0.27	0.16	0.03	-0.24	-0.40	0.86	-0.42	0.17	0.83
Total	-0.13	-0.44	-0.04	-0.12	-0.01	-0.06	-0.02	-0.56	0.87	-0.45	0.23	0.75

Source: Beaulieu and Miron (1990a), p. 24.
Notes: The sample period is 1967:5–1987:12.
Data are in log growth rates.

Table 3.18
Seasonal patterns, U.S. manufacturing, prices

	Seasonal coefficients											
	JAN	FEB	MAR	APR	MAY	JUN	JUL	AUG	SEP	OCT	NOV	DEC
Food	0.42	0.20	-0.43	-0.19	0.40	0.10	0.41	0.12	-0.55	-0.48	-0.25	0.23
Tobacco	0.29	0.09	-0.65	-0.26	-0.10	0.40	0.49	-0.51	0.02	-0.07	0.14	0.15
Textiles	0.18	-0.04	-0.06	0.12	0.01	0.12	-0.01	-0.02	-0.09	-0.01	-0.02	-0.17
Apparel	0.41	-0.10	-0.08	0.10	-0.15	0.21	0.03	-0.02	-0.13	0.02	-0.02	-0.27
Lumber	0.31	1.31	1.23	0.19	-0.39	-0.62	-0.32	0.05	-0.20	-1.33	-0.56	0.34
Furniture	0.37	0.09	-0.14	-0.09	0.01	-0.15	0.02	-0.04	-0.05	0.04	-0.03	-0.04
Paper	0.61	-0.03	0.14	0.33	-0.18	-0.30	-0.04	0.03	-0.16	0.05	-0.23	-0.23
Printing	—	—	—	—	—	—	—	—	—	—	—	—
Chemicals	0.27	0.01	0.41	0.34	0.04	-0.16	-0.11	-0.01	-0.29	-0.04	-0.16	-0.30
Petroleum	0.09	0.22	-0.16	-0.13	0.32	0.43	0.08	0.03	-0.10	-0.49	-0.18	0.07
Rubber	0.17	0.04	0.02	0.20	-0.06	-0.06	0.19	0.24	-0.07	0.01	-0.13	-0.22
Leather	0.57	-0.06	0.33	0.78	0.06	-0.62	-0.22	-0.02	-0.09	-0.25	-0.18	-0.29
Stone, clay, glass	1.06	0.16	-0.04	0.47	-0.16	-0.22	-0.06	-0.24	-0.26	-0.15	-0.29	-0.26
Primary metal	0.40	0.35	0.18	-0.02	-0.25	-0.13	0.17	0.01	-0.03	0.09	-0.41	-0.37
Fabricated metal	0.39	0.29	0.17	0.14	-0.16	-0.23	-0.03	0.10	-0.04	-0.01	-0.36	-0.27
Machinery	0.26	-0.01	-0.04	0.06	-0.02	-0.12	0.06	-0.09	-0.06	0.04	-0.01	-0.07
Electrical machinery	0.26	0.09	0.00	-0.08	-0.09	-0.00	0.09	-0.14	-0.01	-0.03	-0.01	-0.08
Transportation equipment	0.05	-0.39	-0.31	0.04	-0.22	-0.25	-0.17	-0.27	-1.32	3.07	-0.23	-0.01
Instruments	—	—	—	—	—	—	—	—	—	—	—	—
Other	—	—	—	—	—	—	—	—	—	—	—	—
Nondurables	—	—	—	—	—	—	—	—	—	—	—	—
Durables	—	—	—	—	—	—	—	—	—	—	—	—
Total	—	—	—	—	—	—	—	—	—	—	—	—

Source: Beaulieu and Miron (1990a), p. 25.

falls in July, and then recovers in August. Comparing the two measures of employment, production worker employment is more variable than total employment over both the seasonal and the business cycles.

The behavior of manufacturing activity in the fourth quarter appears to differ from that of gross national product (GNP) documented above. Although both peak in the fourth quarter, the peak in manufacturing occurs in October, while that in GNP likely occurs in December, when retail sales increase substantially. The difference between the timing of production in the manufacturing and retail sectors probably occurs because manufactured goods ultimately sold at the retail level (e.g., food, apparel, furniture, paper, printing, leather) take several months to be transported from manufacturers to retailers. For other components of manufacturing (lumber, stone, clay and glass, fabricated metal), the decline in November or December may occur because these industries supply materials to the construction industry, which shuts down in early winter due to weather considerations. In some of the remaining industries, the reason for the slowdown around November is not apparent.

The most interesting feature of the monthly manufacturing seasonal is the dramatic July slowdown and the August–September recovery. Total manufacturing declines 13.0 percent in July and then increases 7.05 percent in August and another 5.4 percent in September. The July slowdown is present across all industries, with only petroleum displaying a decrease in production of less than 4.0 percent. These dramatic changes in the rate of production are masked in the quarterly data. Over roughly the same time period, GNP declines only 0.8 percent from the second quarter to the third.

One class of explanations for the summer slowdown relies on shifts in preferences or technology. For instance, workers may prefer vacations in July. This shift in preferences raises the marginal cost of production, so firms optimally avoid production in July.[3] Similarly, exogenous shifts in the technology may dictate reallocation of production away from low-productivity periods, as in the real business cycle models of Kydland and Prescott (1982), Long and Plosser (1983), or Prescott (1986). Braun and Evans (1994) and Chatterjee and Ravikumar (1992) present models of the seasonal cycle based on these kinds of shifts in preferences and technology and suggest that their models explain many features of the quarterly seasonal patterns. In

particular, Braun and Evans estimate an 8 percent drop in productivity in the first quarter, corresponding to the 8 percent drop
in GNP documented here, while Chatterjee and Ravikumar parameterize their model with a 20 percent drop in productivity in the first
quarter.

These models run into more difficulty when applied to the monthly
results presented above. The only obvious reason for similar seasonal
changes in preferences and productivity across all industries is the
weather, but no aspect of the weather differs as dramatically between
June and August relative to July as do the rates of manufacturing production. It is also difficult to account for the winter slowdown in terms
of the weather, since the declines in output are concentrated in the
fall rather than in the winter, and output increases strongly in February, arguably the month with the worst weather in many parts of the
country.

An examination of average monthly temperature for the forty-eight
continental United States supports this point. Although the highest
temperatures occur in July in all states except Florida (August), the
absolute value of the change in temperature is generally smaller between July and August than between any other adjacent months. On
average, the change is $-1.5°F$ from July to August, while the average
change in months other than January and February is on the order of 8
to $9°F$. The data on precipitation provide even less basis for attributing
the July slowdown to weather, since the pattern of precipitation across
states during June, July, and August is inconsistent. These facts imply
that any function relating productivity to weather would have to be
implausibly nonlinear.

An alternative explanation for the summer slowdown relies on synergies across firms or workers that make it optimal to have all activity
shut down at the same time (Cooper and Haltiwanger 1992, Hall 1991).
These synergies can occur for a number of reasons. Firms may find it
desirable to close at the same time as their upstream or downstream
partners. Under such conditions, two equilibrium outcomes are possible. In one, all firms operate at a relatively low average rate throughout
the year; in the other, all firms close for July but operate at a relatively
high rate the rest of the year. In the second case, each firm closes because otherwise, given that all others have closed, it would have to
stockpile raw materials and inventory intermediate and final goods in
order to operate during the slowdown period. These added costs may
outweigh the benefits of smoothing production. Similarly, firms may

wish to have all workers on vacation at the same time so that retooling or maintenance can take place more easily (Cooper and Haltiwanger 1993a), and different workers in the same family may wish to vacation together.

This perspective does not dismiss any role for the weather in determining the seasonal pattern of production. Although synergies seem likely to be important in explaining the magnitude of the seasonal slowdowns, it is likely that the weather is crucial in determining the timing of the slowdowns. For example, July may well be slightly preferable to August or June as a vacation month. The claim I make is that the magnitude of the downturn in July is greater than can easily be explained simply as the result of exogenous differences between July and other months. Thus, the weather helps pin down the month in which the synergies take place, but the synergies are critical in determining the magnitude of the slowdown.

To the extent that the seasonal cycle in manufacturing represents a synergistic equilibrium cycle, it provides a more readily verifiable example of such a cycle than the business cycle phenomenon that such models were originally designed to explain. The identification of a clear example of this kind of cycle may then shift one's prior as to whether the same kinds of forces are at work in producing the business cycle.[4]

3.3   Other Countries

The U.S. data suggest a number of interesting conclusions but do not provide fully compelling support for these conclusions. To go further, it is necessary to examine data for other countries. This section uses the cross-country variation in seasonal patterns to pin down the ultimate sources of seasonal variation more precisely than is possible from examination of U.S. data alone.

Tables 3.19 through 3.25 present results analogous to those above for the twenty-five OECD countries. As in the United States, deterministic seasonals account for a striking fraction of the total variation in aggregate quantity variables but little of the variation in aggregate price variables. Tables 3.26 through 3.32 present the seasonal patterns in aggregate variables for these countries.

The results for real GDP show that the overall patterns of seasonal variation are strikingly similar across countries. Output falls sharply from the fourth quarter to the first quarter, grows strongly from the

Table 3.19
Summary statistics, OECD countries, real GDP

	Sample period	Standard deviation of seasonals	Standard deviation of residuals	R^2
Argentina	1977:2–1987:2	3.87	3.53	.546
Australia	1960:2–1987:3	9.02	2.31	.938
Austria	1973:2–1987:3	9.07	1.12	.985
Canada	1961:2–1987:3	6.17	2.07	.899
Finland	1970:2–1987:2	7.40	2.95	.863
Germany	1960:2–1987:3	4.75	2.51	.782
Italy	1970:2–1984:4	5.68	1.62	.924
Japan	1965:2–1987:1	10.83	2.19	.961
Netherlands	1977:2–1987:4	5.39	2.52	.821
Norway	1978:2–1987:4	3.28	1.93	.742
Sweden	1970:2–1987:3	11.56	1.87	.974
Taiwan	1961:2–1987:3	3.56	3.44	.517
United Kingdom	1955:2–1987:3	3.46	2.15	.721
United States	1948:2–1985:4	5.13	1.84	.886

Source: Beaulieu and Miron (1990b), p. 15.

first to the second quarter, grows further going into the third quarter, and peaks in the fourth quarter. A few exceptions to this general pattern occur. In three countries (Australia, Japan, Sweden), output does not recover in the second quarter but remains near its low first quarter level. In other countries output does not change much from the second to the third quarter (Argentina, Italy, United States), and in three countries (Netherlands, Sweden, Taiwan), output falls significantly in the third quarter. Finally, in the fourth quarter output declines strongly in Canada and weakly in Germany. Nevertheless, the patterns are extremely similar across countries, particularly the fourth quarter increases and first quarter declines.

The seasonal patterns in GDP suggest two conclusions about the causes of seasonal fluctuations. The fourth quarter boom in output implies a role for Christmas. In contrast to what was suggested above, however, the presence of a first quarter trough in output across Northern and Southern Hemisphere countries casts doubt on the likely role of the weather in explaining this trough.

The patterns in retail sales (table 3.27) provide strong confirmation for both of the conclusions suggested by the data on GDP. The

Table 3.20
Summary statistics, OECD countries, real retail sales

	Sample period	Standard deviation of seasonals	Standard deviation of residuals	R^2
Australia	1961:5–1987:11	12.73	3.17	.942
Austria	1960:2–1987:10	17.80	5.53	.912
Belgium	1969:2–1987:9	11.92	3.73	.911
Canada	1960:2–1987:11	12.72	4.00	.910
Denmark	1967:2–1987:11	12.83	5.57	.841
Finland	1960:2–1987:9	15.71	6.21	.865
France	1960:2–1987:12	20.32	6.32	.912
Germany	1960:2–1987:11	15.02	4.60	.914
Greece	1974:7–1987:10	10.62	5.29	.801
Italy	1970:2–1987:8	19.26	5.52	.924
Japan	1960:2–1987:10	16.50	2.93	.969
Netherlands	1960:2–1987:11	8.76	5.89	.689
Norway	1960:2–1987:11	15.56	4.94	.908
New Zealand	1970:2–1987:10	11.32	6.57	.748
Spain	1965:2–1987:9	23.20	8.35	.885
Sweden	1973:2–1987:10	14.19	4.50	.909
Switzerland	1960:2–1987:10	13.99	5.14	.881
United Kingdom	1960:2–1987:11	11.40	2.25	.963
United States	1960:2–1987:12	11.03	2.83	.938
Yugoslavia	1960:2–1987:11	14.24	10.19	.662

Source: Beaulieu and Miron (1990b), p. 16.

most dramatic feature of the patterns is a large positive growth rate in December followed by a large negative growth rate in January, with this pattern consistent across Northern and Southern Hemisphere countries. This December to January behavior, even more than the fourth quarter to first quarter behavior of GDP, indicates a Christmas shift in consumption demand.[5] The fact that both Australia and New Zealand exhibit seasonal patterns strikingly similar to those of most Northern Hemisphere countries makes the potential role of the weather, at least for this component of economic activity, highly implausible.

The seasonal patterns in industrial production also provide important information. The first significant characteristic is a winter slowdown, with production falling on average 8 percent over the December

Chapter 3

Table 3.21
Summary statistics, OECD countries, industrial production

	Sample period	Standard deviation of seasonals	Standard deviation of residuals	R^2
Australia	1963:2–1987:9	12.29	2.72	.953
Austria	1960:2–1987:11	6.56	3.37	.791
Belgium	1960:2–1987:9	10.49	4.55	.841
Canada	1960:2–1987:11	5.71	2.37	.847
Finland	1960:2–1987:11	16.44	5.08	.913
France	1960:2–1987:11	17.41	4.47	.938
Germany	1960:2–1987:11	7.02	3.56	.795
Greece	1962:2–1987:10	4.38	4.35	.503
Ireland	1975:8–1987:10	8.53	3.94	.824
Italy	1960:2–1987:10	22.53	9.23	.856
Japan	1960:2–1987:11	5.30	1.95	.880
Luxembourg	1960:2–1987:9	7.84	6.23	.613
Netherlands	1960:2–1987:11	6.74	3.64	.774
Norway	1960:2–1987:11	18.13	8.18	.831
Portugal	1968:2–1987:8	9.01	6.58	.652
Spain	1961:2–1987:9	13.94	8.38	.735
Sweden	1960:2–1987:11	32.95	5.61	.972
United Kingdom	1960:2–1987:11	6.85	2.92	.846
United States	1960:2–1987:12	2.45	1.17	.813
Yugoslavia	1960:2–1987:11	9.00	3.37	.877

Source: Beaulieu and Miron (1990b), p. 17.

to January period and then recovering in February. The second important feature is an extreme slowdown in either July or August in almost all Northern Hemisphere countries, with this slowdown followed by an increase of approximately the same magnitude the following month. In fifteen of twenty countries, production declines by at least 10 percent in either July or August, and in seven countries the decline is over 20 percent. Integration of the seasonals in the log growth rates confirms that the level of production is dramatically lower in July or August than in adjacent months in many of the countries considered.

These results provide even more compelling evidence for the existence of synergies than the result for the United States taken in isolation. Not only is the July or August slowdown even more extreme in

Table 3.22
Summary statistics, OECD countries, manufacturing hours

	Sample period	Standard deviation of seasonals	Standard deviation of residuals	R^2
Austria (HH)	1969:2–1987:3	2.79	2.05	.649
Austria (EST)	1965:2–1987:3	3.48	1.82	.785
Canada	1960:2–1987:3	2.16	1.80	.588
Germany	1965:2–1987:3	2.85	2.67	.533
Greece	1962:2–1987:3	2.13	3.18	.310
Japan	1960:2–1987:3	5.17	1.37	.934
Norway (males)	1960:2–1970:4	7.61	3.13	.855
Sweden (HH)	1968:2–1986:2	11.83	3.13	.935
Sweden (EST)	1968:2–1986:2	11.82	3.16	.933
United States	1960:2–1987:4	1.67	1.82	.457

Source: Beaulieu and Miron (1990b), p. 18.

comparison to any difference in weather between the two months, but some countries experience July declines while others experience August declines even though July is the warmest month in all the Northern Hemisphere countries considered here. Explaining these patterns solely via exogenous shifts in technological opportunities appears extraordinarily difficult.

3.4   Summary

The analysis in this chapter is more suggestive than definitive. It has not considered explicit models or hypotheses, so some degree of ambiguity and uncertainty must arise. Nevertheless, the results provide several robust conclusions and a number of tentative ones.

Most important, the results suggest that a small number of readily observable phenomena, namely Christmas and summer vacations, play a key role in determining the patterns of aggregate seasonal variation. In addition, it appears unlikely that all of the variation can be explained in models that rely solely on shifts of preferences and technology, as opposed to models that involve significant synergies. These results do not by themselves shed light on how business cycles are propagated, but they constitute useful examples and show that seasonal cycles are interesting in and of themselves.

Table 3.23
Summary statistics, OECD countries, money stock

	Sample period	Standard deviation of seasonals	Standard deviation of residuals	R^2
Australia	1960:7–1987:11	1.64	1.23	.638
Austria	1960:2–1987:11	2.16	1.94	.554
Belgium	1976:1–1987:12	2.31	1.31	.757
Canada	1960:2–1987:12	1.96	1.50	.631
Denmark	1970:3–1987:11	4.26	2.99	.671
Finland	1960:2–1987:11	2.53	3.39	.358
France	1970:1–1987:11	2.65	1.61	.731
Germany	1960:2–1987:12	2.76	1.26	.827
Greece	1960:2–1987:10	3.73	2.91	.622
Iceland	1960:2–1987:10	2.20	4.46	.195
Ireland	1976:11–1987:12	2.91	1.81	.721
Italy	1962:1–1987:11	2.35	1.77	.638
Japan	1960:2–1987:11	3.90	1.57	.859
Netherlands	1960:2–1987:10	1.77	1.58	.557
Norway	1966:2–1987:10	2.23	1.96	.566
New Zealand	1977:4–1987:10	4.51	3.09	.680
Spain	1960:2–1987:11	3.31	1.17	.890
Switzerland	1960:2–1987:11	1.74	1.41	.604
Taiwan	1968:2–1987:12	3.60	3.17	.563
Turkey	1977:1–1987:12	5.74	5.07	.562
United Kingdom	1971:7–1987:12	1.31	1.82	.340
United States	1960:2–1987:12	1.47	.61	.852
Yugoslavia	1964:11–1987:10	1.02	2.47	.147

Source: Beaulieu and Miron (1990b), p. 19.

Table 3.24
Summary statistics, OECD countries, nominal interest rates

	Sample period	Standard deviation of seasonals	Standard deviation of residuals	R^2
Belgium	1960:2–1987:12	.01	.05	.039
Canada	1960:2–1987:12	.01	.05	.018
France	1971:2–1987:12	.01	.06	.049
Germany	1971:7–1987:12	.01	.02	.070
Ireland	1971:4–1987:12	.02	.07	.103
Japan	1971:4–1987:12	.00	.01	.027
Netherlands	1960:2–1987:12	.01	.05	.069
Sweden	1960:2–1987:12	.01	.06	.042
Switzerland	1970:5–1986:3	.01	.04	.068
United Kingdom	1960:2–1987:12	.01	.06	.067
United States	1960:2–1987:12	.01	.06	.009

Source: Beaulieu and Miron (1990b), p. 28.

Table 3.25
Summary statistics, OECD countries, prices

	Sample period	Standard deviation of seasonals	Standard deviation of residuals	R^2
Austria	1960:2–1987:12	.32	.57	.239
Belgium	1960:2–1987:12	.10	.38	.060
Canada	1960:2–1987:12	.12	.38	.087
Denmark	1967:2–1987:12	.25	.66	.122
Finland	1960:2–1987:12	.23	.97	.052
France	1960:2–1987:12	.09	.38	.051
Germany	1960:2–1987:12	.21	.29	.345
Greece	1960:2–1987:12	.99	.99	.500
Italy	1960:2–1987:11	.15	.59	.060
Japan	1960:2–1987:12	.51	.69	.357
Luxembourg	1960:2–1987:12	.10	.44	.048
Netherlands	1960:2–1987:12	.35	.61	.246
Norway	1960:2–1987:12	.41	.80	.213
Portugal	1960:2–1987:10	.53	1.44	.119
Spain	1960:2–1987:12	.22	.76	.078
Sweden	1960:2–1987:12	.22	.90	.054
Switzerland	1960:2–1987:12	.17	.38	.164
Turkey	1969:5–1987:12	1.56	3.29	.184
United Kingdom	1962:2–1987:12	.35	.61	.246
United States	1960:2–1987:12	.07	.35	.036
Yugoslavia	1960:2–1987:12	.85	3.19	.066

Source: Beaulieu and Miron (1990b), p. 29.

Table 3.26
Seasonal patterns, OECD countries, real GDP

	Q1	Q2	Q3	Q4
Argentina	−6.09	2.53	−.39	3.95
Australia	−14.37	.09	4.05	10.23
Austria	−15.60	6.52	5.66	3.42
Canada	−6.76	4.59	7.49	−5.32
Finland	−12.38	4.50	1.39	6.49
Germany	−7.61	3.24	4.64	−.27
Italy	−9.57	4.72	.78	4.07
Japan	−17.22	.05	5.40	11.77
Netherlands	−4.04	6.41	−6.31	3.93
Norway	−4.17	−2.18	2.78	3.57
Sweden	−9.38	.42	−9.81	18.76
Taiwan	−3.54	1.02	−2.87	5.39
United Kingdom	−5.90	1.65	1.22	3.03
United States	−8.17	3.96	−.56	4.77

Source: Beaulieu and Miron (1990b), p. 15.

Table 3.27
Seasonal patterns, OECD countries, real retail sales

	JAN	FEB	MAR	APR	MAY	JUN	JUL	AUG	SEP	OCT	NOV	DEC
Australia	−33.77	−5.70	7.15	−.41	6.63	−7.80	2.27	.66	−1.03	4.40	2.82	24.77
Austria	−52.38	−2.66	13.54	.05	−.08	−.77	4.80	−1.46	−.47	6.81	3.08	29.53
Belgium	−27.28	−3.88	14.56	.12	.34	1.46	−11.67	−.50	7.37	3.62	−6.78	22.65
Canada	−36.61	−4.27	14.59	4.66	6.41	−1.71	−4.95	−1.99	−.89	5.57	2.49	16.70
Denmark	−30.17	−10.79	9.00	1.04	4.89	−1.86	2.48	−1.64	−4.14	4.49	−2.40	29.11
Finland	−43.50	1.22	3.54	11.27	4.97	−2.69	−8.85	−.73	2.76	2.25	.47	29.29
France	−47.02	−18.32	15.94	−2.34	4.00	−.13	−5.15	−8.67	21.62	3.18	−3.02	39.92
Germany	−42.20	−3.34	17.26	−.20	−2.21	−4.44	3.90	−7.65	3.75	11.13	3.44	20.56
Greece	−23.18	2.11	−9.24	12.38	−9.35	−2.89	−4.28	4.98	.53	7.28	1.75	19.91
Italy	−47.07	−6.65	16.36	−1.42	.30	−1.12	−2.69	−13.25	19.20	8.16	−8.36	36.53
Japan	−43.12	−3.42	17.94	−2.89	−2.48	−.39	7.85	−7.95	−2.36	4.96	.80	31.06
Netherlands	−16.19	−13.87	15.78	.84	3.79	−4.48	.48	−6.50	4.45	7.74	.01	7.97
Norway	−44.96	−2.94	9.45	1.97	6.13	3.51	−4.46	.58	−.89	6.33	−1.92	27.21
New Zealand	−31.44	.13	11.18	−2.99	6.75	−8.34	3.43	.75	−.71	.63	2.57	18.02
Spain	10.61	−54.83	.14	2.03	7.13	1.83	28.90	−34.23	4.51	18.23	−11.41	27.10
Sweden	−38.99	−6.10	10.81	3.96	1.21	−1.98	−3.50	.90	−.11	8.98	−1.99	26.79
Switzerland	−33.40	−12.79	13.53	1.28	−1.69	−3.32	−3.19	−7.54	3.32	9.56	8.36	25.89
United Kingdom	−32.78	−3.85	4.07	1.37	.67	−.92	3.18	−3.09	.57	4.32	6.14	20.30
United States	−30.65	−3.50	13.12	1.16	3.85	−.58	−2.04	1.08	−4.44	4.42	.27	17.31
Yugoslavia	−43.59	2.74	15.76	9.24	−8.48	6.80	1.62	3.28	1.53	.61	.02	10.46

Source: Beaulieu and Miron (1990b), p. 16.

Table 3.28
Seasonal patterns, OECD countries, industrial production

	JAN	FEB	MAR	APR	MAY	JUN	JUL	AUG	SEP	OCT	NOV	DEC
Australia	-21.41	33.47	-.16	-3.00	.19	-.59	1.44	.28	2.83	-.18	1.64	-14.50
Austria	-13.12	5.32	2.13	1.78	2.80	.18	-13.22	.57	10.00	2.36	3.80	-2.59
Belgium	-1.29	5.90	.24	1.70	-.65	-.84	-27.11	17.67	10.78	.05	3.07	-9.50
Canada	.07	6.72	-.40	-1.72	-.65	3.38	-13.70	4.36	7.78	.01	1.79	-7.66
Finland	-.03	1.29	-.07	2.29	-.46	-5.61	-41.79	36.99	6.96	1.68	1.63	-2.89
France	-.51	1.77	-.39	-.55	-2.84	1.68	-12.12	-36.54	45.68	3.76	1.83	-1.76
Germany	-8.62	6.32	1.50	1.88	-1.18	.61	-11.79	-4.58	15.84	1.74	4.29	-5.99
Greece	-7.19	4.93	2.30	-.69	1.96	4.76	-1.75	-3.46	8.50	-4.69	-1.55	-3.13
Ireland	-3.61	7.87	3.94	-.49	1.70	3.44	-9.84	-13.96	18.86	-.55	1.81	-9.16
Italy	1.46	4.37	.66	.25	.49	-.29	-4.30	-52.17	56.58	-1.04	1.48	-7.48
Japan	-10.88	5.78	7.93	-5.56	-2.21	3.27	.44	-5.91	5.84	-.60	-.67	2.57
Luxembourg	.26	4.98	.45	2.39	1.91	-.70	-6.02	-16.56	18.50	-.53	1.45	-6.12
Netherlands	-5.75	2.51	-.64	-.63	-3.62	-1.00	-17.11	5.59	10.28	6.64	3.74	-.01
Norway	4.61	5.74	-4.41	-6.69	-2.09	8.40	-44.76	38.75	7.64	2.33	2.64	-12.17
Portugal	-1.16	2.48	1.46	.97	-2.64	.55	-4.92	-19.23	23.62	1.72	-.34	-2.50
Spain	-.43	-.78	4.01	-3.33	2.83	-2.05	-2.68	-32.74	33.97	4.16	-.24	-2.72
Sweden	-4.38	1.60	1.17	5.05	-2.38	1.13	-84.48	75.17	6.65	2.95	1.34	-3.81
United Kingdom	.24	6.27	1.42	-7.09	.92	.24	-9.40	-5.80	16.09	2.97	2.55	-8.42
United States	.15	2.60	.27	-.39	.11	2.35	-5.19	3.42	2.36	-.35	-2.22	-3.10
Yugoslavia	-17.29	4.30	10.82	-3.32	-1.22	2.89	-17.07	9.21	7.30	4.00	-5.71	6.09

Source: Beaulieu and Miron (1990b), p. 17.

Table 3.29
Seasonal patterns, OECD countries, manufacturing hours

	Q1	Q2	Q3	Q4
Austria (HH)	−1.75	−.11	−2.70	4.56
Austria (EST)	−1.52	−1.53	−2.90	5.95
Canada	−.75	2.93	.76	−2.95
Germany	−2.66	−1.08	−1.10	4.83
Greece	−3.58	1.81	1.39	.38
Japan	−6.48	7.62	−2.10	.96
Norway (males)	−1.36	−5.86	−5.30	12.52
Sweden (HH)	−3.19	−2.68	−13.27	19.14
Sweden (EST)	−3.17	−2.75	−13.23	19.98
United States	−2.87	1.39	.82	.66

Source: Beaulieu and Miron (1990b), p. 18.

Table 3.30
Seasonal patterns, OECD countries, money stock

	JAN	FEB	MAR	APR	MAY	JUN	JUL	AUG	SEP	OCT	NOV	DEC
Australia	-.79	-.33	.01	-.81	-3.28	-.26	-.92	-.47	.58	1.35	.92	4.01
Austria	-3.78	.69	-.41	.97	1.18	1.80	-.26	.49	1.16	-4.42	3.64	-1.06
Belgium	-1.54	-2.39	1.77	1.63	1.35	3.46	-4.25	-2.25	.71	-1.56	-.10	3.18
Canada	-3.97	-3.17	.03	1.42	.22	1.28	1.43	-.47	.30	.15	-.90	3.67
Denmark	-9.37	-1.11	3.52	1.10	-.67	5.64	-6.73	-1.38	3.09	.00	.56	5.35
Finland	-4.55	-.97	-.76	.54	1.27	1.65	-2.67	-.45	.48	-1.73	.83	6.37
France	-3.98	-1.94	1.26	.31	-1.17	2.31	.52	-3.28	1.45	.26	-2.08	6.32
Germany	-7.51	.05	-.34	.74	1.27	1.16	-.36	-.64	-.42	-.25	5.59	.71
Greece	-8.21	-1.38	-1.35	4.17	-2.71	1.97	1.34	.69	.38	-1.22	-1.65	7.97
Iceland	-1.80	-.48	2.47	4.17	2.50	-1.85	.72	-3.40	-.57	.83	.22	-2.83
Ireland	-5.36	-3.51	2.84	-1.92	-.44	2.65	-1.21	.98	2.29	-2.04	.43	5.30
Italy	-4.05	-1.79	-.03	-.12	-.26	.28	.31	-1.67	.64	.04	-.05	6.68
Japan	-7.57	-2.67	4.00	.29	-.99	.84	-1.69	-2.25	1.26	-2.01	1.58	9.22
Netherlands	-.41	-.75	.80	2.09	4.38	-.12	-2.00	-2.44	-.47	-1.38	.44	-.11
Norway	-.48	-2.35	-2.25	-.02	-1.63	4.90	-.41	-1.70	.89	2.22	-2.13	2.97
New Zealand	-7.88	5.59	-6.40	2.77	-.27	-1.31	-1.33	1.93	-5.24	1.87	2.08	8.19
Spain	-7.51	-1.20	.75	-.20	-.45	2.18	1.40	-2.73	1.02	-.75	-.26	7.76
Switzerland	-3.44	-1.66	1.16	-.46	-.45	.79	-2.13	-.79	1.67	.90	1.34	3.07
Taiwan	3.43	-6.36	-3.53	-.59	.95	4.42	-4.28	.33	-.84	-.04	-.57	7.08
Turkey	-13.62	-1.89	-1.44	1.11	-.12	-.13	2.38	1.91	-1.78	1.95	-1.81	13.44
United Kingdom	-3.51	-1.03	1.32	1.71	-.07	.10	.88	-.93	-.11	.13	.74	.77
United States	-.71	-3.23	.08	1.91	-2.20	1.08	.39	-.79	.49	.46	.69	1.84
Yugoslavia	.53	-.99	-.83	.59	-.90	-1.00	2.50	1.05	-1.39	-.29	-.25	.08

Source: Beaulieu and Miron (1990b), p. 19.

Table 3.31
Seasonal patterns, OECD countries, nominal interest rules

	JAN	FEB	MAR	APR	MAY	JUN	JUL	AUG	SEP	OCT	NOV	DEC
Belgium	-.02	-.01	.01	-.01	-.01	-.00	.01	.00	.01	.01	-.01	.02
Canada	-.00	.01	-.01	.01	-.01	.01	.01	-.01	.00	-.01	-.00	.01
France	-.00	-.00	.00	-.02	.02	.02	-.02	-.00	.03	-.02	-.01	.00
Germany	.00	-.00	-.00	-.01	.01	.01	.01	-.00	.00	-.00	.01	-.01
Ireland	.00	-.02	-.02	-.05	.00	.00	.00	.02	-.02	.02	.03	.04
Japan	.00	-.00	-.00	.01	.00	-.00	.00	.00	-.00	.00	-.00	.00
Netherlands	-.03	-.01	-.01	-.01	.01	.01	.01	.01	.01	.02	-.01	.01
Sweden	.01	-.01	-.01	.04	-.01	.00	-.01	-.01	.01	-.01	-.01	-.01
Switzerland	-.03	-.00	-.00	.00	.01	.01	-.01	-.01	.01	.01	.01	.00
United Kingdom	-.01	-.00	-.03	-.02	.00	.01	.02	-.01	.00	.01	.02	.00
United States	.00	.00	-.00	-.01	.00	-.00	.01	.01	-.01	-.00	.00	.00

Source: Beaulieu and Miron (1990b), p. 28.

Table 3.32
Seasonal patterns, OECD countries, prices

	JAN	FEB	MAR	APR	MAY	JUN	JUL	AUG	SEP	OCT	NOV	DEC
Austria	.58	-.02	-.06	.05	-.07	.72	-.32	-.35	-.35	-.12	-.03	-.03
Belgium	.21	.07	-.14	.02	-.04	-.00	.11	-.15	.06	-.04	-.05	-.05
Canada	-.06	-.02	.04	.01	.04	.18	.18	-.05	-.30	.00	.04	-.08
Denmark	-.29	-.16	.20	.13	.45	-.18	.08	-.18	.22	-.01	.20	-.45
Finland	.50	.04	.08	.27	.00	.09	-.01	-.28	.00	-.09	-.23	-.38
France	.17	-.08	.01	.07	-.02	-.06	.07	-.07	.01	.11	-.05	-.16
Germany	.52	.06	-.00	.04	.03	.03	-.18	-.43	-.18	-.03	.10	.04
Greece	.07	-1.29	1.35	.53	-.30	-.28	-1.39	-1.63	1.45	.84	.04	.61
Italy	.14	.15	-.07	.00	-.01	-.25	-.25	-.14	.12	.21	.14	-.03
Japan	.56	-.20	.07	.62	-.09	-.60	-.32	-.35	.95	.33	-.90	-.05
Luxembourg	.11	.04	-.23	.05	.11	-.00	.01	-.17	.01	-.01	.03	.04
Netherlands	.17	.21	.23	.73	-.40	-.25	-.57	.03	.38	-.03	-.25	-.25
Norway	1.02	-.11	.34	-.32	-.21	.01	.48	-.57	.11	-.18	-.19	-.38
Portugal	.19	.19	.80	-.31	-1.13	-.83	-.29	.41	.46	.21	.14	.17
Spain	.27	-.40	.09	.15	-.12	-.49	.15	.08	-.01	-.02	.16	.12
Sweden	.55	.24	-.15	.09	-.30	.04	-.13	.10	-.05	-.09	-.18	-.12
Switzerland	.07	-.05	-.11	-.21	.24	.04	-.20	.05	-.09	-.03	.39	-.10
Turkey	2.04	.12	1.53	1.29	.64	-3.76	.34	-1.18	1.12	.29	-.70	-1.71
United Kingdom	.14	-.05	-.04	1.06	-.08	-.06	-.34	-.32	-.28	.08	.00	-.10
United States	-.07	.06	-.01	.08	.03	.10	.07	-.05	.04	-.06	-.09	-.09
Yugoslavia	1.15	-.08	-.02	-.35	.04	.09	-1.82	-1.15	.12	1.08	1.13	-.17

Source: Beaulieu and Miron (1990b), p. 29.

4   The Similarity of Seasonal Cycles and Business Cycles

The material presented so far has documented the quantitative importance of seasonal fluctuations in aggregate variables and demonstrated that identifying restrictions about the causes of aggregate fluctuations are more readily available for seasonal fluctuations than for business cycle fluctuations. This evidence is inherently interesting because it demonstrates that business cycles are only one kind of aggregate fluctuation and that seasonal fluctuations display interesting phenomena, such as preference shifts and production synergies.

This chapter begins the process of using seasonal fluctuations to learn about business cycles. The approach here is to determine whether the cross-correlations between the seasonal components of aggregate variables display the business cycle "stylized facts."[1] The chapter demonstrates that the seasonal cycle displays the same stylized facts as the business cycle, in some cases even more dramatically. Thus, over the seasonal cycle as well over the business cycle, output moves together across broadly defined sectors, production and sales coincide closely, labor productivity is procyclical, and nominal money and real output are highly correlated. A seasonal business cycle is present in the U.S. and other economies, and its characteristics mirror closely those of the conventional business cycle.

This set of facts is intriguing because of the identifying restrictions available for seasonal cycles. Given these restrictions, it is easier to take a strong stand on the explanation for the seasonal stylized facts than for their business cycle counterparts. This does not in and of itself determine the explanation for the business cycle stylized facts, but it is suggestive and provides examples of certain key phenomena. Chapter 5 addresses explicitly the question of whether conclusions derived about the nature of seasonal cycles apply to the business cycle.

4.1   The Comovement of Output across Sectors

The most basic feature of the business cycle is the first one discussed by Lucas (1977) in his now-famous article on understanding business cycles: output movements across broadly defined sectors move together, implying a substantial cycle in aggregate output. A quantitatively important aggregate seasonal cycle is also present in the United States and other countries. Indeed, the seasonal cycle is more pronounced than the business cycle for most quantity variables. Although the timing of the seasonal peaks and troughs differs to some extent across different components of output, the overall tendencies are sufficiently similar that a large seasonal cycle remains, especially the large decline from the fourth quarter to the first quarter.

A priori reasoning leaves some doubt as to whether one would expect aggregate seasonal cycles of the magnitude documented to be a characteristic of modern economies. Although an agricultural economy might be dominated by a weather-induced cycle, it seems implausible that weather effects would be important enough to drive most sectors of, say, the post–World War II U.S. economy. Some activities, such as residential construction, can proceed at least cost when the weather is good. For many other activities, however, the temperature extremes associated with summer or winter are costly (e.g., air-conditioning or heating), so these activities might have spring or autumn peaks.

The large seasonal in activity is particularly surprising relative to models that assume convex costs of production. If production functions are everywhere concave and seasonals are absent from technology and preferences, output should be produced evenly throughout the year (subject to discounting). If the technology or taste for work is seasonal, then production should be seasonal, ceteris paribus, even with concave within-period production functions. It is far from obvious, however, what might constitute aggregate seasonals in technology.

As with the comovement of output over the business cycle, the comovement over the seasonal cycle suggests the presence of aggregate shocks to economic activity. Given the patterns, the most likely aggregate seasonal shocks are demand shifts related to Christmas and summer vacations combined with synergies across agents that make bunching of activity privately desirable. Aggregate technology shifts appear unlikely to be significant determinants of the aggregate seasonal cycles documented here.

4.2   The Comovement of Production and Sales

A second key stylized fact about the business cycle is the high comovement of production and sales (Blinder 1986). Indeed, production is usually more variable than sales, and the covariance of production and inventory investment is often positive, contrary to the implications of the production-smoothing model.[2]

The behavior of production and sales over the seasonal cycle is strikingly similar to its behavior over the business cycle. Figures 4.1A through 4.1D present estimates of the seasonals in production and shipments for all twenty-three two-digit industries and aggregates in the United States, and figures 4.2A and 4.2B present the seasonal patterns in manufacturing production and shipments for a number of other countries. Each picture plots the seasonals in the log growth rate of shipments and of production. The figures show that the seasonals in production and shipments are strongly similar in almost every two-digit industry in the United States and in overall manufacturing in several other countries. Production is about as variable as sales, and the timing of peaks and troughs is virtually identical in the two series.[3]

As with the business cycle, the similar behavior of production and sales over the seasonal cycle appears problematic for the production-smoothing model of inventory accumulation. In contrast to analyses involving business cycle data, however, many of the standard explanations can be eliminated relatively easily. Most important, the large declines in output and sales in July or August are difficult to reconcile as pure technology shocks, so this class of models appears unlikely to be an adequate explanation for the seasonal facts presented above. Chapter 6 provides a rigorous analysis of issued raised by these facts.

4.3   Procyclical Labor Productivity

Another important stylized fact about business cycles is the procyclicality of labor productivity. The empirical elasticity of output with respect to labor input (measured in hours) is not only greater than labor's share in output (the value implied by constant returns and competition) but is actually somewhat greater than unity. For example, Prescott (1986) reports an elasticity of 1.1 for the United States, and Summers and Wadhwani (1987) estimate elasticities between 1.0 and 2.0 for most OECD countries.[4]

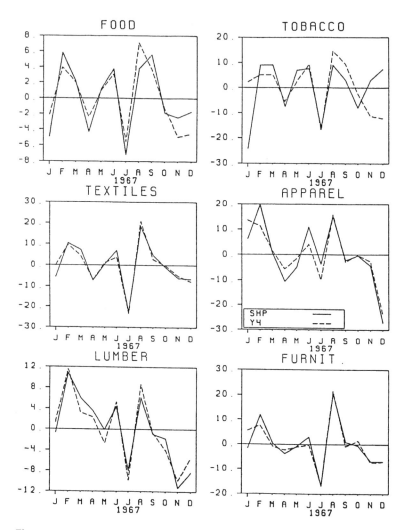

Figure 4.1
Seasonals in production and shipments, United States. Source: Beaulieu and Miron
(1990a), pp. 28–31.

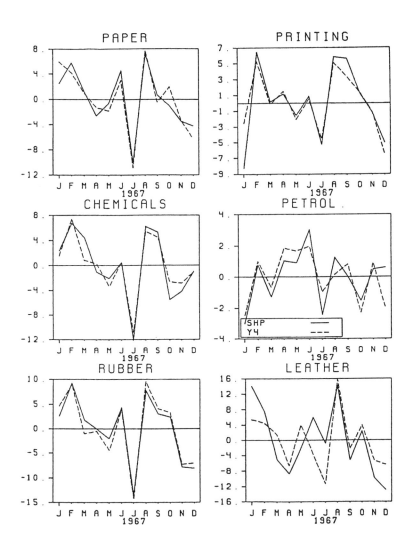

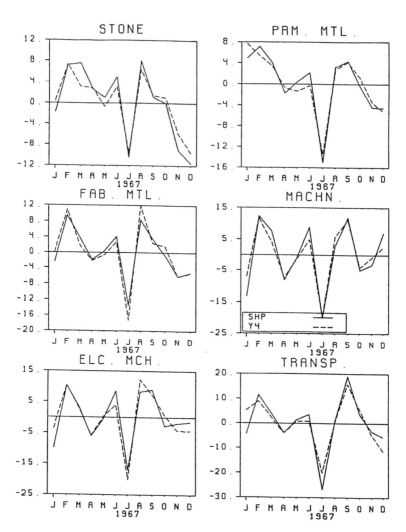

Figure 4.1 *(continued)*

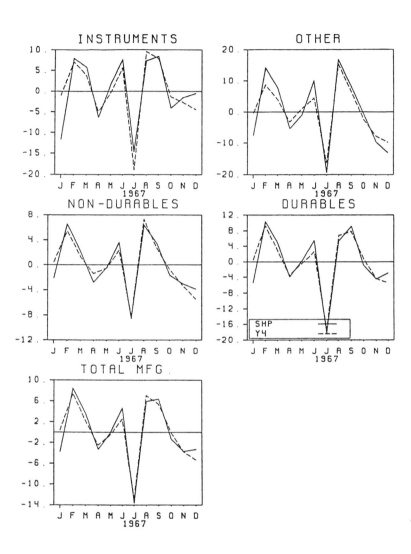

64   Chapter 4

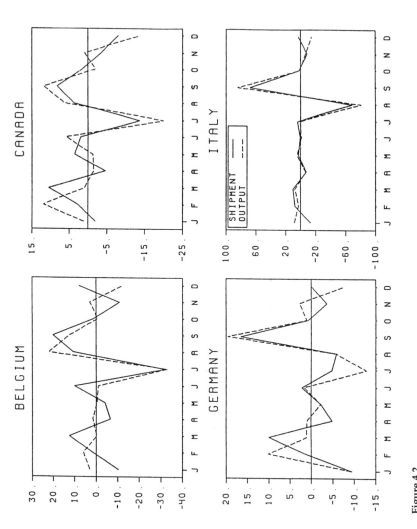

Figure 4.2
Seasonals in production and shipments, other countries. Source: Beaulieu and Miron (1990b), pp. 21, 22.

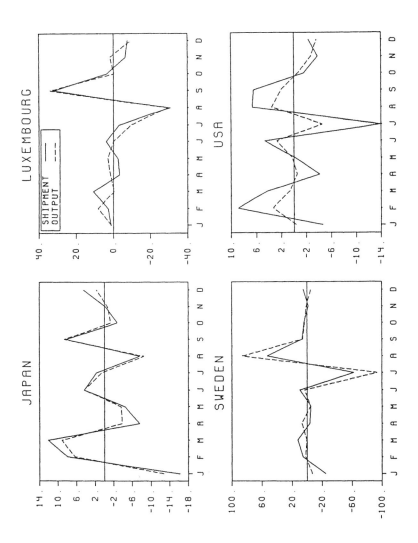

To examine the cyclicality of labor input over the seasonal cycle, one can estimate instrumental variables (IV) regressions of the log growth rate of output on the log growth rate of labor input, using seasonal dummies as the only instruments. For comparison, one can also estimate the elasticity of output with respect to labor input over the business cycle by regressing the log growth rate of output on the log growth rate of labor input, with seasonal dummies included in the regression. Output is defined as shipments plus the change in inventories (Y4, as defined in Miron and Zeldes 1989). Labor input is defined as average weekly hours of production workers times the number of production workers.[5]

Table 4.1 displays the results of this exercise. The seasonal variation in output is highly elastic with respect to the seasonal variation in production worker hours for manufacturing as a whole, as well as for the subcategories of durables and nondurables. The result is robust across industries, with twelve industries displaying an elasticity significantly above 1. Even in industries where labor productivity is not procyclical, the elasticity of output with respect to labor input generally exceeds labor's share in output (Hubbard 1986), in contradiction to the implications of constant returns combined with perfect competition. In all but a few cases, the elasticity over the seasonal cycle is greater than that over the business cycle. Indeed, the estimates do not generally show that labor productivity is procyclical over the business cycle, although they usually show the elasticity to be in excess of labor's share.

One can also examine the seasonal and business cycle behavior of labor productivity using analogous data for other countries. As noted in Beaulieu and Miron (1992), the seasonal patterns in labor input match the patterns in manufacturing output in most countries, but with considerably smaller amplitude, suggesting that labor productivity is procyclical over the seasonal cycle.[6] Table 4.2 demonstrates this conclusion formally by reporting the seasonal elasticities of industrial production with respect to hours worked in manufacturing. The coefficients typically exceed 1, indicating strong procyclicality of labor productivity over the seasonal cycle for most countries.

Interpretation of these results is aided by recalling the seasonal patterns in industrial production. Since it is difficult to rationalize the behavior of production as resulting from changes in technology, it is unlikely that procyclical productivity over the seasons reflects shifts in technology, as in seasonal real business cycle models such as Braun

Table 4.1
Elasticity of output (Y4) with respect to labor input

	Seasonal		Nonseasonal	
	Coefficient	Standard deviation	Coefficient	Standard deviation
Food	0.568	.065	0.369	.112
Tobacco	0.779	.166	0.468	.170
Textiles	3.394	.333	0.211	.066
Apparel	1.591	.193	0.499	.191
Lumber	1.413	.151	0.487	.234
Furniture	1.610	.230	0.527	.163
Paper	0.154	.191	0.521	.183
Printing	0.367	.260	−0.188	.436
Chemicals	2.204	.367	1.263	.205
Petroleum	0.416	.138	0.026	.033
Rubber	2.102	.230	0.358	.094
Leather	1.210	.277	0.160	.278
Stone, clay, glass	0.886	.094	0.526	.085
Primary metal	1.366	.212	1.400	.168
Fabricated metal	1.961	.275	0.549	.161
Machinery	4.084	.361	0.595	.206
Electrical machinery	3.600	.039	0.372	.141
Transportation equipment	0.967	.012	0.819	.102
Instruments	3.347	.382	0.970	.309
Other	1.911	.193	0.092	.215
Nondurables	1.297	.091	0.461	.104
Durables	2.077	.157	0.898	.085
Total	1.736	.125	0.689	.088

Source: Beaulieu and Miron (1990a), p. 26.
Notes: The sample period is 1967:5–1987:12.
The data are in log growth rates.
Seasonal coefficients are from an IV regression of output on total production worker hours using seasonal dummies as the only instruments. Standard errors are corrected.
Nonseasonal coefficients are from a regression of output on labor hours and seasonal dummies. Standard errors are corrected.

Table 4.2
Elasticity of output with respect to labor input

	Sample period	Coefficient	Standard error
Austria (HH)	1969:2–1987:3	2.91	.18
Austria (EST)	1965:2–1987:3	1.95	.10
Canada	1960:2–1987:3	−0.02	.15
Germany	1965:2–1987:3	2.36	.12
Greece	1962:2–1987:3	1.68	.23
Japan	1960:2–1987:3	0.31	.06
Norway (males)	1960:2–1970:4	1.13	.07
Sweden (HH)	1968:2–1986:2	1.53	.04
Sweden (EST)	1968:2–1986:2	1.53	.04
United States	1960:2–1987:4	0.51	.10

Source: Beaulieu and Miron (1992), p. 782.
Notes: The standard errors have been corrected using the Newey and West (1987) procedure.
Employment data are from establishment surveys unless otherwise noted.

and Evans (1995) and Chatterjee and Ravikumar (1992). Instead, it is plausible that the failure of labor input to move sufficiently with output over the seasons reflects labor hoarding, particularly that associated with vacations, combined with variation in capital utilization. In the third quarter, many workers on paid vacations are counted as employed, and the hours for which firms pay are counted as hours worked. In comparing the third and the fourth quarters, therefore, measured labor input does not change much, but true labor input does, so output fluctuates more than measured labor input. Rather than paying workers to stay at the firm and not work or incurring the costs associated with labor turnover, firms "store" hoarded labor at the beach.

4.4   The Relation between Money and Output

A final key stylized fact characterizing the business cycle is that nominal money and real activity are highly positively correlated. Whether this correlation reflects a causal mechanism running from money to output, and if so which mechanism, is a matter of much dispute. In Keynesian models such as Fischer (1977), the correlation reflects causation that relies on sticky nominal prices. In the rational expectations with misperceptions models (Lucas 1972, 1973, 1977), the correlation

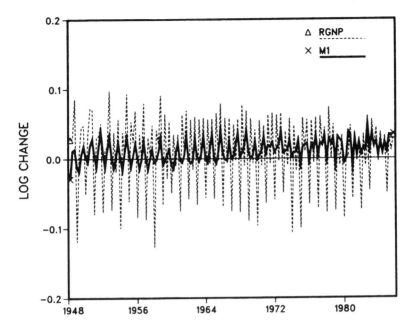

Figure 4.3
Output and money, United States. Source: Barsky and Miron (1989), p. 524.

also reflects causation from money to output but results from informa-tion imperfections. King and Plosser (1984) illustrate in a real, equi-librium business cycle model that the correlation may reflect reverse causality from output to money, a point made earlier by Keynesian op-ponents of monetarism (Tobin 1970).

Figure 4.3 shows a plot of quarterly real GNP growth against the growth of M1. This plot provides for the seasonally unadjusted data an analogue to those in Friedman and Schwartz (1963a, 1982), which, using annual and seasonally adjusted data, demonstrate the tendency toward comovement of real output and nominal money over the busi-ness cycle. The plot suggests that the money-output correlation is as impressive over the seasonal cycle as over the business cycle.[7]

Interpretation of figure 4.3 is facilitated by a joint examination with the seasonal factors presented in table 3.2. Both money and output show strong growth between the third and fourth quarters. The lev-els of both peak in the fourth quarter and then fall markedly going into the first quarter. Money and output do not move together between the first and second quarters. Clearly the fourth quarter comovement dominates. The regression of the seasonal pattern in real output growth on the seasonal pattern in nominal money growth gives a coefficient of 2.84, with a standard error of .38.[8] The standard deviation of the seasonal fluctuations in output is consistently greater (by a factor of 4) than that in money. Friedman and Schwartz (1963b) found that over the business cycle, the magnitude of the fluctuations in output exceeds that in money by a factor of 2.

The data in table 3.30 on the seasonal behavior of money address this issue for a range of other countries. The most dramatic aspect of the seasonal patterns is large, positive growth rates in December followed by large, negative growth rates in January. This behavior mimics the most dramatic fluctuations in GDP and especially retail sales, suggesting a strong comovement of money and output over the seasonal cycle. Table 4.3 demonstrates this more formally by presenting seasonal dummy IV regressions of money on retail sales in OECD countries. Money is highly correlated with retail sales in all instances but one.

The most obvious interpretation of these results is that the relation between money and output over the seasonal cycle represents a prime

Table 4.3
Money and output, OECD countries

	Sample period	Coefficient	Standard error
Argentina	1977:2–1987:2	.45	.33
Australia	1960:2–1987:3	.23	.03
Austria	1973:2–1987:3	.31	.04
Canada	1961:2–1987:3	.36	.04
Finland	1970:2–1987:2	.65	.12
Germany	1968:2–1987:3	.68	.06
Italy	1970:2–1984:4	.68	.08
Japan	1965:2–1987:1	.39	.02
Netherlands	1977:2–1987:3	.52	.06
Norway	1978:2–1987:3	.35	.22
Sweden	1970:2–1987:3	.12	.05
Taiwan	1968:2–1987:3	−.36	.11
United Kingdom	1963:2–1987:3	.54	.14
United States	1948:2–1985:4	.13	.02

Source: Beaulieu and Miron (1990b), p. 20.
Note: The standard errors have been corrected using the Newey and West (1987) procedure.

example of the endogenous money mechanism discussed by King and Plosser (1984). In the fourth quarter, an exogenous increase in consumption spending drives up the demand for money, and both private banks and central banks respond by expanding the money stock.[9] This hypothesis is consistent with the observed absence of seasonals in nominal interest rates (Beaulieu and Miron 1990b, table B11). The conclusion that money must be endogenous rather than exogenous with respect to the seasonal fluctuations in output is reinforced by the view that a regular, fully anticipated change in the money stock is unlikely to have real effects (Lucas 1972).

As discussed in Mankiw and Miron (1991), however, seasonal changes in money may have real effects on the economy if prices are sticky with respect to seasonal fluctuations in demand. As shown above, seasonals in prices are small in most countries, which is consistent with, but does not imply, sticky prices. Mankiw and Miron provide evidence that the change in seasonal monetary policy associated with the founding of the Federal Reserve is also associated with a significant change in the seasonal behavior of real output. This suggests the Fed's accommodation of seasonal asset demands has an independent effect on the seasonal behavior of output. The interpretation of the seasonal correlation between money and output is therefore still open to question.

4.5   Summary

Seasonal cycles and business cycles are similar in many respects. Both display an important set of stylized facts, including the comovement of output across sectors, the comovement of production and sales, the excess elasticity of output with respect to labor input, and the comovement of money and output. Interpretation of these stylized facts over the seasonal cycle is easier than interpretation over the business cycle because the necessary identifying restrictions are more readily available. For example, the high seasonal elasticity of output with respect to labor input likely reflects labor hoarding, since paid vacations are a known, readily verifiable phenomenon and appear to coincide almost exactly with the periods of excess elasticity.

The natural question to ask, in the light of these results, is whether the conclusions presented above about the reasons for particular stylized facts over the seasonal cycle apply to the business cycle as well. For example, does the conclusion that labor hoarding explains the high elasticity of output with respect to labor input over the seasonal cycle imply that labor hoarding explains the high elasticity over the business cycle?

As a matter of logic, the answer to this question is no. It is possible to construct models, for example, in which the high elasticity reflects labor hoarding over the seasonal cycle but technology shocks, say, over the business cycle. The presence of labor hoarding with respect to some types of fluctuations might shift one's priors about the likelihood of such behavior with respect to other fluctuations, but it does not definitively require such a conclusion. The next chapter addresses the question of whether conclusions derived about seasonal cycles apply to business cycles as well.

5   Interactions between Seasonal Cycles and Business Cycles

This chapter discusses evidence that suggests a general similarity of the economic propagation mechanisms for seasonal cycles and business cycles (Beaulieu, MacKie-Mason, and Miron 1992). It begins by documenting a strong, positive correlation across countries and industries between the standard deviation of the seasonal component and the standard deviation of the nonseasonal component of aggregate variables such as output, labor input, interest rates, and prices. It then explains why the most plausible explanation for this finding is that the economic propagation mechanism transmitting seasonal fluctuations from exogenous to endogenous variables is systematically related to that transmitting business cycle fluctuations. Finally, it develops a simple model that embodies this characteristic and presents suggestive evidence for this model.

5.1   Methods and Data

Does a correlation exist across sectors between the amount of seasonal variation and the amount of business cycle variation in macroeconomic time series? This question can be formalized as follows.

Assume one has time-series observations on a variable X for each of I sectors, where sector denotes either a country or an industry within a country. Let X_t^i denote the observation in sector i at time t. For instance, X_t^i might denote output in the ith U.S. manufacturing industry at date t. As above, assume

$$x_t^i = \sum_{k=1}^{12} \xi_k^i d_t^k + \epsilon_t^i \,, \tag{5.1}$$

where x_t^i is the first difference of the log of X_t^i, d_t^k is a dummy for month k, and ϵ_t^i is covariance stationary. Define the seasonal and nonseasonal components of x_t^i as

$$x_t^{i,s} = \sum_{k=1}^{12} \xi_k^i d_t^k \tag{5.2}$$

$$x_t^{i,n} = x_t^i - \sum_{k=1}^{12} \xi_k^i d_t^k \tag{5.3}$$

The two components are orthogonal according to this decomposition. Under this decomposition, the amounts of seasonal and nonseasonal variation can be measured by the standard deviations of the seasonal and nonseasonal components of the variables:

$$\sigma_i^s(x) = (\text{var}(x_t^{i,s}))^{\frac{1}{2}} \tag{5.4}$$

$$\sigma_i^n(x) = (\text{var}(x_t^{i,n}))^{\frac{1}{2}} \tag{5.5}$$

The question is, then, whether the amounts of seasonal and nonseasonal variation are correlated across sectors—that is, whether β_2 is nonzero in the equation

$$\sigma_i^n = \beta_1 + \beta_2 \sigma_i^s + v_i , \tag{5.6}$$

where $i = 1, \ldots, I$ denotes either countries or industries. Nothing in the assumption about the data-generating processes implies a correlation in either direction.

The strategy for estimating β_2 is as follows:

1. Estimate the seasonal dummy coefficients, ξ_k, in equation 5.1 with OLS for each variable in each sector.

2. Compute measures of the seasonal and nonseasonal standard deviations by substituting the estimates of the ξ_k into equations 5.2 and 5.3 and taking standard deviations over time.[1]

3. Estimate the cross-sectional regression,

$$\hat{\sigma}_i^n = \beta_1 + \beta_2 \hat{\sigma}_i^s + \zeta_i ,$$

by least squares.[2]

The resulting estimates of β_2 might be biased because $\hat{\sigma}_i^s$ and $\hat{\sigma}_i^n$ are estimated and therefore measured with error. This measurement error, and thus the bias in estimates of β_2, disappears as the number of time-series observations on the x_t^i approaches infinity, but the estimates might still be biased in finite samples. Beaulieu, MacKie-Mason, and Miron use a Monte Carlo experiment, however, to show that the amount of such bias is insignificant in most cases.[3]

The analysis that follows uses two different data sets. The first consists of time-series observations on six aggregate variables—real retail sales, industrial production, the nominal money stock, the consumer price index (CPI), nominal interest rates, and ex post real interest rates—from twenty-five OECD countries (see Beaulieu and Miron 1990b for details).[4] Most series are available monthly, seasonally unadjusted, for the period 1960:1 through 1987:12, although some are available for only a subsample.

The second data set consists of time-series observations on ten different variables in each of twenty two-digit U.S. manufacturing industries (see Beaulieu and Miron 1990a for details). The variables are two measures of production—shipments plus the change in inventories (Y4) and industrial production—shipments, inventories, four measures of labor input—production worker employment, total employment, average production worker hours, and total production worker hours—nominal wages, and prices. Each series is available monthly, seasonally unadjusted for all twenty industries for the period 1967:4 through 1987:12, except for the price series, which is available for only a subset of industries and in one case—transportation—for only a shorter sample period.

5.2   Cross-Sectional Correlation Results

Consider the cross-country evidence first. Figures 5.1 through 5.6 plot the nonseasonal standard deviation versus the seasonal standard deviation for real retail sales, industrial production, the nominal money stock, the price level, the nominal interest rate, and the real interest rate.[5] The figures also show the OLS regression of the nonseasonal standard deviation on the seasonal standard deviation and a constant.

Table 5.1 reports weighted least-squares regressions. The table gives the coefficient and t-statistic from the regression of the nonseasonal standard deviation on the seasonal standard deviation across countries for each of the six variables. The results in the table confirm that a strong, positive correlation is present across countries between the amount of business cycle variation and the amount of seasonal variation. The correlation is statistically significant at better than the 3 percent level for all six variables.

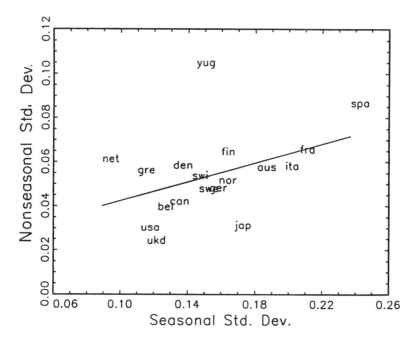

Figure 5.1
Real retail sales. Source: Beaulieu, MacKie-Mason, and Miron (1992), p. 626.

Figures 5.7 through 5.16 plot the standard deviation of the non-seasonal component against the standard deviation of the seasonal component for the ten measures of economic activity in two-digit U.S. manufacturing industries. Table 5.2 reports OLS estimates of the regressions illustrated in the figures. For both measures of output, shipments, and inventories, the amounts of seasonal and business cycle variation are strongly, positively correlated across industries. The same result holds for total hours, average hours, total employment, and production worker employment. The cross-sectional correlation is quite strong for wages but only modest for prices.

The results reported here are robust along several dimensions. In particular, they are not sensitive to the exclusion of apparent outliers, and they are not sensitive to the inclusion of various country or industry characteristics as controls.[6] Further, they are independent of stationary stochastic seasonality, and they hold separately for the first and second halves of the sample period. Beaulieu, MacKie-Mason, and Miron (1991) provide detailed documentation for these results.

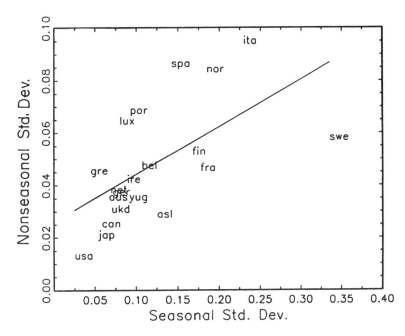

Figure 5.2
Industrial production. Source: Beaulieu, MacKie-Mason, and Miron (1992), p. 627.

5.3   Explanations for the Cross-Sectional Correlations

Taken together, the cross-country and cross-industry correlations constitute a robust stylized fact: countries and industries with large seasonal cycles also have large business cycles. This section discusses possible explanations for this finding. It first indicates in a general framework the factors that can account for the cross-sectional correlations and then uses this framework to discuss the implications of the results for the relation between seasonal cycles and business cycles.

5.3.1   A General Framework

Suppose the reduced-form equation for an endogenous variable, y, relates it to two exogenous variables x_1 and x_2,

$$y = f(x_1, x_2),$$

where time and sector subscripts are suppressed for convenience. Each of x_1, x_2 is the sum of a stationary nonseasonal component and a deterministic seasonal component,

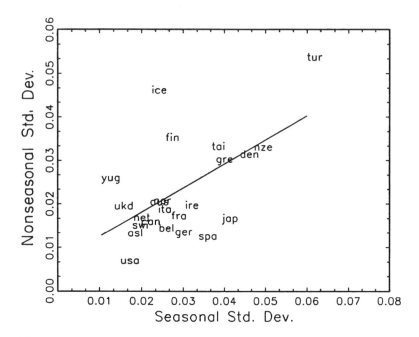

Figure 5.3
Nominal money stock. Source: Beaulieu, MacKie-Mason, and Miron (1992), p. 628.

$$x_1 = x_1^n + x_1^s,$$

$$x_2 = x_2^n + x_2^s.$$

This specification is consistent with a large range of models. For example, x_2 may represent lagged x_1. Alternatively, x_1 may be the seasonal component of a series, while x_2 is the nonseasonal component of the same series (i.e., $x_1^n = x_2^s = 0$).

Define $\bar{x}_i$ as the unconditional mean of x_i^n plus the mean of x_i^s. Let $\tilde{x}_i^n$ and $\tilde{x}_i^s$ be the deviations from the respective means. The second-order Taylor expansion of $f(\cdot, \cdot)$ around $(\bar{x}_1, \bar{x}_2)$ is

$$y \approx f(\bar{x}_1, \bar{x}_2) + \sum_{i=1}^{2} f_i(\bar{x}_1, \bar{x}_2)(\tilde{x}_i^n + \tilde{x}_i^s)$$

$$+ \frac{1}{2} \sum_{i=1}^{2} \sum_{j=1}^{2} f_{ij}(\bar{x}_1, \bar{x}_2)(\tilde{x}_i^n + \tilde{x}_i^s)(\tilde{x}_j^n + \tilde{x}_j^s),$$

where subscripts on $f(\cdot, \cdot)$ denote differentiation.[7] Since x_1^s and x_2^s are deterministic, the seasonal and nonseasonal components of y are

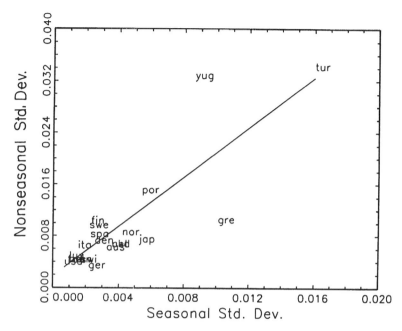

Figure 5.4
Price level. Source: Beaulieu, MacKie-Mason, and Miron (1992), p. 629.

$$y^s = f(\bar{x}_1, \bar{x}_2) + \sum_{i=1}^{2} f_i(\bar{x}_1, \bar{x}_2)\tilde{x}_i^s + \frac{1}{2}\sum_{i=1}^{2}\sum_{j=1}^{2} f_{ij}(\bar{x}_1, \bar{x}_2)\left(\tilde{x}_i^s \tilde{x}_j^s + E[\tilde{x}_i^n \tilde{x}_j^n | t]\right),$$

$$y^n = y - y^s,$$

where $E[\tilde{x}_i^n \tilde{x}_j^n | t]$ denotes the expectation of the product conditional on the season. Assuming that such a decomposition holds in each of I countries or industries, the question is under what conditions the standard deviations of y^n and y^s are correlated across sectors.

Cross-sectional correlation between the seasonal and nonseasonal standard deviations of the endogenous variable y can arise in three ways. First, the seasonal and nonseasonal standard deviations of the exogenous variables might be correlated cross-sectionally. In the above framework, this means $\sigma(x_i^s)$ is correlated with $\sigma(x_i^n)$. Second, nonlinearities in the relationship between the endogenous and exogenous variables can generate the cross-sectional results. In taking the standard deviations of y^s and y^n above, the nonlinearities in $f(\cdot, \cdot)$ produce a correlation between $\sigma(y^s)$ and $\sigma(y^n)$ because of the term $E[\tilde{x}_i^n \tilde{x}_j^n | t]$. Third, the parameters transmitting seasonal fluctuations

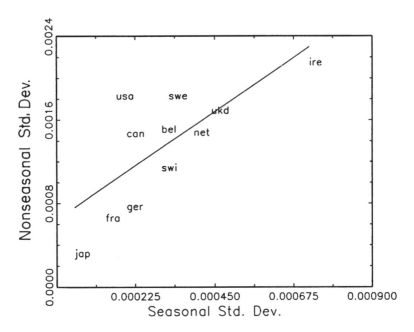

Figure 5.5
Nominal interest rates. Source: Beaulieu, MacKie-Mason, and Miron (1992), p. 630.

from exogenous to endogenous variables might be systematically related to those transmitting nonseasonal fluctuations. For example, the
parameters $f_i(\bar{x}_1, \bar{x}_2)$ might multiply both the seasonal and nonseasonal components of the x_i. The three possibilities are not mutually
exclusive.

The analysis that follows does not pursue the possibility that the seasonal and nonseasonal standard deviations of the exogenous variables
are correlated cross-sectionally. The attractiveness of this explanation
depends on the context. Sometimes the exogenous shocks are unobservable, so explaining the observed correlation in this way is neither
testable nor enlightening. The second possibility—nonlinearities—
is potentially part of the explanation for the empirical results, but
nonlinearities can produce a correlation in either direction so it is important to isolate the particular nonlinearities that are relevant.

Section 5.4 presents a model that explains the empirical findings by
incorporating a link between the parameters relating seasonal and nonseasonal fluctuations. The particular model considered incorporates a
nonlinearity, but this is not crucial for the results. Before presenting the

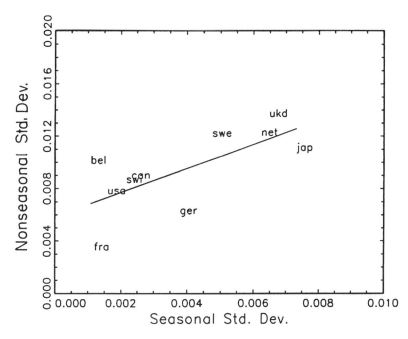

Figure 5.6
Real interest rates. Source: Beaulieu, MacKie-Mason, and Miron (1992), p. 631.

Table 5.1
Cross-country regressions

	Retail sales	Industrial production	Money	Prices	Nominal rate	Real rate
Coefficient	0.22	0.18	0.51	1.91	2.27	0.86
t-statistic	(2.36)	(2.42)	(2.93)	(4.74)	(3.83)	(3.18)
$\bar{R}^2$		0.13	0.34	0.17	0.66	0.47	0.52
Sample size	18	20	23	21	11	10

Source: Beaulieu, MacKie-Mason, and Miron (1992), p. 631.

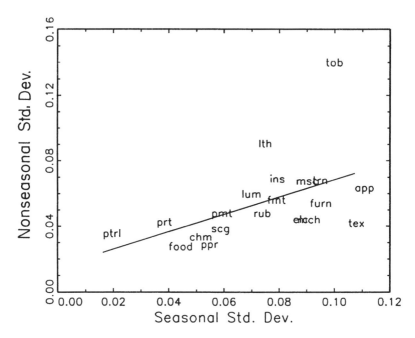

Figure 5.7
Shipments plus change in inventories. Source: Beaulieu, MacKie-Mason, and Miron
(1992), p. 632.

model, however, the next section uses the framework described to discuss the implications of the empirical findings for understanding the
relation between seasonal cycles and business cycles.

5.3.2   The Seasonal Cycle and the Business Cycle

It is common practice in economic modeling to abstract from seasonal
variation, presumably because such variation is "irrelevant" for the
study of what is interesting: the nonseasonal variation. The irrele-
vance of seasonal variation may occur because seasonal fluctuations
result from different exogenous sources than nonseasonal fluctuations
do. For instance, seasonality may result from holidays, while business cycles result from monetary surprises. More important, seasonal
variation might be irrelevant to the study of business cycle variation
because the mechanism by which impulses are propagated treats seasonal shocks differently from nonseasonal shocks. One reason for this
second condition may be that seasonals are anticipated.

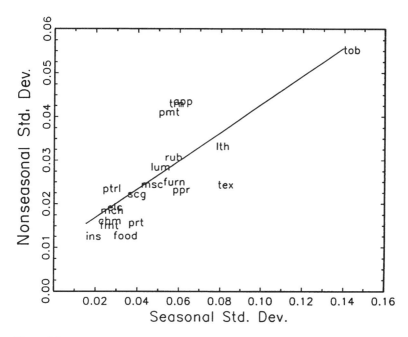

Figure 5.8
Industrial production. Source: Beaulieu, MacKie-Mason, and Miron (1992), p. 633.

These assumptions about the nature of seasonal cycles relative to business cycles imply two restrictions on the analytic framework described above. The first amounts to saying that seasonal cycles are due, say, to x_1, while business cycles are due to x_2 (*i.e.*, $x_1^n = x_2^s = 0$, $\forall t$). The second assumption implies that the parameters transmitting seasonal fluctuations from exogenous to endogenous variables have no connection to those transmitting business cycle fluctuations; for example, $f_1(\bar{x}_1, \bar{x}_2)$ is unrelated to $f_2(\bar{x}_1, \bar{x}_2)$ in the case where $x_1^n = x_2^s = 0$.

If both these conditions hold, the model does not imply a cross-sectional correlation between the seasonal and nonseasonal standard deviations of y, assuming the other possible sources of this correlation are absent.[8] This means that when models assume significantly different sources and propagation mechanisms for seasonal cycles and business cycles, it is more difficult for those models to accommodate the empirical facts presented here. The examples presented next demonstrate these points. The examples are simple, but they help fix ideas.

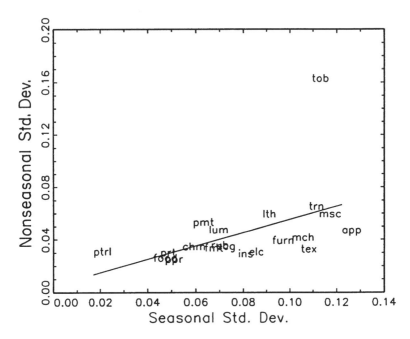

Figure 5.9
Shipments. Source: Beaulieu, MacKie-Mason, and Miron (1992), p. 634.

Consider first the textbook aggregate supply–aggregate demand model due to Lucas (1973):

$$m_t - p_t = y_t \tag{5.7}$$

$$y_t = \theta(p_t - E_{t-1}p_t) + s_t , \tag{5.8}$$

where s_t is a seasonal dummy shifter in the technology (the natural rate), m_t is the nominal money stock, p_t is the price level, y_t is real output, and θ is a parameter. All variables are measured in logs. Equation 5.7 is a standard aggregate demand curve, and equation 5.8 is a standard Lucas supply function, with the natural rate replaced by the seasonal dummy shifter s_t.

The solution for output is

$$y_t = \frac{\theta}{1+\theta}(m_t - E_{t-1}m_t) + s_t .$$

This example embodies in a simple way both of the two notions described above. First, the sources of seasonal and business cycle fluctuations are different. Seasonal variation is due to technology shifts, and business cycle variation is due to monetary surprises. Second, the

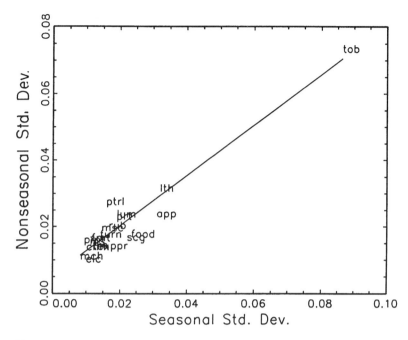

Figure 5.10
Inventories. Source: Beaulieu, MacKie-Mason, and Miron (1992), p. 635.

mechanism transmitting shocks from exogenous to endogenous variables is different as well. No parameter multiplies both the technology
shocks and the money shocks. The model cannot explain the cross-
sectional correlation in output across countries unless those countries
in which the variance of the anticipated technology seasonal is large
are also those in which the monetary authority puts a large variance
into the money stock surprises. This condition need not hold.

A second useful example is the standard permanent income model
of consumption. Assume that a representative consumer faces the
problem

$$\max_{C_t} E_t \sum_{t=0}^{\infty} \beta^t U_t(C_t) \tag{5.9}$$

subject to

$$A_{t+1} = R(A_t + y_t - C_t) \tag{5.10}$$

$$A_0 = \bar{A}_0 \tag{5.11}$$

$$R\beta = 1, \tag{5.12}$$

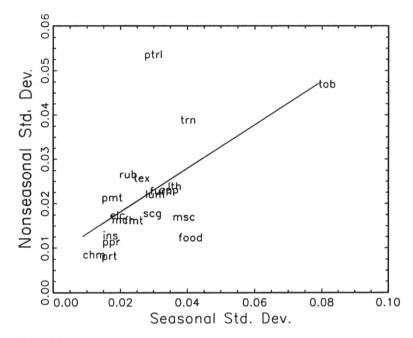

Figure 5.11
Production worker hours. Source: Beaulieu, MacKie-Mason, and Miron (1992), p. 636.

where C_t is consumption, y_t is income, A_t is beginning-of-period wealth, R is the constant, gross real interest rate, and β is the consumer's rate of time preference.

Suppose the utility function is quadratic with a seasonal shifter in the intercept of the marginal utility function,

$$U_t(C_t) = \alpha_t C_t - \gamma C_t^2,$$

where α_t is a seasonal dummy process. Then the solution for the change in consumption is

$$C_t - C_{t-1} = \frac{1}{2\gamma}(\alpha_t - \alpha_{t-1}) + \frac{R-1}{R}\sum_{s=t}^{\infty} R^{-(s-t)}\left(\mathrm{E}_t y_s - \mathrm{E}_{t-1} y_s\right).$$

The variance of the nonseasonal change in consumption depends only on R and the properties of y_t. The variance of the seasonal change in consumption depends only on γ and the properties of α_t.

This example shows why the sharp distinction between anticipated and unanticipated shocks makes the empirical findings hard to explain.

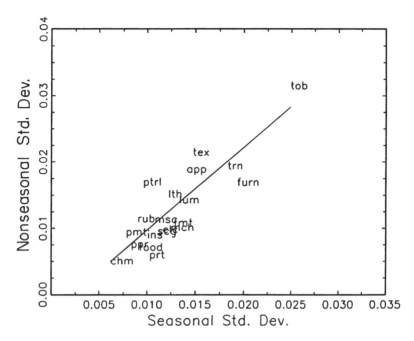

Figure 5.12
Average production worker hours. Source: Beaulieu, MacKie-Mason, and Miron (1992), p. 637.

Changes in consumption are driven by revisions in forecasts of perma-nent income, and such revisions are themselves unforecastable under rational expectations. If income is the only possible source of seasonal-ity in this model, consumption is not seasonal. In order to explain the observed seasonality of consumption, it is necessary to postulate a sea-sonal in preferences. Then, in order for the model to accommodate the cross-sectional results, a cross-sectional correlation must exist between the variance of the seasonal shift in preferences and the variance of the shock to income. Again, this condition need not hold.

This discussion does not prove that the exogenous variables produc-ing business cycles are the same as those producing seasonal cycles, nor does it prove that seasonal and nonseasonal shocks, whatever their source, propagate through the economy in the same manner. The dis-cussion does show that models of aggregate fluctuations in which the sources and impact of seasonal fluctuations are fundamentally differ-ent from those of business cycle fluctuations have difficulty encom-passing the empirical findings above.

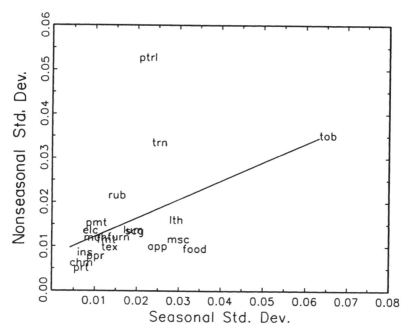

Figure 5.13
Production worker employment. Source: Beaulieu, MacKie-Mason, and Miron (1992), p. 638.

5.4   Capacity Choice and Output Fluctuations

This section presents a model that generates some of the cross-sectional correlations documented above. This model is not the only way to explain the correlations, but it illustrates that a model consistent with the findings can produce interesting results.[9] Moreover, the main innovation in this model is important and worth pursuing in its own right.

The basic idea is illustrated in figure 5.17, which shows a firm's marginal cost curve along with the demand curves faced by that firm in various states of the world. The diagram portrays two seasons with the state of demand uncertain around its mean level in each season. The MC curve begins to rise steeply at some point, which can loosely be thought of as "capacity." The firm obtains flexibility by purchasing "excess" capacity, so the firm can expand output over a larger range without a substantial increase in marginal cost. In the top panel, the firm faces a demand curve that does not shift much seasonally. It therefore chooses a level of capacity that is close to the average level of output. In

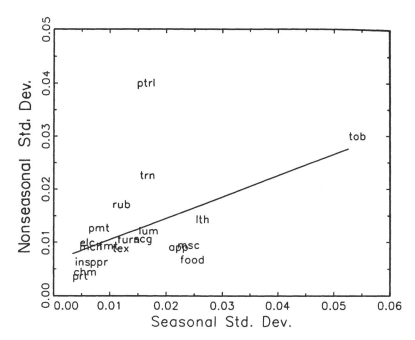

Figure 5.14
Total employment. Source: Beaulieu, MacKie-Mason, and Miron (1992), p. 639.

the bottom panel, the firm faces a much greater seasonal variance in demand, so optimal capacity choice is greater, implying that nonseasonal shocks in the low-demand season have a bigger effect on output than they would in the world described in the top panel. The seasonal variation in demand is not special; an increase in the amount of nonseasonal variation also leads to an increase in optimal capacity.

5.4.1   The Basic Model

The simplest model of capacity has a firm with constant marginal costs up to the capacity limit, giving a backward L-shaped marginal cost curve. Such a model typically yields a corner solution for output, since the solution to the first-order conditions may be greater than capacity before imposing the inequality constraint. To ensure interior solutions, the derivations that follow assume a hyperbolic marginal cost function for which the vertical asymptote can be thought of as the binding capacity constraint.[10]

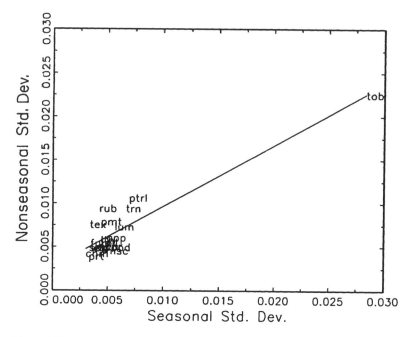

Figure 5.15
Wages. Source: Beaulieu, MacKie-Mason, and Miron (1992), p. 640.

The firm's marginal cost curve is given by:

$$MC = cx_s \frac{\phi}{\phi - x_s},$$

where x_s is the firm's output in season s, c is a fixed parameter, and ϕ is a parameter (the vertical asymptote) chosen ex ante by the firm at some cost per unit of "flexibility." Purchasing more ϕ lengthens the range over which the marginal cost curve is relatively flat and hence increases the firm's output response to demand shifts.

Suppose the firm chooses its technology once a year. During the year, it produces for one high and one low season, after which the technology disintegrates. The inverse demand curve is linear,

$$p_s = a_s - \frac{b}{2}x_s,$$

where $a_s = a + \delta\sigma + \tilde{\epsilon}$ with a fixed, $\tilde{\epsilon}$ is a white noise demand shock, $\delta = \{-1, 1\}$ in the low and high seasons, respectively, and σ is the magnitude of the seasonal shift in demand.

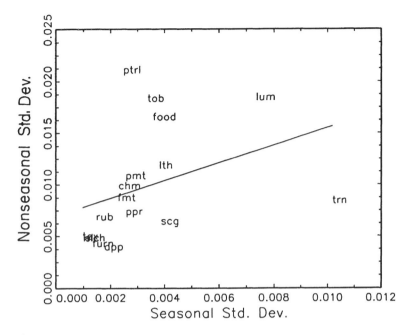

Figure 5.16
Prices. Source: Beaulieu, MacKie-Mason, and Miron (1992), p. 641.

If output decisions are made after the realization of the current period's shock, then given technology, ϕ, optimal output in a period s is

$$x_s^* = \frac{(a_s + [b+c]\phi) - \left[(a_s + [b+c]\phi)^2 - 4ba_s\phi\right]^{\frac{1}{2}}}{2b} \qquad (5.13)$$

and maximized period profits are

$$\pi_s^* = (a_s - \frac{b}{2}x_s^*)x_s^* - c\phi[\phi \ln \phi - \phi \ln(\phi - x_s^*) - x_s^*]. \qquad (5.14)$$

Both seasons are the same length, and the firm does not discount across
the two seasons. Then the firm's optimal ex ante capacity choice is
obtained by maximizing the expected sum of period profits, minus
the cost of purchasing capacity, $q\phi$. No explicit solution to this model
exists, but numerical solutions can illustrate its properties.

For all parameter values tested, the model yields a positive correlation between the seasonal and nonseasonal standard deviations of output as the seasonal demand shift changes. Two typical sets of results
are given in tables 5.3A and 5.3B. The correlation coefficient between

Table 5.2
Cross-industry regressions

	Y4[a]	IP	Shipments	Inventories	Production worker hours
Coefficient	0.53	0.32	0.50	0.76	0.49
t-statistic	(2.55)	(9.50)	(2.05)	(25.85)	(7.39)
$\bar{R}^2$	0.22	0.60	0.18	0.91	0.35
Sample size	20	20	20	20	20

	Average hours	Production workers	Total employment	Wages	Prices
Coefficient	1.25	0.42	0.40	0.70	0.88
t-statistic	(8.00)	(5.45)	(6.39)	(28.19)	(1.34)
$\bar{R}^2$	0.73	0.20	0.22	0.86	0.09
Sample size	20	20	20	20	17

Source: Beaulieu, MacKie-Mason, and Miron (1992), p. 642.
Note: OLS regression results except for prices, which is estimated by weighted least squares.
a. Y4 is shipments plus the change in inventories.

the standard deviations of the seasonal and nonseasonal components of output is greater than 0.9 in both cases. Thus, the model is consistent with the facts presented here.[11]

5.4.2   Empirical Verification

Thorough empirical testing of the model is beyond the scope of this book, in large part because the model is too preliminary to withstand detailed scrutiny. To illustrate the model's potential, however, this section examines one simple implication that is likely robust to the most obvious theoretical extensions. The prediction is that output exhibits a particular form of seasonal heteroskedasticity.

Imagine nonseasonal stochastic shifts in the intercept of the demand curve in each season (see figure 5.17). The low season will exhibit substantially more variation in realized output than the high season because of the effective truncation of high-season output by the capacity constraint as well as because of the greater slope of the MC curve up to the level of capacity. One should therefore see seasonal heteroskedasticity in the nonseasonal output residuals—that is, different

Low Seasonal Variance

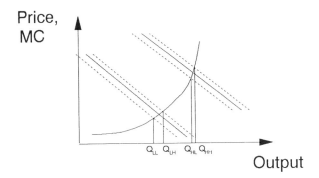

High Seasonal Variance

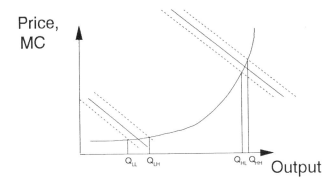

Figure 5.17
Fluctuations in demand and the choice of capacity. Source: Beaulieu, MacKie-Mason, and Miron (1992), p. 645.

nonseasonal variances in different seasons. The prediction is stronger than merely saying that output will be seasonally heteroskedastic; the model implies that the variance in the high season is lower than in the low season.

Testing this proposition is complicated when production might contain a unit root, since under that condition, the theoretical variance of the level of output conditioned only on the season is infinite. Although the variance of growth rates is finite, the model does not predict a pattern relating heteroskedasticity in the growth rate variances to the seasonals in the growth rates. The variance of the growth rates,

Table 5.3A
Simulated capacity model

Seasonal shift	Optimal "capacity"	Standard deviation of output		Nonseasonal standard deviation of output	
σ	ϕ^{*a}	Seasonal	Nonseasonal	Low season	High season
0.0	5.661	0.000	0.169	0.029	0.029
0.5	5.676	0.085	0.170	0.032	0.026
1.0	5.722	0.173	0.174	0.037	0.024
1.5	5.798	0.263	0.179	0.042	0.022
2.0	5.905	0.359	0.186	0.048	0.021
2.5	6.044	0.462	0.195	0.056	0.020
3.0	6.216	0.573	0.205	0.065	0.019
3.5	6.419	0.694	0.217	0.075	0.019
4.0	6.654	0.825	0.230	0.087	0.019
4.5	6.920	0.966	0.244	0.100	0.019
5.0	7.214	1.119	0.258	0.113	0.020
5.5	7.536	1.282	0.272	0.128	0.020
6.0	7.882	1.455	0.286	0.142	0.021
6.5	8.249	1.637	0.299	0.157	0.021
7.0	8.636	1.828	0.312	0.172	0.022
7.5	9.039	2.026	0.324	0.186	0.023
8.0	9.457	2.231	0.335	0.200	0.024
Correl.[b]			0.997		

Source: Beaulieu, MacKie-Mason, and Miron (1992), p. 648.
Note: Each row contains the results from a different simulation, with the seasonal shift parameter indicated. For all simulations, the other parameter values are $e = \pm 1$; $a = 10$; $b = 1$; $c = 1$; $\delta = 0.5$; $q = 1$.
a. ϕ^* is the optimal choice of the flexibility parameter ("capacity").
b. Correl. gives the correlation between the seasonal standard deviation of output and the nonseasonal standard deviation of output.

however, should be related to the seasonal in the level of output. Assume that the process for output is integrated because the process for demand is integrated. The firm adjusts output more in response to a shock to demand growth if capacity is slack than if capacity is tight because when capacity is slack, MC is relatively flat. The nonseasonal output growth rate variance should be high when the level of output is low.

Beaulieu, MacKie-Mason, and Miron (1992) verify this intuition with a twenty-year simulation of the model in which the stochastic demand shock is integrated. This produces integration in pro-

Table 5.3B
Simulated capacity model

Seasonal shift	Optimal "capacity"	Standard deviation of output		Nonseasonal standard deviation of output	
σ	ϕ^{*a}	Seasonal	Nonseasonal	Low season	High season
0.0	2.475	0.000	0.051	0.003	0.003
0.5	2.480	0.027	0.053	0.004	0.002
1.0	2.494	0.055	0.057	0.005	0.002
1.5	2.518	0.087	0.065	0.007	0.001
2.0	2.554	0.124	0.077	0.011	0.001
2.5	2.604	0.170	0.093	0.016	0.001
3.0	2.670	0.226	0.112	0.024	0.001
3.5	2.754	0.296	0.133	0.035	0.001
4.0	2.858	0.382	0.156	0.048	0.001
4.5	2.982	0.484	0.177	0.062	0.001
5.0	3.123	0.602	0.195	0.076	0.001
5.5	3.277	0.734	0.210	0.088	0.001
6.0	3.443	0.876	0.222	0.098	0.001
6.5	3.615	1.025	0.231	0.106	0.001
7.0	3.794	1.181	0.238	0.112	0.001
7.5	3.976	1.340	0.244	0.117	0.002
8.0	4.161	1.502	0.248	0.122	0.002
Correl.[b]			0.945		

Source: Beaulieu, MacKie-Mason, and Miron (1992), p. 649.
Note: Each row contains the results from a different simulation, with the seasonal shift parameter indicated. For all simulations, the other parameter values are $e = \pm 1$; $a = 10$; $b = 2.5$; $c = 0.25$; $\delta = 0.5$; $q = 2.5$.
a. ϕ^* is the optimal choice of the flexibility parameter ("capacity").
b. Correl. gives the correlation between the seasonal standard deviation of output and the nonseasonal standard deviation of output.

duction, and all of the results already discussed still hold. In particular, the log growth rate of output is seasonally heteroskedastic, with the growth rate variances decreasing in the seasonal level of output.

The prediction of seasonal heteroskedasticity is tested in the three measures of output considered above: industrial production (IP) across countries, IP across U.S. manufacturing industries, and Y4 across U.S. manufacturing industries. Tables 5.4 through 5.6 report White (1980) tests for any form of seasonal heteroskedasticty under the column labeled "Heteroskedasticity." At the 5 percent level, the data reject the

Table 5.4
Tests for heteroskedasticity: IP, OECD countries

	Heteroskedasticity		Pattern	
Country	χ^2_{11} [a]	p-value	Correlation[b]	p-value
Australia	9.83	0.546	0.420	0.913
Austria	12.69	0.314	−0.147	0.324
Belgium	36.30	0.000	−0.734	0.003
Canada	87.35	0.000	−0.469	0.062
Finland	85.71	0.000	−0.650	0.011
France	77.14	0.000	−0.874	0.000
Germany	58.54	0.000	−0.608	0.018
Greece	59.93	0.000	0.720	0.996
Ireland	20.52	0.039	−0.685	0.007
Italy	67.71	0.000	−0.413	0.091
Japan	30.96	0.001	−0.538	0.035
Luxembourg	140.33	0.000	−0.650	0.011
Netherlands	92.90	0.000	−0.280	0.189
Norway	64.64	0.000	−0.685	0.007
Portugal	52.38	0.000	−0.105	0.373
Spain	86.55	0.000	−0.559	0.029
Sweden	112.89	0.000	−0.455	0.069
United Kingdom	98.26	0.000	−0.161	0.309
United States	32.07	0.001	−0.580	0.024
Yugoslavia	41.13	0.000	−0.329	0.148

Source: Beaulieu, MacKie-Mason, and Miron (1992), p. 651.
Notes: a. χ^2_{11} are statistics for the hypothesis that all monthly variances are the same. P-values are the significance levels for the chi-square statistics.
b. Correl. gives the Spearman Rank Correlation between the monthly variances of the growth rates and the average level of the series in that month. P-values are for test that the correlation ≤ 0 using a t-test approximation.

null of no seasonal heteroskedasticity for eighteen of twenty countries (IP) and fourteen (IP) or seventeen (Y4) of twenty U.S. manufacturing industries. The tables also report test statistics for three U.S. industry aggregates. The results are consistent with those for the individual two-digit industries.

The next test is whether the variance of the growth rate conditional on the month is negatively correlated with the level of production in that month. To calculate the seasonals in the level of production, regress the log level of an industry's or country's production on twelve

Table 5.5
Tests for heteroskedasticity: IP, U.S. manufacturing

Industry	Heteroskedasticity		Pattern	
	χ^2_{11} [a]	p-value	Correlation[b]	p-value
Food	77.67	0.000	−0.154	0.317
Tobacco	23.79	0.014	−0.287	0.183
Textiles	24.19	0.012	−0.776	0.001
Apparel	202.64	0.000	−0.685	0.007
Lumber	26.64	0.005	−0.455	0.069
Furniture	27.85	0.003	−0.315	0.160
Paper	31.50	0.001	−0.301	0.171
Printing	39.61	0.000	0.175	0.707
Chemicals	17.58	0.092	−0.448	0.072
Petroleum	25.23	0.008	−0.531	0.038
Rubber	21.05	0.033	−0.224	0.242
Leather	45.30	0.000	−0.909	0.000
Stone, clay, glass	26.41	0.006	−0.713	0.005
Primary metals	14.60	0.202	−0.517	0.042
Fabricated metals	10.77	0.463	−0.371	0.118
Machinery	11.31	0.417	0.063	0.577
Electrical machinery	34.63	0.000	−0.385	0.109
Transportation equipment	59.71	0.000	−0.804	0.001
Instruments	12.58	0.321	−0.154	0.317
Miscellaneous manufacturing	9.28	0.596	−0.587	0.022
Nondurables	32.47	0.001	−0.007	0.491
Durables	66.01	0.000	−0.671	0.008
Total manufacturing	66.24	0.000	−0.573	0.026

Source: Beaulieu, MacKie-Mason, and Miron (1992), p. 652.
a. See note a to table 5.4.
b. See note b to table 5.4.

Table 5.6
Tests for heteroskedasticity: Y4, U.S. manufacturing

Industry	Heteroskedasticity		Pattern	
	$\chi^{2\,a}_{11}$	p-value	Correlation[b]	p-value
Food	51.01	0.000	−0.294	0.177
Tobacco	25.71	0.007	−0.154	0.317
Textiles	33.66	0.000	0.329	0.852
Apparel	15.40	0.165	−0.580	0.024
Lumber	49.94	0.000	−0.448	0.072
Furniture	11.03	0.441	−0.182	0.286
Paper	47.63	0.000	−0.448	0.072
Printing	23.96	0.013	−0.357	0.128
Chemicals	35.02	0.000	0.070	0.585
Petroleum	16.14	0.136	−0.273	0.196
Rubber	34.69	0.000	−0.629	0.014
Leather	28.49	0.003	−0.182	0.286
Stone, clay, glass	31.58	0.001	−0.392	0.104
Primary metals	29.34	0.002	−0.035	0.457
Fabricated metals	35.30	0.000	−0.734	0.003
Machinery	37.54	0.000	−0.357	0.128
Electrical machinery	45.11	0.000	−0.329	0.148
Transportation equipment	28.19	0.003	−0.629	0.014
Instruments	31.16	0.001	−0.028	0.466
Miscellaneous manufacturing	38.03	0.000	−0.329	0.148
Nondurables	17.07	0.106	−0.175	0.293
Durables	42.73	0.000	−0.385	0.109
Total manufacturing	33.18	0.000	−0.343	0.138

Source: Beaulieu, MacKie-Mason, and Miron (1992), p. 653.
a. See note a to table 5.4.
b. See note b to table 5.4.

monthly dummies and a quadratic trend. The estimates of the seasonal in the level of output are then the twelve coefficients on the monthly dummies. For each country and industry, then calculate the Spearman rank correlation between the variance of the production growth rate in a month and the average level of production in that month. One can also calculate the significance level for the one-sided alternative that the correlation is negative.[12]

The Spearman rank correlations are reported in tables 5.4 through 5.6 under the column headed "Pattern." For all three production series, eighteen of the twenty countries or industries display negative correlations. For countries, with output measured by IP, ten of the correlations are significant at the 5 percent level and three more are significant at the 10 percent level. For industries with output measured by IP, eight of the correlations are significant at 5 percent and two more are significant at 10 percent. For industries with output measured by Y4, four of the correlations are significantly negative at 5 percent and another two at 10 percent. The percentage of negative rank correlations is substantially larger than under the null of no relationship. This conclusion applies even if countries or industries are correlated so that the observed seasonal variance–production level pairs are not independent observations.[13]

These results support the premise in the model that capacity constraints affect production more in high- versus low-demand seasons. They do not show that capacity constraints are chosen endogenously, as suggested above. This is an interesting topic for future work.

5.5   Conclusions

This material presented in this chapter is important at two levels. More important, it makes a compelling case that the economic propagation mechanism responsible for seasonal fluctuations is likely to be closely related to that for business cycle fluctuations. Thus, conclusions derived about aggregate seasonal fluctuations are probably applicable to aggregate business cycle fluctuations.

In addition, the material offers one specific model consistent with the main empirical finding. The explanation clearly requires significant further development at the theoretical level, as well as additional testing of its empirical implications. These are tasks for future work. Nevertheless, this chapter closes with a discussion of some implications of the capacity story for understanding aggregate fluctuations.

The first and perhaps most important implication is that endogenous control of technological flexibility links seasonal cycles and business cycles, so it is not possible to study correctly the two types of fluctuations separately. In the model, the amount of seasonal variation in demand is a crucial determinant of the firm's nonseasonal output variability, and the nonseasonal variation in demand partly determines the firm's seasonal pattern of production. Seasonal and nonseasonal fluctuations therefore interact and jointly determine the mechanisms by which both seasonal cycles and business cycles are propagated.

A corollary is that both anticipated and unanticipated shocks can have real effects, and these effects cannot always be sharply distinguished. Over horizons that matter, firms in the model respond similarly to all shifts in demand, regardless of how well anticipated. The degree of flexibility chosen ex ante affects the ex post response to both anticipated and unanticipated shocks. Of course, if policymakers systematically attempt to exploit the medium-term fixity of technological flexibility, firms will adjust their choice of flexibility (the Lucas 1976 critique). Nevertheless, policies that smooth anticipated fluctuations can have real effects.

A second implication of the model is that the technology is not something that can be treated as exogenously determined, as it is in the real business cycle models of Prescott (1986) and others. Instead, the degree of technological flexibility is chosen endogenously by firms in response to the degree of demand and cost variability. Of course, exogenous technology shocks may be one source of aggregate fluctuations, but the model suggests that the path of technology should not be taken as determined entirely outside the model. As long as output can be produced in more than one way, firms' choice of method is affected by the stochastic environment in which they operate, and this implies interactions between the nature of demand shocks and supply shocks.

Finally, the model is potentially consistent with the view (De Long and Summers 1988) that the stabilization of output has first-order effects on welfare by raising the average level of output in addition to reducing its variance. Over fifty years ago Kuznets (1933) suggested this as a reason for stabilizing the seasonal cycle. Since nothing here models the general equilibrium of the economy, the analysis has no policy implications taken by itself; in particular, unused capacity is not equivalent to socially "excessive" capacity. It does follow, however, even in this simple model, that stabilizing demand—either seasonally or nonseasonally—would reduce the amount of resources invested in capacity and thus have a first-order effect on output.

6

Seasonal Fluctuations and
the Production-Smoothing
Model of Inventories

The material presented so far has described empirical regularities that characterize aggregate seasonal fluctuations, and it has argued that these regularities suggest interesting conclusions about the structure of the macroeconomy and the mechanisms producing both business cycles and seasonal cycles. This material has not, however, used seasonal fluctuations to evaluate an explicit economic model. This chapter is the first of several that attempts this task.

The chapter analyzes the production-smoothing model of inventory accumulation, using the analysis found in Miron and Zeldes (1988). A great deal of research on the empirical behavior of inventories examines some variant of the production-smoothing model of finished goods inventories, but most of the empirical work uses seasonally adjusted data and omits analysis of seasonal fluctuations.[1]

For several reasons, however, the use of seasonally adjusted data to test inventory models is problematic. First, seasonal fluctuations account for a major portion of the variation in production, shipments, and inventories. Thus, any analysis that ignores seasonality has omitted a quantitatively important part of the story. Second, seasonal fluctuations are anticipated and thus seem particularly likely, a priori, to be consistent with the production-smoothing model. Finally, the use of adjusted data is likely to lead to rejection of the model even when it is correct (Summers 1981), since standard adjustment procedures make the adjusted data a two-sided moving average of the underlying unadjusted data.[2] Therefore, the key implication of most rational expectations models—that the error term should be uncorrelated with lagged information—need not hold in the adjusted data even if it does hold in the unadjusted data (Sargent 1978).

The analysis that follows posits a simple version of the production-smoothing model that explicitly accounts for the seasonal fluctuations in production and sales. It then tests this model using seasonally un-adjusted data for six two-digit manufacturing industries. Seasonal-ity enters the model through seasonal shifts in technology, seasonal movements in factor prices, or seasonal shifts in sales. The key re-sult is that the model can account for the high comovement in pro-duction and sales only if the seasonal pattern in sales is virtually identical to that in the technology. Since no obvious reason exists for this condition to hold, the model appears inconsistent with the data.

6.1   The Model

Consider a profit-maximizing firm. Sales by the firm, the price of the firm's output, and the firm's capital stock may be exogenously or endogenously determined. The firm may be a monopolist, a perfect competitor, or something in between. The firm is a competitor in the markets for inputs.

The firm's intertemporal cost minimization problem is

$$\min_{y_{t+j}} E_t \sum_{j=0}^{T} \Gamma_{t,t+j} C_{t+j}(y_{t+j}) \tag{6.1}$$

subject to

$$n_{t+j} = n_{t+j-1}(1 - s'_{t+j-1}) + y_{t+j} - x_{t+j}, \tag{6.2}$$

$$n_{t+j} \geq 0 \ \forall j, \tag{6.3}$$

where y_t is production in period t, x_t is sales in period t, and n_t is the stock of inventories at the end of period t, all measured in units of the output good. The end of the firm's horizon is period T. C_t is the firm's one-period nominal cost function, to be derived shortly. $\Gamma_{t,t+j}$ is the nominal discount factor, defined as the present value at t of one dollar at $t + j$. Thus,

$$\Gamma_{t,t+j} \equiv [\prod_{s=0}^{j-1}(\frac{1}{1 + \tilde{R}_{t+s}})], \tag{6.4}$$

$$\Gamma_{t,t} \equiv 1, \tag{6.5}$$

and

$$\tilde{R}_{t+s} \equiv (1 - m_{t+s+1})R_{t+s}. \tag{6.6}$$

R_t is the pretax cost of capital for the firm, and m_t is the marginal tax rate. E_t indicates the expectation conditioned on time t information.

The term s'_t is the fraction of inventories lost due to storage costs. In the case of linear storage costs, s'_t is a constant, say, s_1. Some researchers assume storage costs are convex in the level of inventories. For example, convex inventory costs are the key factor driving Blinder and Fischer's (1981) model of the real business cycle. The analysis below captures these costs here by writing $s'_t = s_1 + (s_2/2)n_t$.[3]

For any cost-minimizing firm that carries inventories between two periods, the marginal cost of producing an extra unit of output this period and holding it in inventory until next period must equal the expected marginal cost of producing an extra unit of output next period. This first-order condition can be written as

$$MC_t = E_t \left[\frac{MC_{t+1}(1 - s_t)}{1 + \tilde{R}_t} \right] \tag{6.7}$$

or

$$E_t \left[\frac{MC_{t+1}}{MC_t} \frac{(1 - s_t)}{1 + \tilde{R}_t} \right] = 1. \tag{6.8}$$

Rational expectations implies

$$\frac{MC_{t+1}}{MC_t} \frac{(1 - s_t)}{1 + \tilde{R}_t} = 1 + \epsilon_{t+1}, \tag{6.9}$$

where $E_t[\epsilon_{t+1}] = 0$, that is, ϵ_{t+1} is orthogonal to all time t information. The marginal storage cost, s_t, equals $s_1 + s_2 n_t$.[4] The Euler equation is not satisfied when desired inventories are zero.

The production-storage problem of a cost-minimizing firm parallels the consumption-saving problem of a utility-maximizing consumer. The firm's problem is to minimize the expected discounted value of a convex cost function, subject to an expected pattern of sales and costs of holding inventories. The consumer's problem is to maximize the expected discounted value of a concave utility function, subject to an expected pattern of income and return to holding wealth.

The solution to cost minimization yields a first-order condition analogous to the first-order condition implied by the stochastic version of the permanent income hypothesis (Hall 1978), so one can apply the methods of that literature to the production-smoothing model. Production, sales, inventories, the interest rate, and storage costs are analogous to consumption, income, wealth, the rate of time preference, and the return on wealth, respectively. The nonnegativity condition on inventories is analogous to a borrowing constraint in the consumption literature. In the simplest version of this model, the real interest rate, the growth in the capital stock, and productivity growth are all constant. Given the production function above, these assumptions imply that real output follows a geometric random walk with drift. This is analogous to Hall's (1978) condition that consumption follow a random walk with drift.

To implement the model described above requires a specific cost function. Assume a Cobb-Douglas production function with m inputs (q_i, $i = 1, \ldots, m$). Let the last input (q_m) be the capital stock. In each period, the firm thus solves the constrained problem

$$\min_{q_1, q_2, \ldots, q_{m-1}} \sum_{i=1}^{m} w_i q_i \tag{6.10}$$

subject to

$$f(q_1, \ldots, q_m) = \mu \prod_{i=1}^{m} q_i^{a_i} = \bar{y}, \tag{6.11}$$

$$q_m = \bar{q}_m, \tag{6.12}$$

where w_i and q_i are the price and quantity, respectively, of input i, and f is the production function. The production function includes a productivity measure μ that may shift in deterministic or stochastic ways.

Define $A \equiv \sum_{i=1}^{m-1} a_i$. The one-period (constrained) cost function from this problem is

$$C(y) = w_m q_m + A q_m^{(A-1)/A} \left[\prod_{i=1}^{m-1} \left(\frac{w_i}{a_i} \right)^{a_i/A} \right] \mu^{-1/A} y^{1/A}, \tag{6.13}$$

and the marginal cost function is

$$q_m^{A-1/A} \left[\prod_{i=1}^{m-1} \left(\frac{w_i}{a_i} \right)^{a_i/A} \right] \mu^{-1/A} y^{(1-A)/A}. \tag{6.14}$$

Equation 6.14 can be used to calculate the ratio of marginal costs in t and $t+1$:

$$\ln\left(\frac{MC_{t+1}}{MC_t}\right) = \left[\sum_{i=1}^{m-1}(a_i/A)\ln\left(\frac{w_{it+1}}{w_{it}}\right)\right] -$$

$$\left(\frac{1-A}{A}\right)\ln\left(\frac{q_{mt+1}}{q_{mt}}\right) +$$

$$\left(\frac{1-A}{A}\right)\ln\left(\frac{y_{t+1}}{y_t}\right) -$$

$$\frac{1}{A}\ln\frac{\mu_{t+1}}{\mu_t}. \tag{6.15}$$

To derive an expression for the growth rate of output, take logs of equation 6.9, impose a first-order Taylor expansion of $\ln(l - s_t)$ around $n_t = k$ for an arbitrary value of $k \geq 0$ and a second-order Taylor expansion of $\ln(1 + \epsilon_{t+1})$ around $\epsilon_{t+1} = 0$, and substitute in equation 6.15 to get

$$Gy_{t+1} = \left[\frac{A}{1-A}(-\ln(1-s_1-s_2k) - \frac{ks_2}{1-s_1-s_2k} - \frac{1}{2}\sigma_\epsilon^2\right]$$

$$+ \left(\frac{A}{1-A}\right)\left[\ln(1+\tilde{R}_t) - \sum_{i=1}^{m-1}(a_i/A)Gw_{it+1}\right] + Gq_{mt+1} +$$

$$\frac{s_2}{1-s_1-s_2k}\left(\frac{A}{1-A}\right)n_t + \left(\frac{1}{1-A}\right)G\mu_{t+1} +$$

$$\left(\frac{A}{1-A}\right)\left[((1/2)\sigma_\epsilon^2 - (1/2)\epsilon_{t+1}^2) + \epsilon_{t+1}\right], \tag{6.16}$$

where for any variable Z, $GZ_{t+1} \equiv \ln(Z_{t+1}/Z_t)$. The term $(A/(1 - A))(1/2)\sigma_\epsilon^2$ has been added and subtracted from the equation, so the last term has a mean of zero.

Equation 6.16 is the basis of the estimation reported below. It says that the growth rate of output is a function of the real interest rate (where the inflation rate used to calculate the real rate is a weighted average of the rates of inflation of factor prices), the growth in the capital stock, the level of inventories, productivity growth, and a surprise term. The key implication tested here is that no other time t information should help predict output growth.[5]

This model accommodates seasonal fluctuations in output growth in several ways. First, the observable or unobservable component of productivity might shift seasonally. Second, the relevant input prices might be seasonal. Of course, it is not entirely accurate to describe these as determining the seasonal fluctuations in output growth, since in general equilibrium the seasonals in output growth and input prices are determined simultaneously. For an individual firm, however, and even for a two-digit industry, the degree of simultaneity is likely to be small.

The productivity shifter μ is a function of some observable seasonal variables and some unobservable ones. The observable variables are current temperature, current precipitation, and the squares and cross-products of these two variables. Thus, $\mu = e^{Z\gamma + \eta}$, where Z is a matrix of observable weather variables and μ is the unobservable productivity shifter.

In the absence of shifts in the cost function (i.e., changes in μ), the model exhibits production smoothing. For a given time path of the capital stock, the derived cost function is convex, inducing firms to spread production evenly over time.[6] When productivity can vary, the result is no longer a pure production-smoothing model (i.e., the variance of production can exceed the variance of sales), but the convexity of the cost function remains and provides a motive for production smoothing.

6.2 Identification and Testing

Before estimating the model it is necessary to make explicit the identifying assumptions. Equation 6.16, augmented to include the weather variables, can be written as:

$$
Gy_{t+1} = \left(\frac{A}{1-A} \right) \left[-\ln(1 - s_1 - s_2 k) - \frac{k s_2}{1 - s_1 - s_2 k} - \frac{1}{2}\sigma_\epsilon^2 \right]
$$

$$
+ \left(\frac{A}{1-A} \right) \left[\ln(1 + \tilde{R}_t) - \sum_{i=1}^{m-1}(a_i/A)Gw_{it+1} \right] + Gq_{mt+1}
$$

$$
+ \frac{s_2}{1 - s_1 - s_2 k} \left(\frac{A}{1-A} \right) n_t + \left(\frac{1}{1-A} \right)(Z_{t+1} - Z_t)\gamma
$$

$$
+ \left(\frac{1}{1-A} \right) G\eta_{t+1}
$$

$$
+ \left(\frac{A}{1-A} \right) \left[((1/2)\sigma_\epsilon^2 - (1/2)\epsilon_{t+1}^2) + \epsilon_{t+1} \right]. \qquad (6.17)
$$

Since the right-hand-side variables are in general correlated with the expectation error, one must use an instrumental variables procedure to estimate the equation. The instruments must be correlated with the included variables but not with the error term.

Recall that the error includes expectations errors and the growth in the unobserved productivity shifter. Any variable known at time t is, by rational expectations, orthogonal to ϵ_{t+1}.[7] However, rationality of expectations does not imply that $G\eta_{t+1}$ is orthogonal to time t information; productivity growth might have a predictable component. If productivity follows a geometric random walk, growth in productivity is independent and identically distributed (i.i.d.) and therefore orthogonal to lagged information.

Garber and King (1984) note that many studies effectively ignore the identification issue by assuming no shocks in the sector being estimated. The approach here allows some measurable shocks to this sector and makes the following identifying assumptions about the relationship between the unobserved cost shifter and the included instruments:

1. The unobserved productivity shifter (η) is uncorrelated with lagged values of sales and with the part of current sales that was predictable based on lagged information.

2. The growth of the productivity shifter is uncorrelated with lagged growth rates of input prices, lagged growth rates of output, and lagged interest rates.

The following variables are therefore orthogonal to the error term in the regression: lagged growth in sales, lagged growth in output, lagged interest rates, lagged growth in factor prices, and lagged inventories. Some sets of results relax the assumption that the lagged growth rate of output is uncorrelated with the growth in the productivity shifter. The tests of the model involve estimating equation 6.17 with instrumental variables, including the variables in the above list as instruments.

Since the number of instruments is greater than the number of right-hand-side variables, the equation is overidentified. One can test the overidentifying restrictions by regressing the estimated residuals on all the instruments, including the predetermined right-hand-side variables. The quantity T times the R^2 from this regression is distributed χ^2_j, where T is the number of observations and j is the number of overidentifying restrictions. One possible alternative hypothesis is that firms simply set current output in line with current sales. In this case, the lagged growth rate of sales should enter significantly in tests of the overidentifying restrictions.

It is possible that weather variables do not capture all the seasonality in productivity. The estimation procedure allows for this by making the productivity measure an arbitrary function of seasonal dummies in equation 6.17. This gives the same results as first regressing all of the variables on seasonal dummies and then using the residuals from these regressions for estimation purposes; thus, it is equivalent to using seasonal dummy-adjusted data.

To determine whether the use of Census X-11 adjusted data (Hylleberg 1986) has been responsible for the previous rejections of the production-smoothing model, the results compare tests using seasonally unadjusted data with seasonal dummies included in the regression to tests using X-11 seasonally adjusted data.

When unconstrained seasonal dummies are included in equation 6.17, the regression results contain no information on whether the seasonal movements in the data are consistent with the model. An additional set of results therefore assumes that the seasonal shifts in productivity not captured by weather variables are uncorrelated with instruments used to estimate equation 6.17. Under this assumption, seasonal dummies can be excluded from the equation and the seasonal fluctuations used to conduct two further tests. The first is that once the other factors in the cost function are taken into account, the remaining movements in output should be uncorrelated with the seasonal movements in sales. The second test is whether the seasonal movements taken by themselves are consistent with the model. The next section describes these tests in detail.

6.3   Data and Basic Results

The data set used to estimate the model consists of monthly observations on production, shipments, inventories, and input prices for the six two-digit production-to-stock industries for May 1967 through December 1982. Miron and Zeldes (1988) provide details of the construction of the data set.

The empirical results use two different measures of production. The first comes from the identity that production of finished goods equals sales plus the change in inventories of finished goods. Commerce Department data for sales and the change in inventories are used to compute this production measure (Y4). The second measure of production used is the Federal Reserve Board's index of industrial production (IP), also available at the two-digit SIC level. In principle, the two production series measure the same variable and should therefore behave similarly over time. As documented in Miron and Zeldes (1989), however, the two series are in fact quite different.

This section examines the basic results from estimating equation 6.17 and testing the implied overidentifying restrictions. The estimation and testing are carried out with (1) the standard X-11 seasonally adjusted data and (2) seasonally unadjusted data plus seasonal dummies.

Table 6.1 presents a summary of the results, consisting of estimation with both unadjusted and adjusted data for both Y4 and IP.[8] The first line of each set of results lists the variables that entered equation 6.17 at a significance level of 5 percent. The second line presents the R^2 from the regression of the residuals on all the instruments. The same line reports the marginal significance level of the test statistic TR^2. The last line lists the variables that entered this auxiliary test significantly.

The results in the table show the following. First, in no case does the interest rate or the growth rate in energy prices enter equation 6.17 significantly. In about one-third of the cases, the growth in raw materials prices enters significantly, but usually with the wrong sign. Wage growth enters significantly only four times—twice with the wrong sign. Thus, the signs and statistical significance of the coefficient estimates are not supportive of the model.

Second, the data reject the overidentifying restrictions on the model in all cases using the Y4 data and in two-thirds using the IP data. For the Y4 data, the rejections are about as strong using seasonally adjusted as seasonally unadjusted data. For the IP data, the rejections are not quite as strong overall using the seasonally unadjusted data. On the whole, the use of unadjusted data with seasonal dummies does not provide better results than using seasonally adjusted data.

Thus far, the data provide a negative assessment of the model for two reasons. First, the data typically reject the overidentifying restrictions. Second, the signs of the coefficient estimates are not sensible and are rarely significant. These negative results can be challenged in two ways, however. First, the instrument list might include variables that are correlated with the error term even under the null hypothesis, thus invalidating the tests of the overidentifying restrictions. Second, the

Table 6.1
Regression results, equation 6.17

	Food	Tobacco	Apparel	Chemicals	Petroleum	Rubber
Y4, NSA What enters eq. 6.17 significantly?	sd, $-rm$	tem, $-tem2$	sd	$-sd$, tem $-tem2$, $-pre$	$-w$, $-day$ $-tem2$, $-pre2$	sd
R^2, significance level	.17, .000	.23, .000	.09, .050	.15, .001	.13, .004	.16, .000
What is significant in test of OIRs?	we_{-1}, $-we_{-2}$	tem_{-1}	—	$-y_{-1}$, x_{-1}, $-n_{-2}$, n_{-3}, sd	we_{-2}	w, sd
Y4, SA What enters eq. 6.17 significantly?	—	rm, tem, $-tem2$	$-n_{-1}$, rm	rm	$-w$, $-day$ $-pre2$, tpr	w
R^2, significance level	.10, .027	.14, .002	.11, .014	.14, .002	.14, .002	.11, .014
What is significant in test of OIRs?	—	—	—	—	—	—
IP, NSA What enters eq. 6.17 significantly?	sd	$-sd$, w, $-pre2$	sd, day_{-1}	sd, rm	sd, $-pre2$	rm
R^2, significance level	.16, .000	.16, .000	.09, .050	.04, .583	.08, .090	.02, .926
What is significant in test of OIRs?	$-y_{-1}$, $-w_{-2}$	$-y_{-1}$, sd	$-y_{-1}$	—	—	—

IP, SA						
What enters eq. 6.17 significantly?	—	$-pre2$	$-pre2, day_{-1}$	$tem, -tem2$	$-day_{-1}$	$rm, tem, -tem2$
R^2, significance level	.15, .001	.28, .000	.09, .050	.13, .004	.09, .050	.06, .257
What is significant in test of OIRs?	$-y_{-1}, -we_{-2}$	$-y_{-1}, -y_{-2}$ $-tem_{-1}, tpr_{-1}$	$-y_{-1}$	x_{-1}, x_{-2}	—	$-n_{-1}$

Source: Miron and Zeldes (1988), p. 892.

Notes: The sample period is 1967:5–1982:12. NSA = not seasonally adjusted; SA = seasonally adjusted; OIR = overidentifying restrictions.

The first line of each set of results lists the variables that entered equation 6.17 at the 5 percent significance level. We list seasonal dummies if one or more of the eleven dummies entered significantly.

The second line gives the R^2 from the regression of the residuals on the instruments, as well as the marginal significance level of this statistic. The quantity $T \times R^2$ is distributed x_j^2, where j is the number of overidentifying restrictions and T is the number of observations. In the results presented here, there are nine such restrictions.

The third line lists the variables that entered the regression of the residuals on the instruments at the 5 percent significance level.

w = wage growth, sd = seasonal dummies, y = output growth, x = sales growth, day = number of production days, we = energy price growth, rm = raw materials price growth, n = inventories, r = interest rate, pre = change in precipitation, $pre2$ = change in precipitation squared, tem = change in temperature, $tem2$ = change in temperature squared, tpr = change in temperature * precipitation.

A ($-$) before variable indicates that the sign of the coefficient was negative.

A subscript of $-l$ on a variable means that it is dated l periods earlier than the dependent variable.

instruments might be poorly correlated with the right-hand-side variables. In this case, the parameter estimates are not likely to be statistically significant, even under the null.

In order to account for these possibilities, one can estimate equation 6.17 using two alternative instrument lists. The first excludes production from the instrument list and includes extra lags of sales. The second list excludes all variables dated time t and includes extra lags of the variables at earlier dates.

With both alternative instrument lists, the data reject the overidentifying restrictions significantly less often than with the list used in the basic results. In both cases, however, the input price variables, the interest rate, and the level of inventories rarely enter statistically significantly with the correct sign.

This raises the second issue. Expected changes in input prices might not appear to affect the timing of production because expected changes in input prices do not occur. That is, the instruments may have no explanatory power for the right-hand-side variables. In this case, the failure of these input prices to explain the pattern of production is not evidence against the model. Direct examination shows, however, that the instruments have statistically significant explanatory power in most cases.

To summarize, the basic instrument list provides evidence against the production-smoothing model, even when it incorporates a stochastic interest rate, measurable and unmeasurable cost shocks, and nonquadratic technology. With two weaker sets of identifying restrictions, the data provide substantially less statistical evidence against the model but still no evidence that it describes an important aspect of firm behavior. Using seasonally unadjusted data and seasonal dummies does little better than using X-11 adjusted data.

The results presented incorporate seasonal fluctuations into the analysis by using seasonally unadjusted data and including seasonal dummies and weather variables in the equations. This approach does not determine to what extent the seasonal movements in interest rates or input prices determine the seasonal movements in output growth, nor does it show whether the seasonal movements in the data themselves satisfy the production-smoothing model. To answer these questions, one cannot include seasonal dummies in equation 6.17 and must therefore assume that any seasonal or other fluctuations in productivity not captured by the weather variables are orthogonal to the instruments.

Table 6.2
Variance of production divided by variance of sales

		Food	Tobacco	Apparel	Chemicals	Petroleum	Rubber
Y4	Nonseasonal	1.22	1.84	1.32	1.01	0.91	1.13
	Seasonal	1.71	4.71	0.58	0.72	2.73	0.99
	Total	1.50	2.53	0.80	0.89	0.94	1.09
IP	Nonseasonal	0.48	0.58	1.20	0.83	0.48	0.95
	Seasonal	1.64	6.28	0.21	0.18	7.91	0.61
	Total	1.14	1.95	0.50	0.55	0.59	0.86

Source: Miron and Zeldes (1988), p. 895.
Notes: The sample period is 1967:5–1982:12.
The estimation procedure is the following. For both shipments and production, the log level is regressed on a constant, time and a time trend that is one beginning in October 1973. The coefficients are estimated by generalized least squares (GLS), assuming a second-order autoregressive process for the error term. The antilogs of the fitted values of this regression are then subtracted from the actual data, in levels, to define the detrended data. The seasonal and nonseasonal variances are calculated as the variance of the fitted values and residuals, respectively, of a regression of the detrended series on seasonal dummies.
We convert the IP measure from an index to a constant dollar figure by multiplying it by the ratio of average Y4 to average IP.

Before describing the formal tests, it is useful to consider a set of stylized facts about the seasonality in production, inventories, and sales. Table 6.2 presents estimates of the ratio of the variance of production to the variance of sales, including estimates based separately on the seasonal and nonseasonal variation. Following Blinder (1986), these numbers are based on detrended levels rather than growth rates.[9] If cost shocks are assumed to be small, the production-smoothing model restricts these ratios to be less than 1. For three of the six industries, this ratio for the seasonal components is greater than 1.

While one could interpret a ratio greater than 1 as rejecting the production-smoothing model, the ratio need not be less than 1 if the cost function shifts seasonally. Even in this case, however, the seasonal movements contain information. Whether seasonal shifts in productivity affect the seasonal pattern of production, the seasonal pattern in production need not match the seasonal pattern of sales.

Figures 6.1 through 6.6 show the seasonal patterns in output and shipments for the six industries examined and document behavior potentially problematic for the production-smoothing model.[10] The seasonal movements in output and sales are in fact very similar. The

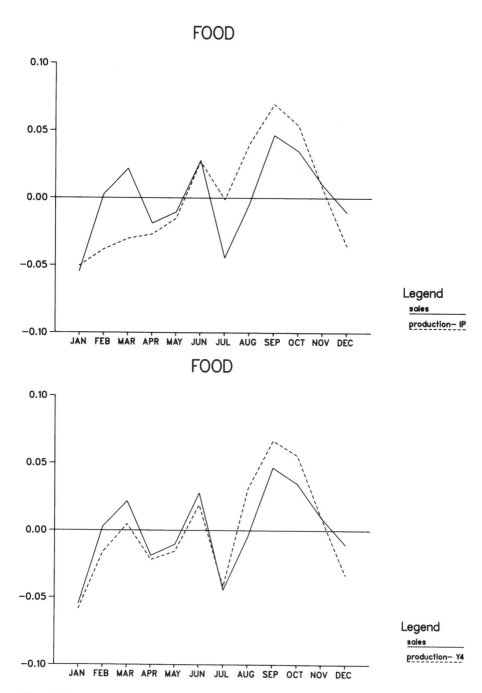

Figure 6.1
Seasonal pattern in production and shipments, food. Source: Miron and Zeldes (1988), p. 896.

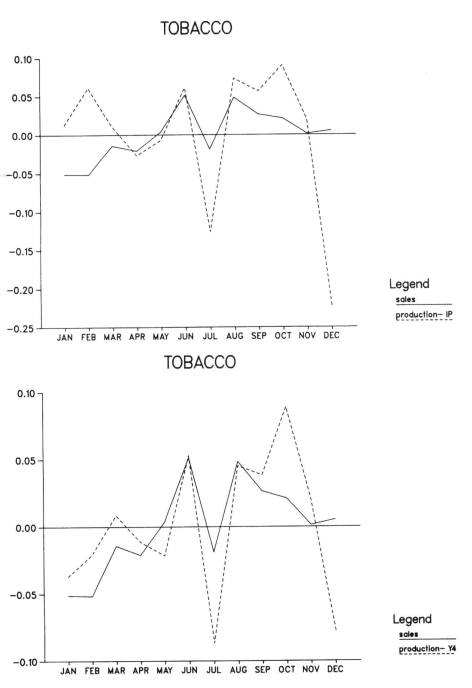

Figure 6.2
Seasonal pattern in production and shipments, tobacco. Source: Miron and Zeldes (1988), p. 897.

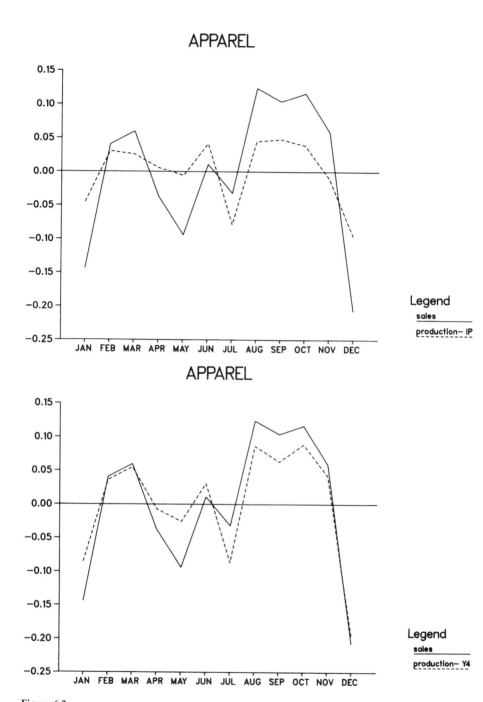

Figure 6.3
Seasonal pattern in production and shipments, apparel. Source: Miron and Zeldes (1988), p. 898.

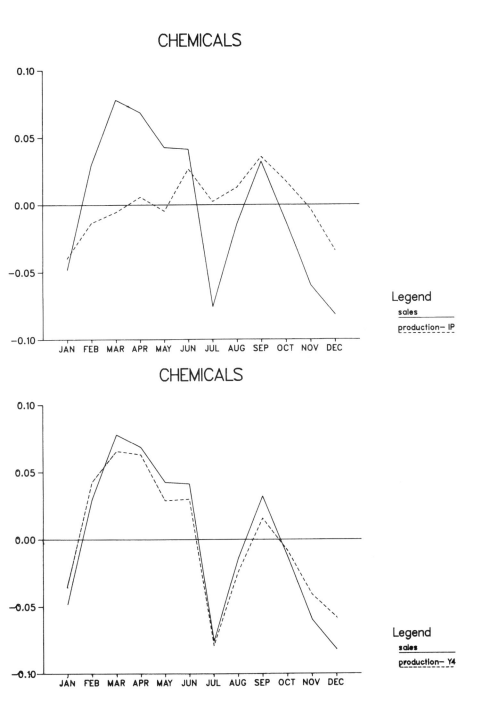

Figure 6.4
Seasonal pattern in production and shipments, chemicals. Source: Miron and Zeldes (1988), p. 899.

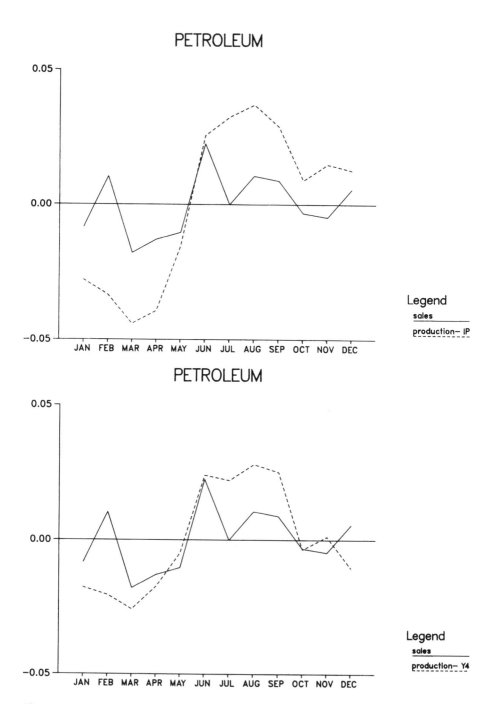

Figure 6.5
Seasonal pattern in production and shipments, petroleum. Source: Miron and Zeldes (1988), p. 890.

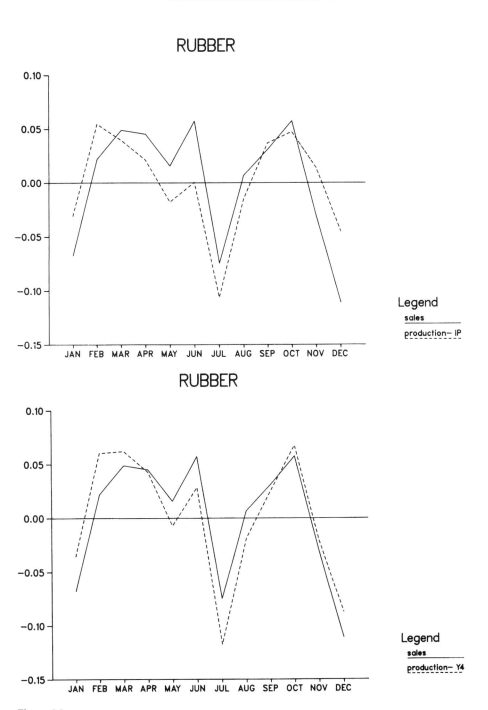

Figure 6.6
Seasonal pattern in production and shipments, rubber. Source: Miron and Zeldes (1988), p. 891.

implication of these graphs is that inventories do not appear to be play-ing the role of smoothing seasonal fluctuations in sales.

The tests presented in this section formalize this observation. First, they examine whether the contemporaneous seasonal movement in sales growth helps predict residual output growth, once the move-ments in factor prices, the weather, and lagged inventories are taken into account. To do this, the seasonal component of contemporaneous sales growth is added to the instrument list. It is unusual when running this type of orthogonality test to include as an instrument a contempo-raneous variable, but since this series is deterministic, it is part of the lagged information set. Since it is also assumed orthogonal to the un-observable productivity shifter, it is a valid instrument.[11]

The interpretation of this procedure is the following. Because sea-sonal dummies are excluded from the equation, the seasonal and nonseasonal movements in the right-hand-side variables must affect output growth via the same coefficients. Given this restriction, the test determines whether the part of output growth not explained by these variables is correlated with the seasonal component of sales growth. The test therefore compares the seasonal component in sales and out-put, after taking into account the measured seasonality in factor costs, the weather, and the level of inventories.

This test of the production-smoothing model using seasonal fluctu-ations involves one important maintained hypothesis: that the coeffi-cients on the seasonal and nonseasonal components of input prices and the weather are the same. A last set of tests relaxes this assumption and tests whether the seasonal movements in the data, taken by them-selves, are consistent with the model. This is accomplished as follows:

1. Construct the seasonal component of each of the relevant variables (output growth, input prices, weather variables, etc.) by regressing them on seasonal dummies and calculating the fitted values of these regression.

2. Regress the seasonal component of output growth on the seasonal in input prices, weather, the level of inventories, and the contempora-neous seasonal component of sales and test the restriction that this last coefficient is zero.[12]

Tables 6.3 and 6.4 summarize the results. Table 6.3 presents the same type of information as table 6.1, but it includes the t-statistic on the seasonal component of contemporaneous sales in the test of the over-

Table 6.3
Regression results, seasonal dummies excluded, seasonal component of sales in instrument list

		Food	Tobacco	Apparel	Chemicals	Petroleum	Rubber
Y4, NSA	What enters eq. 6.17 significantly?	−w, tem −tem2	−w	w, tem −tem2	−w, tem, −pre, −tem2	−w, −pre2, −day,	−w, tem, −tem2, −pre
	R², significance level	.52, .000	.16, .001	.14, .003	.31, .000	.18, .000	.26, .000
	What is significant in test of OIRs?	tem−1, −tem2−1, −x−2, −rm−1, xseas	tem−1	xseas	tem−1, xseas	we−2	xseas
	t-stat on xseas	3.51	0.51	2.84	4.14	1.87	3.41
IP, NSA	What enters eq. 6.17 significantly?	−w, tem, −tem2	−w	w, rm, tem, −tem2	tem, −tem2, −pre	−w, −pre2	tem, −tem2
	R², significance level	.30, .000	.14, .003	.12, .012	.15, .002	.13, .007	.24, .000
	What is significant in test of OIRs?	−y−1, y−2, −w−2, xseas	−y−1, w−2	−y−1, xseas	—	−y−1, x−1, xseas	xseas
	t-stat on xseas	2.86	0.99	2.62	1.82	3.39	3.41

Source: Miron and Zeldes (1988), p. 903.
Notes: The sample period is 1967:5–1982:12. NSA = not seasonally adjusted.
The first line of each set of results lists the variables that entered equation 6.17 at the 5 percent significance level.
The second line gives the R^2 from the regression of the residuals on the instruments, as well as the marginal significance level of this statistic.
The quantity $T \times R^2$ is distributed χ^2_j, where j is the number of overidentifying restrictions and T is the number of observations. In the results presented here, there are ten such restrictions.
The third line lists the variables that entered the regression of the residuals on the instruments at the 5 percent significance level.
w = wage growth, y = output growth, x = sales growth, day = number of production days, we = energy price growth, rm = raw materials price growth, n = inventories, r = interest rate, pre = change in precipitation, $pre2$ = change in precipitation squared, tem = change in temperature, $tem2$ = change in temperature squared, tpr = change in temperature* precipitation, $xseas$ = seasonal component of sales growth (defined as the fitted values from a regression on seasonal dummies).
A (−) before variable indicates that the sign of the coefficient was negative.
A subscript of $−l$ on a variable means that it is dated l periods earlier than the dependent variable.

Table 6.4
Regression results, seasonal components only

		Food	Tobacco	Apparel	Chemicals	Petroleum	Rubber
Y4	What enters eq. 6.17 significantly?	$-n, x$	x	x	x	—	x
	t stat on x	9.21	4.91	1.98	11.69	1.10	19.99
IP	What enters eq. 6.17 significantly?	x	$-pre, x$	—	x	—	x
	t stat on x	3.19	3.39	1.14	2.31	.62	3.97

Source: Miron and Zeldes (1988), p. 904.
Notes: The sample period is 1967:5–1982:12.
The coefficients were obtained by estimating equation 6.17, with sales growth included, using seasonal dummies only as instruments. This gives coefficient estimates numerically identical to the procedure described in the text, but it produces correct standard errors. The t statistic on sales growth reported in the table is from this instrumental variables regression.
The first line of each set of results lists the variables that entered equation 6.17 at the 5 percent significance level.
w = wage growth, y = output growth, x = sales growth, day = change in number of production days, n = inventories, pre = change in precipitation, $pre2$ = change in precipitation squared, tem = change in temperature, $tem2$ = change in temperature squared, tpr = change in temperature $*$ precipitation.
A $(-)$ before variable indicates that the sign of the coefficient was negative.

identifying restrictions. Table 6.4 is also set up similarly to table 6.1, but it simply reports whether the seasonal component in sales significantly affects the seasonal component in output growth, after controlling for the seasonal movements in input prices, the weather, and the level of inventories.

The results in both tables provide striking evidence against the production-smoothing model. In table 6.3, the data reject the overidentifying restrictions in every instance. In most cases, the seasonal component of sales is significantly correlated with output, even after taking account of any seasonals in input prices, lagged inventories, and the weather. This is true for five out of six industries using at least one of the output measures and for three of the six industries using both output measures. When the instrument list omits time t variables and lagged output growth, the data again reject the overidentifying restriction, and the seasonal in sales growth is significantly correlated with residual output growth in most cases.

In table 6.4 (the seasonal-only results) the seasonal in the sales growth is statistically significant in five out of six cases for the Y4 measure of output and in four out of six cases for the IP measure. Variables other than sales almost never enter significantly.

These results on the seasonal behavior of production and sales are highly problematic for the production-smoothing model. To a large extent, firms appear to choose their seasonal production patterns to match their seasonal sales patterns, rather than using inventories to smooth production over the year. Moreover, since the seasonal variation in production and sales growth generally accounts for more than 50 percent of the total variation in these variables, this problematic behavior is a quantitatively important feature of the data.

A key assumption made here is that the seasonal in the productivity shifter is uncorrelated with the seasonal in demand. Are there circumstances under which this assumption would not hold? An example that comes to mind is the case of an economy-wide seasonal in labor supply due to preferences for vacations in certain months. This would induce a corresponding seasonal in output. If each industry's output is an input into another industry, shipments might display a corresponding seasonal, leading optimally to the same seasonal patterns in output and shipments.

Theoretically, the approach here accounts for this by including the wage as a determinant of desired production. However, if the measured wage differs from the shadow cost of labor, the residual will include the seasonal in labor supply and therefore still be correlated with the seasonal in shipments. This explanation suggests that one should see the same seasonal movements in output in all industries. Figures 6.1 through 6.6 indicate that seasonal patterns in production are similar but hardly identical in different industries.

It is not clear what conclusion to draw from this discussion. Possibly the hypothesis proposed here is the explanation for the seasonal results. If so, the question is whether the same argument applies to nonseasonal movements—that is, whether the failure of the production-smoothing model over the business cycle is due to economy-wide changes in desired labor supply that are not captured by measured wages.

6.4   Conclusions

The results presented show a strong rejection of the production-smoothing model. Most notably, the seasonal component of output growth is highly correlated with the seasonal component of sales growth, even after adjusting for the seasonality in interest rates, wages, energy prices, raw materials prices, and the weather. A strong similarity of the seasonality in production and sales also characterizes a high fraction of the industries for which physical units data are available (Krane 1991, Kahn 1990, Kashyap and Wilcox 1993, Beason 1993), so the key result here is robust and not merely an artifact of imperfect data.

In addition to contradicting the basic production-smoothing model, the results shed light on a number of hypotheses that have been advanced as explanations for the model's failures. First, these results provide direct evidence on whether the inappropriate use of data seasonally adjusted by X-11 has been responsible for the failure of the model. X-11 data are (approximately) a two-sided moving average of the underlying seasonally unadjusted data. This means that such data are likely to violate the crucial orthogonality conditions that are tested in these kinds of models, even if the unadjusted data satisfy them. Although it seemed likely on a priori grounds that the use of X-11 adjusted data was a major problem, the results indicate otherwise. The particular method of treating seasonal fluctuations does not appear crucial to an evaluation of the model.

Another issue illuminated by these results is that of costs of changing production. The model here omits these costs (or, more generally, costs of changing inputs); their addition might "help the data fit the model." This tactic seems unsatisfactory, however, since the magnitude of the seasonal changes in production makes it unlikely that adjustment costs are large, although these costs might be lower when they are anticipated.

Finally, the seasonal-specific results help rule out a concern regarding the choice of appropriate instruments. The estimation here assumes that firms know current demand, and therefore time t sales is a valid instrument. Other work on this topic, however, assumes that firms do not know the level of current period demand when they choose the current period level of production (e.g., Kahn 1987). If this assumption is more appropriate, the general results above are inconsistent, but it is still valid to include the seasonal component of contemporaneous sales growth, since the seasonal component of demand would be known even if the overall level were not. Since the results from this test show a strong rejection of the model, this suggests that the assumption that firms observe demand before choosing output is not, by itself, to blame.

What remains, then, as possible explanations for the failure of the production-smoothing model? One possibility concerns the maintained assumption that firms always hold positive inventories, which implies that firms do not stock out. Total inventories for each industry are always positive in the data considered here, but this is probably not the case for each individual firm or product. Kahn (1987) presents a model in which, because stockouts are costly, firms may not smooth production. However, relatively little direct evidence indicates that stockout costs are high or that firms cannot simply hold unfilled orders as a type of negative inventories. This line of research deserves further attention—in particular, direct empirical testing.

Perhaps the simplest possible explanation for the results is that marginal cost curves are flat, which means firms have little incentive to smooth production even if inventory holding costs are low. This explanation appears inconsistent with evidence summarized here (Beaulieu, MacKie-Mason, and Miron 1992; Cecchetti, Kashyap, and Wilcox 1995, 1996) that capacity constraints seem to bind in many manufacturing industries. Yet if capacity is chosen so that it binds only rarely, firms operate below capacity most of the time. Thus, evidence of production smoothing might be difficult to locate even though capacity models indeed imply production smoothing. This interpretation says that production smoothing is present but irrelevant much of the time.

7

Financial Panics,
the Seasonality of
Nominal Interest Rates,
and the Founding of
the Fed

The chapter provides a second example of an analysis in which focusing on seasonal fluctuations sheds light on the seasonal and nonseasonal structure of the economy. The basic claim is that concern about seasonality constituted a primary reason for the establishment of the Federal Reserve system. The analysis thus shows that attempting to understand the seasonal as well as business cycle fluctuations in the data can provide insights into the nature of all types of fluctuations (Miron 1986a).

The chapter discusses the relation between seasonal fluctuations in nominal interest rates, financial panics, and the establishment of the Federal Reserve. After the founding of the Fed in 1914, the frequency of financial panics and the size of the seasonal movements in nominal interest rates declined substantially. Since the Fed was established in part to "furnish an elastic currency," it is natural to hypothesize that the Fed caused these changes in the behavior of financial markets. A number of other major changes took place in the economy and in the financial system during this period, however, including World War I, the shift from agriculture to manufacturing, and the loosening of the gold standard, so the role of the Federal Reserve is not immediate. This chapter argues nevertheless that the Fed, by carrying out the seasonal open market policy that eliminated the seasonal in nominal interest rates, caused the decrease in the frequency of panics.

7.1 A Model of the Banking System

This section presents a model of the banking system in which the magnitude of the seasonal movements in nominal interest rates is positively correlated with the frequency of financial panics. The model shows that the Fed can reduce the frequency of panics by carrying out the seasonal open market policy that eliminates seasonal fluctuations from nominal rates.

The starting point is the Friedman and Schwartz (1963a, pp. 50–53) textbook model of the money supply:

$$H = R + C \tag{7.1}$$

$$M = C + D \tag{7.2}$$

$$L = M - H \tag{7.3}$$

where H is high-powered money, M is money, C is currency, D is deposits, and L is loans. In this framework the money supply is determined by the interaction of the nonbank public (through the desired currency-deposit ratio), banks (through the desired reserve-deposit ratio), and the monetary authority (through high-powered money). The model presented here explicitly examines the bank's choice of reserve-deposit ratio and then makes standard assumptions about the remaining terms.

The banking system consists of a fixed number of identical banks, each of which acts as a price taker. The representative bank holds two types of assets—reserves, R, and loans, L—and has one type of liability—deposits, D. The bank accepts deposits infinitely elastically and pays out currency on demand.[1] The only decision it faces is what proportion of its assets to hold as reserves and what proportion as loans. The larger the proportion of loans, the greater are the costs to the bank of managing its portfolio.

The bank faces costs of holding a large proportion of its assets as loans because it can suffer unexpected deposit withdrawals. Under fractional reserve banking, a sufficiently large amount of withdrawals causes the bank to fail because some of its assets are tied up in loans, and it takes time to convert these into cash. If the bank experiences withdrawals, therefore, it liquidates some of its loans to bolster its reserve position. This imposes costs since the bank accrues capital losses, incurs excess brokerage fees when it calls in loans unexpectedly, or both.

The bank's cost function takes the form

$$c(R/D) = \frac{1}{2}(W - E(W))^2((R/D) - 1)^2, \tag{7.4}$$

where W is the amount of withdrawals the bank experiences. Costs depend on the amount of unexpected withdrawals and on the ratio of reserves to deposits. They increase with the amount of unexpected with-drawals but decrease with the reserve-deposit ratio. The cost function described by equation 7.4 assumes that unexpected withdrawals and unexpected deposits have the same effect on costs. It also assumes that the distribution of withdrawals is independent of the level of deposits. Both of these assumptions are probably unrealistic, but they simplify the presentation of the results. The results do not depend on these two assumptions.

The bank's problem is

$$\max E(iL - c(R/D)),\tag{7.5}$$

subject to

$$R + L = D,\tag{7.6}$$

where i is the nominal interest rate. The solutions for R and L are

$$R^d = D(1 - (iD/s^2))\tag{7.7}$$

$$L^s = D(iD/s^2),\tag{7.8}$$

where $s^2 = E(W - E(W))^2$. These solutions imply a desired loan/re-serve ratio of

$$L^s/R^d = id/(s^2 - iD).\tag{7.9}$$

When the interest rate or the level of deposits is high, the bank would like to hold a small proportion of its assets as reserves and a large proportion as loans. When the variance of withdrawals, s^2, is high, the bank wishes to hold a small proportion as loans and a large proportion as reserves.

To close the model, assume that the demand for loans is negatively related to the real interest rate and that the demand for deposits is interest inelastic:

$$L^d = P(Y - b(i - \pi^*))\tag{7.10}$$

$$D^d = Pd\tag{7.11}$$

where P is the price level and π^* is expected inflation. Real loan demand is negatively related to the real interest rate and positively related to Y, a measure of the real demand for credit in the economy. The demand for deposits, d, does not depend on the interest rate or on the state of the economy.

Assume for now that $P = 1$ and $\pi^* = 0$; this simplifies the presentation without affecting the results. Assume also that the level of high-powered money is fixed and independent of the behavior of the economy. The United States and its major trading partners were on the gold standard during the period 1890–1914, but gold flows were sufficiently sluggish so that the U.S. interest rate could move independently of the world rate in the short run.[2] In addition, as shown by Clark (1986), seasonal movements in the world rate corresponded closely to those in the United States.

Equations 7.7, 7.8, 7.10, and 7.11 jointly determine the equilibrium values of the endogenous variables in the model. The two exogenous variables Y and d parameterize the solutions. By noting how the solutions depend on these variables, one can see how they depend on external conditions, which can be interpreted as the effects of different seasons. Determining the sensitivity of the solutions to Y and d therefore suggests how equilibrium in financial markets depends on the seasonal movements in loan and deposit demand.

The equilibrium value of the interest rate is

$$i = Ys^2/(bs^2 + d^2). \tag{7.12}$$

The interest rate is high in seasons in which loan demand is high or deposit demand is low. When the variance of deposit withdrawals is high, the level of interest rates is also high.

The equilibrium values for loans, reserves, and the loan-reserve ratio are

$$L = \frac{Yd^2}{(bs^2 + d^2)} \tag{7.13}$$

$$R = \frac{(bds^2 + d^3 - d^2Y)}{(bs^2 + d^2)} \tag{7.14}$$

$$\frac{L}{R} = \frac{Yd^s}{(bds^2 + d^3 - d^2Y)}. \tag{7.15}$$

The quantity of loans is high when demand for them is high and when deposits at banks are high; they are low when the variance of withdrawals is high. Reserves are low when loan demand is high and high when deposit demand is high. The ratio of loans to reserves increases with loan demand, decreases with deposit demand, and decreases with the variance of withdrawals.

The seasonal movements in Y and d also affect the distribution of costs of running the banking system:

$$c(R/D) = \frac{(W - E(W))^2}{2} \frac{d^2 Y^2}{(bs^2 + d^2)^2}. \tag{7.16}$$

These costs are high when d is low and when Y is high, given the distribution of W. That is, a withdrawal of a given size imposes higher costs on the banking system in periods when loan demand is high or deposit demand is low.

Panics can be thought of as periods when the costs of running the banking system are especially high. Since the distribution of costs shifts upward with seasonal increases in loan demand and seasonal decreases in deposit demand, the probability that costs exceed any given level is higher in seasons when loan demand is high or deposit demand is low. Thus panics are more likely to occur at these times.

That panics are more likely to occur in seasons with high-loan demand or low-deposit demand is the first key result provided by the model. The explanation is as follows. In some seasons, an exogenous increase in loan demand forces up nominal rates. Banks respond by loaning out a higher proportion of their reserves, which increases expected costs but also produces more revenue. The increase in loan-reserve ratios means a decrease in reserve-deposit ratios, so the distribution of costs, and thus the frequency of panics, is higher, even though the distribution of unexpected withdrawals is unchanged. It is the seasonal increase in loan demand and the resulting decrease in reserve-deposit ratios that causes an increased frequency of panics, not any change in the variance of deposit withdrawals.

Consider now the costs of running the banking system when the Fed intervenes by conducting open market operations. An open market purchase increases the supply of loans by an amount F. Assuming this has no effect on P or π^*, the costs are

$$c\left(\frac{R}{D}\right) = \frac{(W - E(W))^2}{2} \frac{d^2 (Y - F)^2}{(bs^2 + d^2)^2}. \tag{7.17}$$

Costs decrease with F when $F < Y$. Since $c(R/D)$ is convex in F, the Fed can lower the average number of panics per year by conducting an open market policy that is seasonal and averages to zero. If open market operations affect P or π^*, then the derivation above needs to be modified accordingly. In general, however, the Fed can still affect the behavior of nominal interest rates and therefore the frequency of panics (Miron 1984, chap. 4).

The conclusion that the Fed can reduce the frequency of panics by eliminating nominal interest rate seasonality is the second key result of this model. By supplying loans in periods when loan demand is high, the Fed accommodates the increase in demand and lessens the increase in interest rates that would otherwise occur. This lessens both the decrease in the reserve-deposit ratio and the accompanying upward shift in the distribution of costs. Open market purchases in a season with high loan demand thus decrease the probability of a panic.

The model presented provides an explanation for the change in the behavior of panics and interest rates that occurred after 1914. The Fed accommodated the seasonal movements in loan demand, thereby smoothing the seasonal pattern in nominal interest rates. In response to the reduction in the seasonality of interest rates, banks reduced the seasonal variation in their desired reserve-deposit ratios, so in equilibrium these were smoother. Finally, the fact that reserve-deposit ratios were smoother meant that, on average, banks were less exposed to unexpected deposit withdrawals, and so the frequency of panics fell.

The central implication of the hypothesis that the behavior of financial panics and interest rates changed after 1914 because of the Fed's seasonal open market operations is that the amount of credit extended by the Fed should have been seasonal. Additional implications are as follows: the total amount of credit outstanding in the economy should have become more seasonal after 1914, the loan-reserve ratio of banks should have become less seasonal, and the loans made by private banks should have become less seasonal.

7.2 Evidence

This section examines empirically the implications of the model and the hypotheses it suggests about the behavior of the Fed. These results come from a simple model, but they do not depend on the particular assumptions made to keep the analysis simple.

7.2.1 The National Banking System and the Founding of the Federal Reserve System

The period from 1863 through 1913 is known as the national banking period because the provisions of the National Banking Acts of 1863,

1864, and 1865 determined critical features of the banking and financial structure. These acts were both a response to problems of the ante-bellum financial system and a measure designed to raise revenue for the North during the Civil War. The acts successfully generated revenue and cured some prewar financial ills (notably the multiplicity of note issue). During the national banking period, however, those in academia, the banking community, and government still regarded the financial system as fundamentally flawed because of the "perverse elasticity of the money supply" and the high frequency of financial panics.

The term *perverse elasticity of the money supply* referred to the tendency of the money supply to contract in precisely those periods when it was "needed" most: the spring and the fall of each year when seasonal increases in loan and currency demand forced interest rates up and reserve-deposit ratios down. These seasonal movements were attributed mainly to the need for both currency and credit by the agricultural sector of the economy in the spring planting season and the fall crop-moving season and to the need for currency and credit by the corporate sector for quarterly interest and dividend settlements. Additional currency was needed because the volume of transactions was higher in these periods. Credit demand was high because farmers borrowed to finance the planting and harvesting of the crops.[3]

The financial panics that occurred in this period were combinations of bank failures, bank runs, and stock market crashes. A typical panic began after an individual bank was hit by either an unexpectedly large deposit withdrawal or a large loan default. If the bank had a small amount of reserves, it would need to call in loans. This action might concern other banks enough that they too would call in some of their loans, many of which were in stock market call loans, and the cumulative effect of loan recall by many banks tended to depress the stock market. At the same time, the fact that banks were calling in loans caused the nonbank public to increase its desired currency-deposit ratio, and this could cause either individual bank failures or runs on many banks. Eventually the process either reserved itself or ended in a suspension of convertibility (Sprague 1910).

The dynamics of various panics differed, of course. Some began in New York as the result of a large loan default at a New York bank and then were transmitted west as New York banks tried to acquire additional reserves from country banks. Others started in the West when crop failures damaged the liquidity positions of country banks, which then tried to recall balances from reserve cities. Nevertheless, the key element of a panic was similar in all of the major episodes: a generally increased demand for reserves that could not be satisfied for all parties simultaneously in the short run.

The likelihood that an event such as a large loan default would precipitate a panic depended on the initial position of the banking system. If such an event happened when loan demand was high or deposit demand was low, so that the reserve-deposit ratios of banks were low, then the costs imposed by the loan default were higher. Since seasonal movements in loan and deposit demands produced seasonal movements in reserve-deposit ratios, panics tended to occur in the fall and spring, when high loan demand and low deposit demand produced low reserve-deposit ratios. Thus the problems of perverse elasticity and the accompanying financial panics were partly a result of and coincided with seasonal movements in asset demands.

The academicians, bankers, and government officials of the time understood this phenomenon. J. Laurence Laughlin, a professor of economics at the University of Chicago, commented in detail on this relation between panics and seasonality in his 1912 treatise on reform of the banking system (pp. 309–342). Paul Warburg, a Wall Street banker who later served on the Federal Reserve Board, wrote in 1910 that "there can be no doubt whatever that the basis for healthy control by a central bank must exist in a country where regular seasonal requirements cause, with almost absolute regularity, acute increased demand for money and accommodation" (1930, p. 156). Leslie Shaw, secretary of the treasury from 1902 to 1906, attempted to accommodate the seasonal demands in financial markets but was hampered by limited funds for that purpose.[4]

The panic of 1907 precipitated sufficient concern about panics and elasticity that Congress passed the Aldrich-Vreeland Act of 1908. This act addressed the problems of the banking system by granting certain emergency powers to New York City banks and by creating the National Monetary Commission. This commission was assigned to undertake a detailed study of the U.S. banking system. Its *Report*, published in 1910, contained in-depth examinations of every aspect of banking theory and practice in the United States and abroad.

Two parts of the report deserve particular notice. O. M. W. Sprague, a professor of economics at Harvard, wrote *History of Crises under the National Banking System* (1910), examining in detail the operation of the banking system during five of the worst financial crises (1873, 1884, 1890, 1893, and 1907). Sprague wrote that "with few exceptions all our crises, panics, and periods of less severe monetary stringency have occurred in autumn" (p. 157). E. W. Kemmerer of Cornell contributed the volume *Seasonal Variations in the Relative Demand for Money and Capital in the United States* (1910). He noted that "the evidence accordingly points to a tendency for the panics to occur during the seasons normally characterized by a stringent money market" (p. 232). Thus two parts of the report mentioned explicitly the tendency for panics to occur in certain seasons.

The Federal Reserve Act established the Federal Reserve system in 1913, three years after the publication of the commission's *Report*. The preamble to the act states it is "an act to . . . furnish an elastic currency." It was to be expected, therefore, that the Fed would try to eliminate panics by accommodating the seasonal demands in financial markets.

7.2.2 Evidence of the Changes in Financial Markets

The next step is to document that the frequency of financial panics diminished after the founding of the Fed and that the size of the seasonal fluctuations in nominal interest rates diminished substantially.

Table 7.1 shows the starting dates of the financial panics that occurred during the period 1890–1908 according to Sprague and Kemmerer.[5] Sprague classified periods of financial strain as either crises or "periods of financial stringency." A crisis, the more serious situation in his terminology, necessarily involved a suspension of convertibility of deposits into currency. Sprague identified three periods of serious strain, which amounted to one every six and one-third years. Kemmerer's classification system distinguished major from minor panics and included a larger number of episodes than Sprague's. He determined the starting dates by reading the *Commercial and Financial Chronicle* and the *Financial Review*, two important business periodicals of their day. Kemmerer found six major and fifteen minor panics during the 1890–1908 period. If only major panics are included, the frequency was slightly more than one every three years. Including minor panics raises the frequency to more than one per year.

Between 1915 and 1933, the banking system experienced financial panics only during the subperiod 1929–1933.[6] Several recessions occurred during the subperiod 1915–1928 (1918–1919, 1920–1921, 1923–1924, 1926–1927), and one was quite severe. Nevertheless, until 1929, no pre–Fed style financial disruptions occurred, even during the

Table 7.1
Dates of financial panics, United States, 1890–1908

Classification	Year	Month
Sprague		
Financial stringency	1890	August
Crisis	1893	May
Crisis	1907	October
Kemmerer		
Major panics	1890	November
	1893	May
	1899	December
	1901	May
	1903	March
	1907	October
Minor panics	1893	February
	1895	September
	1896	June
	1896	December
	1898	March
	1899	September
	1901	July
	1901	September
	1902	September
	1904	December
	1905	April
	1906	April
	1906	December
	1907	March
	1908	September

Source: Miron (1986a), p. 131. As corrected in Miron (1996).

recessions. The 1921 *Annual Report* of the Fed notes that the financial market failures symptomatic of earlier downturns did not occur during the 1920–1921 recession.[7]

The question of whether the frequency of financial panics diminished after the founding of the Fed therefore consists of determining the probability that it would have taken fifteen years for the economy to experience its first panic after 1914 if in fact the tendency of the economy to panic had been unchanged. The appropriate data to use to estimate the frequency of panics during the pre-Fed period are Kemmerer's on the number of major panics; Sprague's definition of panics omits periods often cited elsewhere, while Kemmerer's data on minor panics include periods that were not noted by many other observers. Assuming that the distribution of panics was Bernoulli, Kemmerer's data provide an estimate of the probability of having a panic in a given year of .316. This implies that the probability of obtaining a sample of fourteen years with no panics was .005. The data therefore reject the hypothesis of no change in the frequency of panics at 1 percent level of confidence.

Figure 7.1 shows the estimated seasonal pattern in the interest rate on stock market call loans for the periods 1890–1908 and 1919–1928.[8] The patterns were calculated using weekly data by computing the unconditional mean in each week, after subtracting a trend. The top portion is for 1890–1908 and the bottom for 1919–1928. Both are plotted in hundreds of basis points per year and show fifty-two coefficients. The patterns are statistically significant in each period.

The size of the seasonal cycle clearly decreases from the earlier period to the later. The standard deviation of the seasonal cycle was 130

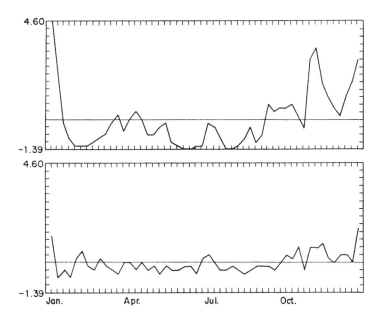

Figure 7.1
Seasonal pattern in nominal rate, before (top) and after (bottom) 1914. Source: Miron (1986a), p. 132.

basis points before 1914 but only 46 basis points afterward. The amplitude of the cycle dropped from 600 basis points before 1914 to 230 after. The change in the patterns is statistically significant.

7.2.3   Implications of the Model for the Pre-Fed Data

The second step in the analysis is to confirm that the model presented is consistent with the data for the pre-Fed period. The central implication of that model is that the distribution of financial panics should have been seasonal, with periods of high frequency corresponding to periods with high interest rates. Table 7.2 summarizes the data in table 7.1 on the starting dates of panics by showing the number of panics that began in each month of the year. The distribution was clearly seasonal, and the periods of high frequency were spring and fall. This result is confirmed by a χ^2 goodness-of-fit test of the null hypothesis that the number of panics in each month was the same—that is, a test of the null hypothesis of no seasonality. The calculated test statistic for the data in the table is 25.91, while the 1 percent critical value of the χ^2 statistic with 11 degrees of freedom is 24.73.

Figure 7.2 provides additional support for the model. It shows the estimated seasonal pattern in the call money loan rate (top) and the loan-reserve ratio (bottom) for the period 1890–1908. (The scale on

Table 7.2
Distribution of financial panics by month, 1890–1908

January	0
February	1
March	3
April	2
May	2
June	1
July	1
August	0
September	5
October	1
November	1
December	4

Source: Miron (1986a), p. 133. As corrected in Miron (1996).

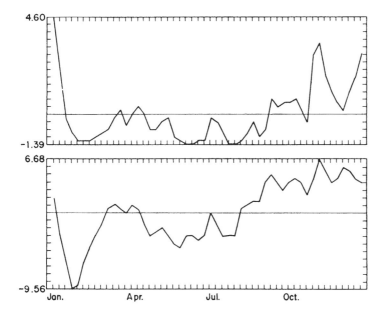

Figure 7.2
Seasonal pattern in nominal interest rate (top) and loan-reserve ratio (bottom) before
1914. Source: Miron (1986a), p. 133.

the bottom is in percent and shows the percentage change in the level
of the loan-reserve ratio in each week.) The peaks in both variables occur in approximately the same two periods of the year, spring and fall,
and the correlation between the estimated seasonal patterns is .63. Both
the timing of the peaks, which coincides with that in financial panics,
and the positive correlation between the seasonal patterns, are results
implied by the model.

Note that the pre-Fed seasonal movements in the loan-reserve ratio
were large, with the standard deviation of the cycle being 3.5 percent
and the amplitude 16.2 percent. In the post–World War II period, the
elasticity of loan supply with respect to the interest rate has been small
(Rasche 1972), and excess reserves have been kept near zero. The explanation for this change in behavior may be either the advent of the
Federal Deposit Insurance Corporation (FDIC) or the smoother behavior of nominal interest rates. To the extent that the explanation is the
lack of seasonal fluctuations in interest rates, this result also confirms
the model.

7.2.4   Implications of the Hypothesis That the Fed Caused the Changes in Financial Markets

The hypothesis that the Fed caused the decrease in both the frequency of financial panics and the size of the seasonal movements in nominal interest rates implies that its actions should have been seasonal, with peaks of accommodation coming in seasons that had previously tended to be ones of financial stress. From 1915 to 1918, the Fed accommodated seasonal strain mainly by subsidizing loans for agricultural purposes, since the problems of financing World War I constrained its ability to conduct discretionary open market operations. Then, in 1918, it began to engage in significant seasonal open market operations.

The Fed established its loan subsidy program during the first full year of its existence, 1915. The program rediscounted bills backed by agricultural commodities at preferential rates to ensure "that whatever funds might be necessary for the gradual and orderly marketing of the cotton crop" would be available. (The subsidy was not limited to bills backed by cotton, however.) The annual reports for the years 1916–1918 all note that the program was working well and that the usual seasonal strain in financial markets had been avoided. The Fed discontinued the program in 1918 when it gained better control over its open market operations due to the end of the war.

Figure 7.3 shows the estimated seasonal pattern in Federal Reserve credit outstanding for the period 1922–1928.[9] The periods of peaks in reserve credit outstanding coincide with periods during which peaks

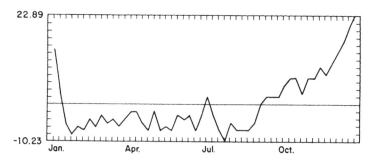

Figure 7.3
Seasonal pattern in federal reserve credit outstanding, 1922–1928. Source: Miron (1986), p. 134.

in interest rates and loan-reserve ratios occurred before the founding of the Fed, and the seasonal pattern is statistically significant. Federal Reserve credit increased 32 percent over the seasonal cycle, which amounted to roughly $400 million in a typical year. Since the total amount of loans outstanding at New York City banks was $6,000 million, this increase was substantial. The actions of the Fed were seasonal and likely to have alleviated the seasonal strain that existed before 1914.

Several additional implications of the hypothesis of Fed responsibility can also be verified quantitatively. The seasonal variation in the total amount of credit outstanding should have increased after 1914 since, according to the hypothesis, the Fed's policy was one of subsidizing loan demand. Also, the seasonal variation in loan-reserve ratios should have decreased because this produced the seasonal variation in bank operating costs that the Fed wished to eliminate. Figure 7.4 shows the seasonal pattern in loans by banks before 1914 and in the total amount of credit outstanding (banks and the Fed) after 1914. The total amount of credit outstanding became more seasonal after the

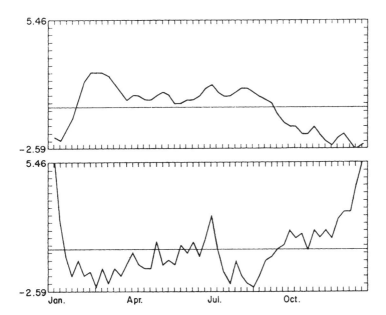

Figure 7.4
Seasonal pattern in total credit outstanding before (top) and after (bottom) 1914. Source: Miron (1986), p. 134.

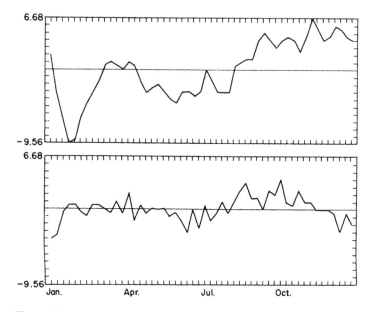

Figure 7.5
Seasonal pattern in loan-reserve ratio before (top) and after (bottom) 1914. Source: Miron (1986), p. 134.

founding of the Fed, with the standard deviation increasing from 1.4 to 1.8 percent and the amplitude rising from 4.8 to 7.7 percent. Figure 7.5 shows the estimated seasonal pattern in the loan-reserve ratio of banks before and after 1914. The figures show that the seasonal pattern diminished considerably, with the amplitude falling from 16.2 to 7.8 percent and the standard deviation dropping from 3.5 to 1.5 percent. Note in particular that the periods that showed the most significant seasonal strain before 1914 in all cases show almost none after 1914.

The other implication of the hypothesis that the Fed caused the changes in financial markets is that the seasonal variation in loans made by private banks should have decreased. The seasonal pattern in loans by banks before and after 1914 is shown in figure 7.6. The amount of seasonal variation diminishes, as implied by the hypothesis of Fed causation. The timing of the seasonal pattern also changes, however, and this is not implied by the hypothesis.

The explanation for the change in timing is probably that the pattern of deposits at banks changed after 1914 because the Treasury began

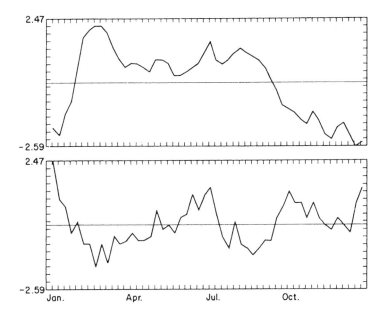

Figure 7.6
Seasonal pattern in loans before (top) and after (bottom) 1914. Source: Miron (1986), p. 135.

keeping some of its deposits at the Fed. Before 1914, the Treasury kept its holdings of currency in either Treasury offices or private banks, and movements of cash between these two places affected the stock of high-powered money. After 1914, the Treasury also kept some of its deposits at the Fed. Since Treasury deposits at the Fed are not part of high-powered money, increases in Treasury deposits decrease high-powered money. If the Treasury kept at the Fed deposits that it had previously kept at private banks, the seasonal movements in the Treasury's holdings of cash would have produced different seasonal movements in high-powered money after 1914.

Figure 7.7 shows the seasonal pattern in Treasury deposits at the Fed for the period 1922:1–1928:12. A large peak occurs at about the time of the year (February–March) when the loan seasonal diminishes. Thus the change in the behavior of the Treasury may explain the change in timing of the loan seasonal.

The quantitative evidence therefore establishes that the Fed caused the changes in the behavior of financial markets. Two quotations from

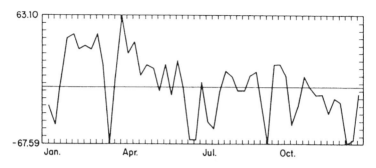

Figure 7.7
Seasonal pattern in treasury deposits at the Fed. Source: Miron (1986), p. 135.

the Fed's first annual report confirm this evidence. In discussing the proper role for monetary policy, the report says,

What is the proper place and function of the Federal Reserve Banks in our banking and credit system? On the one hand, it is represented that they are merely emergency banks to be resorted to for assistance only in the time of abnormal stress; while on the other, it is claimed that they are in essence simply additional banks which should compete with the member banks, especially with those of the greatest power. The function of a reserve bank is not to be identified with either of these extremes. . . . Its duty is not to await emergencies but by anticipation, to do what it can to prevent them. So also if, at any time, commerce, industry or agriculture are, in the opinion of the Federal Reserve Board, burdened unduly with excessive interest charges, it will be the clear and imperative duty of the Reserve Board acting through the discount rate and open market powers, to secure a wider diffusion of credit facilities at a reasonable rate. . . . The more complete adaptation of the credit mechanisms and facilities of the country to the needs of industry, commerce, and agriculture—with all their seasonal fluctuations and contingencies—should be the constant aim of a Reserve Bank's management. [1914, p. 17]

Further, the report states,

It should not, however, be assumed that because a bank is a Reserve Bank its resources should be kept idle for use only in times of difficulty. . . . Time and experience will show what seasonal variates in the credit demand and facilities in each of the Reserve Banks of the several districts will be and when and to what extent a Reserve Bank may, without violating its special function as a guardian of banking reserves, engage in banking and credit operations. [1914, p. 18]

It is clear that the Fed considered the elimination of both seasonal strain and financial panics as essential parts of its function.

The statements of H. Parker Willis and Carter Glass provide additional support for this proposition. Willis, an economist at Columbia University, was an expert consultant to the House Banking and Currency Committee in 1912–1913 while the Federal Reserve Act was being written, and he later became secretary of the Federal Reserve Board. He wrote in 1915 that the potential benefits of the system were that "there will be no such wide fluctuations of interest rates . . . from season to season as now exist . . . and no necessity of emergency measures to safeguard the country from possible results of financial panic or stringency" (p. 75). Carter Glass, who sponsored the Federal Reserve Act as a member of the House of Representatives in 1913, wrote in 1927 (p. 387) that two of the most important accomplishments of the system were removal of panics and the elimination of seasonal interest rate fluctuations.

7.2.5 Seasonality and Financial Panics during the Great Depression

The United States did not experience any financial panics from 1915 through 1928. Five financial panics did occur, however, during the period 1929–1933, and these were among the most severe in the country's history. Since the preceding sections have shown that the Fed successfully eliminated panics from 1915 to 1928, it is necessary to explain why panics recurred during the later period.

Figure 7.8 shows the actual level of Federal Reserve credit outstanding during the year 1929 as well as the level projected on the basis of the pattern that obtained from 1922 through 1928. The actual level is below the projected level starting in March. Further, the points at which the discrepancy increases correspond to periods that experienced peaks in loan demand during the 1890–1908 period. Figure 7.9 shows the estimated seasonal patterns in reserve credit outstanding for the two periods 1922–1928 and 1929–1933. The seasonal pattern is dampened in the later period, with the standard deviation of the cycle falling from 7.5 to 6.9 percent and the amplitude falling from 33.1 to 26.1 percent.

These results show that the Fed accommodated the seasonal demands in financial markets to a lesser extent during the 1929–1933 period than it had previously. This means the frequency of panics should have increased, as it did. It also means that panics should have occurred in the spring and in the fall: three of the panics were in the fall (1929, 1930, 1932), and two were in the spring (1931, 1933).[10] Thus,

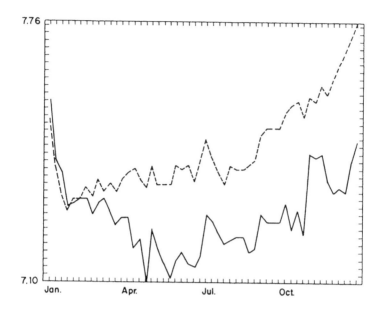

Figure 7.8
Actual (solid line) and forecast (broken line) value of reserve credit outstanding. Source:
Miron (1986), p. 136.

the recurrence of panics during this period corroborates the hypothesis that the Fed caused the reduction in the frequency of panics after
1914.

The decreased accommodation of the seasonals in asset demands
was probably the result of a generally restrictive open market policy that the Fed initiated in late 1928.[11] During much of the 1920s,
some observers feared that stock market speculation was "excessive,"
and those who most objected to the speculation encouraged the Fed
to restrain the growth of credit, particularly loans by banks to stock
market brokers. The officials at the Fed differed in their view of how
much to restrain credit. On balance, however, they opposed restraining speculation so much that it might adversely affect general business
activity.

This policy changed toward the end of 1928. Stock market speculation had been especially virulent, and the Fed responded with a
strongly restrictive policy. The explanation for the change in policy is
that Benjamin Strong, the governor of the New York Fed, died in October 1928. During the period 1915–1928, Strong was a dominant force
in the Federal Reserve system and in the entire financial community.

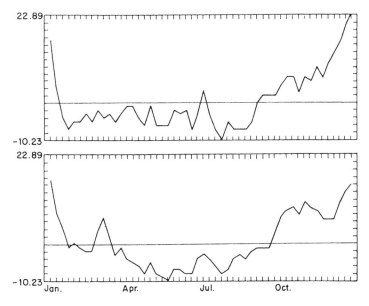

Figure 7.9
Seasonal pattern in reserve credit outstanding, 1922–1928 (Top) and 1929–1933 (Bottom).
Source: Miron (1986), p. 136.

In the words of his biographer, Lester Chandler, Strong was "one of the world's most influential leaders in the fields of money and finance. During the first fourteen turbulent, formative years of the Federal Reserve System, his was the greatest influence on American monetary and banking policies" (1958, p. 3). Strong intensely disliked stock market speculation but was an outspoken critic of restraining speculation at the cost of causing a recession. His death allowed the balance of opinion at the Fed to shift toward greater restraint, and a highly restrictive policy resulted.[12] One of the manifestations of this policy was the incomplete accommodation of the seasonal demands in financial markets.

7.3   Conclusions

The conclusion of this chapter clearly raises the question of what current monetary policy should do about nominal interest rate seasonals. The post–World War II period has witnessed substantial seasonality in both open market operations and the stock of money but virtually no seasonality in nominal rates. This suggests that the Fed has accommodated seasonal fluctuations in asset demands since World War II in much the same way that it did following its inception in 1914. It also suggests that if the Fed produced a nonseasonal money stock, as Friedman (1959, 1982) has suggested it should, interest rate seasonals would return.

A return of nominal interest rate seasonals, however, would not necessarily cause a return of financial panics. Congress imposed deposit insurance on the banking system in 1934, and the presence of deposit insurance might eliminate panics independent of the Fed's seasonal policy. Thus, the analysis here does not by itself imply that continued elimination of interest rate seasonals is desirable. It does show that an important aspect of Fed policy is its seasonal behavior, and it demonstrates that this aspect of policy can have substantial real effects on the economy.

8   The Gold Standard and Interest Rate Seasonality

The analysis in chapter 7 argues that the Fed was created for the purpose of eliminating nominal interest rate seasonals and that the Fed was indeed responsible for a dramatic reduction in nominal interest rate seasonality in the United States after 1914. This conclusion, if accurate, provides an excellent example of how examination of seasonal fluctuations can enhance understanding of the economy generally.

The conclusion that the Fed was responsible for the reduction in interest rate seasonality has not gone unchallenged. Clark (1986), in particular, notes that the disappearance of seasonal fluctuations in nominal interest rates was a worldwide phenomenon. Although the United States was certainly not a small country by 1914, neither was it so dominant that it should have been able, acting on its own, to alter greatly the stochastic processes of world prices and interest rates. Clark suggests it would appear more plausible to attribute the altered behavior of nominal interest rates to the dissolution of the worldwide gold standard at the start of World War I.

This chapter summarizes research that evaluates the role of the destruction of the gold standard and the founding of the Federal Reserve, both of which occurred in 1914, in contributing to seasonal and non-seasonal changes in the behavior of interest rates and prices after 1914. The chapter, based on Barsky et al. (1988), presents a model of policy coordination in which the introduction of the Fed stabilizes interest rates—seasonally and otherwise—even if the gold standard remains intact. It also offers empirical evidence that the dismantling of the gold standard did not play a crucial role in precipitating the changes in interest rate behavior.

8.1   Historical Overview

The period 1879–1914 stands out in the history of the world monetary systems as the time when the world came closest to operating on a textbook version of the gold standard. The period is also unusual, although not unique, in that the United States was the only major economic power without a central bank. The period after 1914 differed drastically from the period before 1914 in several respects. As a result of World War I, the international gold standard was suspended in most countries, and it returned for only a limited time and in much weakened form. The Federal Reserve system began operations in 1914, providing the United States with centralized monetary control for the first time in almost eighty years.[1]

8.1.1   Central Banking before 1914

By the last quarter of the nineteenth century, most of the important economic powers other than the United States had established central banks: the Bank of England, established in 1694; the Bank of France (1800); the State Bank of Russia (1860); the German Reichsbank (1876); and the Bank of Japan (1882).[2] Some of the banks were closer to ordinary (state-sanctioned) commercial banks than to modern central banks, and none engaged in what would today be considered a complete set of central banking activities. The Bank of England was the most developed of these in exercising central banking functions, and it was widely regarded as playing a central role in enforcing the international gold standard.[3]

It was universally recognized during this period that the crucial objective of the central banks was to maintain a supply of gold reserves sufficient to ensure convertibility (Bloomfield 1959, p. 23). Central banks accomplished this task through a number of different means, the most important of which was manipulating the interest rate at which they would discount private debt. Other methods of safeguarding the gold reserve included open market operations and changes in regulations regarding convertibility. The Bank of England relied heavily on changes in the discount rate (bank rate), while the continental central banks made more frequent use of other methods (Eichengreen 1985, p. 13).

Contemporary discussions about how the Bank of England should set bank rate indicate the objectives that pre-1914 central banks pursued when they were not handcuffed by the need to ensure convertibility. Sayers (1936) states that the bank gave weight to the condition of the domestic economy; specifically, the bank anticipated the effects of future events on the interest rates and attempted to set bank rate at the level it expected to maintain. The *First Interim Report* of the Cunliffe Committee (1918) suggested that bank rate be raised in response to permanent but not temporary disturbances in the money market. Jevons (1884) argued that the bank should not raise the bank rate in response to the regular autumnal drains on the bank's reserves since these replenished themselves in the normal course of business. Bagehot claims in *Lombard Street* (1873) that the bank had an "inescapable duty" to act as lender of last resort. Whatever the objectives of the world's central banks, they were either very skillful or very lucky in maintaining convertibility since the period was marked by few exchange crises (Bloomfield 1959, p. 9).

The United States stood out from other economic powers of this period in its lacking a central bank until the founding of the Federal Reserve system in November 1914. The events precipitating the founding of the Fed started with the panic of 1907, which led to the passage of the Aldrich-Vreeland Act, a temporary measure designed to allow New York City banks some leeway in dealing with emergencies and to the creation of the National Monetary Commission, a congressional and academic committee that undertook to study all aspects of the domestic and international banking system. The commission's report, published in 1910, laid the basic blueprint for the Federal Reserve Act, which became law in December 1913. The heads of the twelve banks met in August 1914 to discuss the details of the system's organization, and the banks opened for business in November of that year.

The Fed was created mainly to eliminate dramatic interest rate fluctuations through provision of an "elastic currency" (Laughlin 1912, Willis 1915, Glass 1927, Warburg 1930). The Fed was expected to perferm other central banking activities, of course, particularly the elimination of the interregional interest rate differentials and the associated pyramiding of reserves (Gendreau 1979, 1983; White 1983). The Fed's crucial objective, however, was the accommodation of the regular seasonal fluctuations in money markets as well as the sterilization of more erratic interest rate fluctuations associated with financial panics. It is useful to note that the Fed was conceived and created before the outbreak of World War I and the suspension of the gold standard. The founders of the Fed had no way of knowing that the Fed would find itself, almost precisely at the moment of its birth, in a new kind of international monetary situation. Instead, they expected that the Fed would operate under the gold standard regime that had come to be the accepted system of international monetary arrangements (Friedman and Schwartz 1963a, p. 191).

8.1.2   The Gold Standard and World War I

The exact definition of the gold standard varies considerably among different authors, and the features of the gold standard that are important depend on the question at hand. The discussion here focuses on features that are crucial to determining the conditions under which interest rates and prices are determined both within and across countries.

Eichengreen (1985) ascribes three basic characteristics to the classical gold standard: (1) convertibility between domestic money and gold at a fixed official price; (2) freedom for private citizens to export and import gold; and (3) a set of rules relating the quantity of money in circulation to that country's gold stock.[4] The first two features imply that a gold standard establishes a system of fixed exchange rates between national currencies. This system places strong restrictions on the feasible monetary and fiscal policies available to an open economy operating under a gold standard (Sargent 1986, pp. 45–46).

Three different types of rules relating the quantity of fiat money to gold reserves were common (Bloomfield 1959, p. 18). Fiduciary systems required all notes above a certain limit to be backed 100 percent by legal reserves. Proportional systems required notes to be covered by a minimum proportion of legal reserves. Combination systems involved aspects of both systems. If a central bank (in a closed economy) operated under a fiduciary system and was not at the constraint, it could affect interest rates and the price level by altering the mix of notes relative to gold.

The thirty-five-year period preceding 1914 constituted the world's purest experience with a classical gold standard. All the major economic powers in Europe and Asia, as well as the United States and most Latin American countries, maintained convertibility during this period. Only a few countries on the gold standard devalued, and only a small number of economic powers participated in any other kind of monetary arrangement.[5] The period is also noteworthy for the comparative absence of balance-of-payments crises or other traumatic events associated with the exchange rate regime.

The suspension of the gold standard in 1914 was the direct result of the outbreak of World War I in August 1914. Within a few months of the outbreak of the war (indeed in some cases even before the declaration), most countries had suspended gold payments either de jure or de facto (Brown 1940, pp. 7–26). When the war ended, most countries had experienced such rapid inflation during the previous four years that an immediate return to convertibility at anything like the prewar parities was unthinkable. The announced aim of virtually all countries, however, was a quick return to the gold standard, and the macroeconomic history of the subsequent period can be understood only in this light.[6]

The correct characterization of the system of international monetary arrangements varies considerably over the 1914–1933 period. During the war, the major currencies floated relative to one another, but controls on prices, gold movements, and international capital flows make any simple description of that system inaccurate. The period from 1919 through 1925 appears to be a relatively clean case of floating rates. From 1926 through 1931, several countries resumed convertibility, so the world moved back toward a gold standard. The consensus, however, is that operation of the gold standard during this period did not approximate its smooth operation before 1914. Beginning with Britain's devaluation of sterling in fall 1931, a number of countries left the gold standard, this time for good. The final blow to the international gold standard was the departure of the United States in 1933 (Eichengreen 1985, pp. 19–24).

8.2 Evidence of the Changes in Behavior of Interest Rates and Prices

This section documents the seasonal and other changes in the behavior of the nominal interest rates and inflation rates that occurred after 1914 in the United States and Britain. These two countries were the world's major economic powers, and New York and London were the key financial centers. In addition, consistent data series exist for these two countries.[7] The results examine the behavior of financial markets in both countries for two periods (1890–1910 and 1920–1933) that do not overlap the founding of the Fed or World War I.[8] The objective is to document the change in regime in a way that avoids problems of how the transition took place.

All data series are monthly. The nominal interest rate series for the United States consists of observations from the first week of each month on the three-month time loan rate available at New York City banks.[9] The nominal rate series for Britain consists of observations from the first week of the month on the three-month rate on bankers' bills available in London, as reported in the *Economist*.[10] The price series for the United States is the wholesale price index for all commodities published by the Bureau of Labor Statistics. The numbers are averages of observations collected throughout the month. The price series for Britain is an index of the wholesale prices of forty-five commodities, developed by Augustus Saurbeck and continued after his death by the *Statist*.[11] It is (purportedly) measured during the last week of each month. The series is shifted forward one month in all of the calculations reported here, so it is only one week out of alignment with the interest rate series.

Table 8.1 shows the autocorrelation function for the nominal interest rate in the United States and Britain for the two different sample

Table 8.1
Autocorrelations of the short rate

	United States				Britain			
	1890–1910		1920–1933		1890–1910		1920–1933	
	Level	Change	Level	Change	Level	Change	Level	Change
First	0.75	−0.19	0.96	0.02	0.84	−0.04	0.95	0.06
Second	0.61	0.12	0.92	0.05	0.68	−0.11	0.89	0.14
Third	0.40	−0.20	0.86	−0.10	0.57	−0.05	0.82	0.04
Fourth	0.29	−0.05	0.81	0.09	0.48	−0.18	0.74	0.03
Fifth	0.20	−0.06	0.76	0.10	0.45	−0.02	0.66	−0.07
Sixth	0.14	−0.09	0.70	0.06	0.42	0.01	0.58	−0.02
Seventh	0.12	−0.02	0.64	−0.03	0.39	−0.13	0.50	−0.15
Eighth	0.11	−0.09	0.58	0.01	0.38	−0.13	0.44	−0.02
Ninth	0.13	0.02	0.52	−0.10	0.42	0.02	0.37	−0.00
Tenth	0.15	−0.00	0.48	0.02	0.45	0.10	0.31	−0.05
Eleventh	0.17	0.06	0.42	−0.03	0.45	−0.01	0.25	0.00
Twelfth	0.15	0.15	0.37	0.03	0.45	0.18	0.19	−0.04
Standard Deviation	1.53	1.07	2.11	0.52	1.25	0.70	1.61	0.45

Source: Barsky et al. (1988), p. 1131.
Note: The approximate standard errors for the autocorrelations (under the null that the series is white noise) are 0.06 for the 1890–1910 sample and 0.08 for the 1920–1933 sample.

periods. In both countries the short rate was mean reverting during the 1890–1910 period. The autocorrelations of the level of rates dampen quickly, and the first differences show significant negative autocorrelation. In the 1920–1933 period, the autocorrelations die out less quickly, and the first differences are less highly autocorrelated. In the first sample, the autocorrelations indicate that the short rate is more persistent in Britain than it is in the United States. In the second sample, the autocorrelation functions are almost identical.

Table 8.2 presents regressions of the short rate on the lagged short rate, including and excluding seasonal dummies. These results confirm those in table 8.1. In the early period, the coefficient on the lagged short rate is significantly less than 1 in both countries, and seasonality is quantitatively important. In the later period, the coefficient on the lagged short rate is not significantly different from 1, and seasonality is much less important. In both countries, the short-term nominal interest rate became approximately a random walk.

Figure 8.1 displays estimates of the seasonal pattern in short rates for both countries and sample periods. The seasonal patterns were calculated by regressing the short rate on seasonal dummies only, with the coefficients constrained to change smoothly from one month to the next. This procedure consisted of regressing the short rate on lags one through twelve of the seasonal dummy for January, with the coefficients constrained to follow a fifth-order polynomial distributed lag. The figures present the differences of the twelve coefficients from the average coefficient.

The pattern of seasonality is similar in timing across countries. Rates were high in the fall, especially November, and low in the summer, particularly July. The amplitude of the seasonal pattern is also similar: approximately 200 basis points (at an annual rate) in both countries. The seasonal pattern is statistically significant in both countries in both sample periods, but in the later sample period, the amplitude of the seasonal patterns is much smaller. Tests of the hypothesis that the seasonal patterns are the same before and after 1914 reject the null at the 1 percent level for both the United States and Britain.[12]

The next question is whether the changes in the behavior of the nominal interest rates coincided with changes in the behavior of inflation rates. Tables 8.3 and 8.4 present results for the one-month inflation rate analogous to those in tables 8.1 and 8.2 for the nominal interest rate.

Table 8.2
Regressions of the short rate on lagged short rate

	United States				Britain			
	1890–1910		1920–1933		1890–1910		1920–1933	
Constant	1.01	0.03	0.09	0.05	0.42	0.09	0.11	0.10
	(0.18)	(0.29)	(0.09)	(0.16)	(0.10)	(0.16)	(0.09)	(0.09)
i_{t-1}	0.75	0.77	0.97	0.98	0.84	0.86	0.96	0.97
	(0.04)	(0.04)	(0.02)	(0.02)	(0.03)	(0.03)	(0.02)	(0.02)
d^2		1.05		0.34		0.19		−0.07
		(0.29)		(0.19)		(0.18)		(0.17)
d^3		0.90		−0.10		0.00		−0.23
		(0.29)		(0.19)		(0.18)		(0.17)
d^4		0.55		−0.16		0.39		−0.09
		(0.29)		(0.19)		(0.18)		(0.17)
d^5		0.60		−0.07		−0.08		−0.07
		(0.29)		(0.19)		(0.18)		(0.17)
d^6		0.77		−0.06		−0.20		0.14
		(0.29)		(0.19)		(0.18)		(0.17)
d^7		1.10		0.17		0.60		0.13
		(0.29)		(0.19)		(0.18)		(0.17)
d^8		1.44		0.16		0.48		−0.01
		(0.29)		(0.19)		(0.18)		(0.17)
d^9		1.30		0.12		0.58		0.19
		(0.29)		(0.19)		(0.18)		(0.17)
d^{10}		1.46		−0.12		1.05		−0.06
		(0.29)		(0.19)		(0.18)		(0.17)
d^{11}		0.71		−0.12		0.23		0.06
		(0.29)		(0.19)		(0.18)		(0.06)
d^{12}		1.10		0.17		−0.04		−0.07
		(0.29)		(0.19)		(0.18)		(0.17)
$\bar{R}^2$	0.57	0.62	0.94	0.94	0.71	0.79	0.92	0.92
s.e.e.	1.00	0.94	0.52	0.51	0.68	0.59	0.45	0.45

Source: Barsky et al. (1988), p. 1131.
Note: Standard errors are in parentheses.

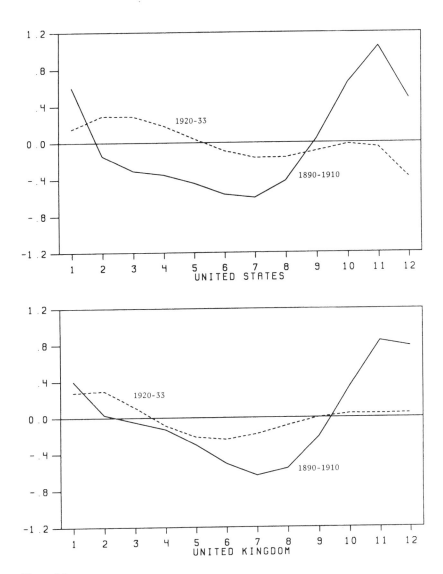

Figure 8.1
Seasonal in nominal interest rates. Source: Barsky, Mankiw, Miron and Weil (1988), p. 1132.

158   Chapter 8

Table 8.3
Autocorrelations of the inflation rate

	United States		Britain	
	1890–1910	1920–1933	1890–1910	1920–1933
First	0.18	0.65	0.32	0.46
Second	0.02	0.56	0.10	0.28
Third	0.03	0.38	0.10	0.17
Fourth	−0.00	0.31	0.05	0.15
Fifth	−0.02	0.13	0.05	0.10
Sixth	−0.02	0.07	0.02	0.09
Seventh	−0.04	−0.00	0.02	0.06
Eighth	0.05	−0.04	0.15	0.09
Ninth	0.02	−0.04	0.13	0.12
Tenth	−0.03	−0.00	−0.03	0.15
Eleventh	−0.02	0.04	0.01	0.08
Twelfth	−0.09	−0.04	−0.02	−0.09
Standard deviation	18.95	23.08	12.02	25.47

Source: Barsky et al. (1988), p. 1133.
Note: The approximate standard errors for the autocorrelations (under the null that the series is white noise) are 0.06 for the 1890–1910 sample and 0.08 for the 1920–1933 sample.

During the early sample period, the autocorrelation function of the United States shows significant correlation at the first lag but little at any other lag. This is exactly what one would expect if the true inflation process were white noise in continuous time but one employed time-averaged price-level data to compute the inflation rates (Working 1960). For the United States, the price-level data are averages over a month, so the results are consistent with a white noise process for the inflation rate. In Britain, the first-order autocorrelation is stronger during the early sample period, and several of the higher-order autocorrelations are significant. Also, the price data for Britain are allegedly from the last week of each month, so the time-average bias should not be severe. The results therefore indicate some positive serial correlation in the inflation rate for Britain. In the post-1914 sample period, inflation is moderately and significantly persistent in both countries.

Table 8.4
Regressions of inflation rate on lagged inflation rate

	United States				Britain			
	1890–1910		1920–1933		1890–1910		1920–1933	
Constant	0.73	−2.90	−1.65	2.22	0.29	0.90	−4.01	4.34
	(1.19)	(4.07)	(1.39)	(4.65)	(0.72)	(2.44)	(1.80)	(5.97)
π_{t-1}	0.18	0.17	0.66	0.68	0.32	0.36	0.47	0.50
	(0.06)	(0.06)	(0.06)	(0.06)	(0.06)	(0.06)	(0.07)	(0.07)
d^2		6.46		−4.33		−2.99		−12.66
		(5.76)		(6.54)		(3.45)		(8.44)
d^3		2.14		−1.92		2.61		−7.11
		(5.76)		(6.54)		(3.56)		(8.43)
d^4		−4.63		−4.90		1.14		−14.98
		(5.76)		(6.54)		(3.45)		(8.43)
d^5		4.34		7.84		−9.04		−16.49
		(5.76)		(6.54)		(3.45)		(8.45)
d^6		10.28		−7.05		3.78		5.06
		(5.76)		(6.60)		(3.49)		(8.48)
d^7		11.49		−0.14		0.29		−12.84
		(5.78)		(6.55)		(3.45)		(8.43)
d^8		6.78		−13.50		−0.03		−4.95
		(5.79)		(6.57)		(3.45)		(8.43)
d^9		−0.64		−6.02		−0.16		−10.21
		(5.77)		(6.53)		(3.45)		(8.43)
d^{10}		5.77		−10.17		−4.88		−5.13
		(5.76)		(6.53)		(3.45)		(8.43)
d^{11}		−0.37		−1.66		−0.72		−13.83
		(5.76)		(6.54)		(3.47)		(8.43)
d^{12}		2.10		−3.64		2.56		−4.77
		(5.76)		(6.53)		(3.45)		(8.44)
$\overline{R}^2$	0.029	0.045	0.433	0.447	0.098	0.139	0.219	0.228
s.e.e.	18.8	18.7	17.5	17.3	11.4	11.3	22.4	22.3

Source: Barsky et al. (1988), p. 1134.
Note: Standard errors are in parentheses. s.e.e. = standard error of estimate.

The regression results tell essentially the same story as the autocorrelations. In the United States, inflation is not persistent in the early sample period but is clearly so in the later sample. In Britain, inflation is somewhat persistent in the first sample and modestly but significantly persistent in the later sample.

Figure 8.2 displays estimates of the seasonal patterns in inflation.[13] The estimates indicate substantial seasonality in the inflation rate in both countries in both time periods: the amplitude is at least 800 basis points in every sample and more than 2,000 basis points in the later samples. The seasonal in the inflation rate is significantly different from zero in all four samples. Although the point estimates suggest that the seasonal patterns are significantly different across sample periods, tests of the hypothesis of no change fail to reject the null at even the 35 percent level for either country.[14]

The results clearly delineate the changes in the stochastic processes for interest rates and prices. In both countries, persistence in the short-term nominal interest rate and the inflation rate increased, and seasonality in the interest rate decreased markedly. One cannot determine whether the seasonality of inflation rates changed significantly. Although the changes that occur in both variables are qualitatively similar across countries, the changes are more pronounced in the United States.

8.3   A Model of Policy Interaction under a Gold Standard

The traditional explanation of the changes in the behavior of interest rates and prices in the United States is that the changes were due to the founding of the Federal Reserve system. Certainly a reader of contemporary periodicals would be drawn to this explanation. The Fed was created primarily to stabilize interest rates and credit markets, so it should not be surprising that interest rates stabilized after its founding. The fact that the change in the behavior of interest rates and prices occurred worldwide, however, calls this traditional explanation into question. One might also make the a priori argument that under a fixed exchange rate system, as existed before 1914, the existence of the Fed should be irrelevant. Under fixed exchange rates, international arbitrage should equate nominal interest rates throughout the world. Therefore, the introduction of a single central bank, such as the Federal Reserve, should have at most minimal effects on interest rates or prices.

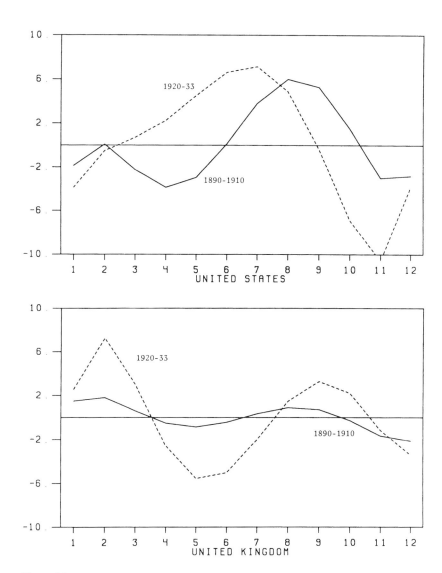

Figure 8.2
Seasonal pattern in inflation rate, United States and United Kingdom. Source: Barsky, Mankiw, Miron and Weil (1988), p. 1135.

The assertion that the Fed could not have been responsible for the changes in the behavior of interest rates and prices obviously raises the question of what did cause these changes. The most obvious alternative explanation is that the changes were caused by the breakdown of the classical gold standard and the fixed exchange rate system at the beginning of World War I. Indeed, it might seem difficult to make an affirmative case for the position that the breakdown of the classical gold standard was not relevant to the changes in the behavior of interest rates and prices.

The purpose of this section is to make theoretically plausible the position that the Fed could have been the cause of the changes in the behavior of interest rates and prices. The analysis argues that the founding of the Fed might have led to the changed behavior of interest rates and prices, even if World War I and the breakdown of the classical gold standard had not occurred. Of course, no purely theoretical discussion can preclude a possibly important role for the destruction of the gold standard in causing the changes in financial markets. Theory can, however, overturn the presumption that the changes could not have been due to the Fed. The following empirical work evaluates the part each of these two events played in bringing about the observed changes in the behavior of interest rates and prices.

8.3.1   The Setup of the Model

This section proposes a simple model in which exchange rates are fixed and the introduction of a single central bank might have worldwide implications for interest rates and prices.[15] The model is highly stylized. It assumes perfect capital markets, perfect purchasing power parity, and a complete dichotomy between real and monetary phenomena. These assumptions are probably incorrect and perhaps patently false. The model is nonetheless useful as an illustration of some of the forces that might have been at work. In particular, the model shows that the introduction of a central bank in one country might have worldwide implications.

Consider a world of two identical countries operating under fixed exchange rates. Each country wishes to stabilize its nominal interest rate and to avoid international gold flows. When only one country has a central bank, it is impossible for that bank to both stabilize interest rates and avoid gold flows. Hence, the bank must trade off the two goals. Once the second country introduces a central bank, both banks together can stabilize interest rates without generating undesirable gold flows. This equilibrium with two central banks achieves the first-best monetary policy, even in the absence of coordination.

In each country, the demand for money is given by the simple quantity equation

$$M_t = P_t \tag{8.1}$$

$$M_t^* = P_t^*, \tag{8.2}$$

where M is the country's quantity of money, P is the price of goods in terms of money, and the asterisk denotes a foreign country variable. Because of purchasing power parity, $P = P^*$.

The supply of money is assumed to consist of monetary gold and fiduciary money—that is, money printed by the central bank that is (in principle) convertible into gold and thus trades one-for-one with gold. The world supply of money is

$$M_t + M_t^* = M_{t-1} + M_{t-1}^* + X_t + X_t^*, \tag{8.3}$$

where X is the quantity of new fiduciary money printed. The bank changes the quantity of fiduciary money within sufficiently narrow bounds that the maintenance of the gold standard is not threatened.[16]

The real interest rate, r_t, is exogenous and common across countries. The nominal rate, i_t, is

$$i_t = r_t + \pi_t, \tag{8.4}$$

where π_t is the world inflation rate. From the simple money demand equations,

$$\pi_t = (M_t - M_{t-1})/M_{t-1} = (M_t^* - M_{t-1}^*)/M_{t-1}^*. \tag{8.5}$$

The rate of inflation equals the rate of money growth in each country.

The central banks wish to achieve a nominal interest rate target and to avoid flows of gold between countries. Define

$$f_t = (M_{t-1} + X_t - M_t)/M_{t-1}, \tag{8.6}$$

$$f_t^* = (M_{t-1}^* + X_t^* - M_t^*)/M_{t-1}^*, \tag{8.7}$$

and

$$x_t = X_t/M_{t-1} \tag{8.8}$$

$$x_t^* = X_t^*/M_{t-1}^*. \tag{8.9}$$

The quantities f_t and f_t^* are the percentage net outflows of gold between the two countries, and the quantities x_t and x_t^* are the percentage production of new fiduciary money.

The choice variables for the two central banks can be viewed as x and x^*. Straightforward algebra verifies that

$$i_t = r_t + (1/2)(x_t + x_t^*), \tag{8.10}$$

and

$$f_t = -f_t^* = (1/2)(x_t - x_t^*). \tag{8.11}$$

The first equation says that the nominal interest rate depends on the exogenous real interest rate and the average rate of money creation in the two countries. The second equation says that the amount of gold flow between the two countries depends on the difference between the amounts of money creation.

8.3.2   The Solution with One Central Bank

Consider first the situation in which only the home country has a central bank. In this case, $x^* = 0$. The home country has one choice variable, x, which affects both the interest rate i and the amount of gold flow f.

Suppose the objective of the central bank is to minimize

$$V = (i_t - \bar{i}_t)^2 + \phi f_t^2. \tag{8.12}$$

That is, the central bank dislikes gold flows and would like to stick close to a target nominal interest rate, $\bar{i}_t$.[17] It faces the constraints

$$i_t = r_t + (1/2)x_t, \tag{8.13}$$

and

$$f_t = (1/2)x_t. \tag{8.14}$$

Minimizing V subject to these constraints yields

$$x_t = \frac{2}{1+\phi}(\bar{i}_t - r_t) \tag{8.15}$$

$$f_t = \frac{1}{1+\phi}(\bar{i}_t - r_t) \tag{8.16}$$

$$i_t = (1/(1+\phi))\bar{i}_t + (\phi/(1+\phi))r_t. \tag{8.17}$$

Note that for large ϕ, the central bank embarks on no policy at all, since doing so generates highly undesirable gold flows. In this limiting case, the nominal interest rate simply equals the exogenous real interest rate.

8.3.3   The Solution with Two Central Banks

Consider now a situation with two central banks. Each central bank has the same objective function and takes the other central bank's creation of money (x or x^*) as given.

The home country's reaction function, determined by choosing x to minimize V for a given x^*, is

$$x_t = (2/(1+\phi))(\bar{i}_t - r_t) + (\phi - 1)/(\phi + 1)x_t^*, \tag{8.18}$$

and the foreign country's reaction function is

$$x_t^* = (2/(1+\phi))(\bar{i}_t - r_t) + (\phi - 1)/(\phi + 1)x_t. \tag{8.19}$$

The Nash equilibrium is therefore

$$x_t = x_t^* = \bar{i}_t - r_t, \tag{8.20}$$

and the equilibrium values of the endogenous variables are

$$i_t = \bar{i}_t, \tag{8.21}$$

$$f_t = 0. \tag{8.22}$$

Thus, the equilibrium with two central banks has no gold flows, and the nominal interest rate always equals its target.[18]

8.3.4   Discussion

At the broad-brush level, the model outlined provides a basis for attributing the changes in the behavior of interest rates and prices to the founding of the Federal Reserve rather than to the dissolution of the gold standard. Before 1914, all countries had both an interest rate target and a desire to minimize gold flows. Because the United States had no central bank, however, and most countries with central banks placed significant weight on their desire to prevent gold flows, it was not optimal for any central bank to attempt to smooth its country's interest rate. After 1914, when the Fed was introduced, it was desirable for each central bank to stabilize rates, knowing that all other banks would do similarly. As a result, interest rates were stabilized. This explanation of the changes in behavior of interest rates and prices gives no role to the destruction of the gold standard. The explanation also provides a basis for believing that the founders of the Fed were rational in thinking that the introduction of the Fed would stabilize interest rates in the United States, even if the world continued to operate on a gold standard.

8.4 What Was Responsible: The Fed or the Gold Standard?

One implication of the line of reasoning in the previous section is that the dissolution of the gold standard and the founding of the Federal Reserve might have been hypothetical substitutes to some extent. Both would tend to have the effect of removing the need to avoid gold flows as a dominant objective of monetary policy, allowing the domestic consideration of interest rate smoothing to come to the forefront. The counterfactual entertained in the theoretical example of policy coordination imagined the operation of the Federal Reserve, in addition to other countries' central banks, within the context of a continuing gold standard. The conclusion of that analysis was that interest rate stabilization in each country would have been an admissible equilibrium outcome in that scenario.

A second counterfactual worth entertaining is to suppose that the gold standard had been suspended but no Federal Reserve had been established. Although freedom from international constraints regarding gold flows would certainly have been achieved, it is by no means clear how, in the absence of a central bank, the United States could have taken advantage of this freedom to stabilize interest rates. No well-articulated story exists in which the dissolution of a gold standard, in and of itself, would lead to smoothed interest rates. This observation makes one suspicious that the break with gold, unaccompanied by the introduction of the Fed, would have done the job. However, some more concrete evidence on the roles of the two historical events is needed. This section presents information that allows an evaluation of whether the Fed or the destruction of the gold standard was more likely responsible for the changes in financial markets.

Before turning to that evidence, it is important to address briefly the issue of whether World War I or some other, unspecified event might have been responsible for the changes in the behavior of interest rates and prices. Note first that the changes documented above appear to have occurred well before 1920; the period 1915–1918 is statistically much more like the 1920–1933 period than the 1890–1910 period. The changes that occurred in financial markets were clearly present during World War I and continued, in even more dramatic form, after the end of the war. This indicates that the war in and of itself was not the source of the changes.

A second piece of evidence that either the Fed or the gold standard was responsible for the changes is switching regressions analogous to those in Mankiw, Miron, and Weil (1987). These allow dating of the most likely point of the changes in the stochastic processes and indicate that for both interest rates and inflation, the switch occurred with high probability sometime between mid-1914 and mid-1915 in both the United States and Britain. Thus, these results support the notion that either the dismantling of the gold standard or the founding of the Fed, rather than some other unspecified event, was responsible for the changes observed in the stochastic behavior of interest rates and prices.[19]

To evaluate the roles of the two major changes in institutions, consider evidence from examining a different historical example of a switch from fixed to flexible exchange rates. Tables 8.5 and 8.6 present autocorrelations of the short rate and the inflation rate for the sample periods 1957–1969 and 1974–1984. The first sample period ends before the breakdown of the Bretton Woods fixed rate regime, and the second begins after initiation of current flexible rate period.[20]

The results make two points. First, seasonal or other transitory variation in interest rates did not return in either country when the world returned to a system of fixed exchange rates. The 1957–1969 period exhibits essentially none of the mean reverting variation in interest rates displayed by the 1890–1910 period. Second, the change from fixed to flexible rates in the early 1970s was accompanied by at most minor changes in the persistence of interest rates in each of the two countries.[21] If the exchange rate regime rather than the Fed was the key consideration in 1914, one would expect to see some signs of similar changes in interest rate processes accompanying the inception and demise of the Bretton Woods regime.

The evidence on inflation shows that the degree of persistence during the Bretton Woods period is more like the pre-Fed period than the 1920–1933 period. Also, the increased persistence of inflation at the

Table 8.5
Autocorrelations of the short rate

	United States				Britain			
	1957–1969		1974–1984		1957–1969		1974–1984	
	Level	Change	Level	Change	Level	Change	Level	Change
First	0.95	0.21	0.95	0.09	0.94	0.11	0.94	0.11
Second	0.90	0.05	0.87	−0.09	0.86	0.04	0.87	0.13
Third	0.84	0.15	0.84	−0.05	0.78	−0.09	0.79	−0.04
Fourth	0.78	−0.04	0.79	−0.14	0.71	0.01	0.71	−0.12
Fifth	0.72	−0.07	0.76	0.01	0.64	0.05	0.65	0.12
Sixth	0.67	−0.06	0.72	−0.19	0.56	−0.07	0.57	0.01
Seventh	0.63	−0.27	0.71	−0.15	0.49	−0.14	0.49	−0.03
Eighth	0.60	−0.11	0.71	0.15	0.43	−0.24	0.42	−0.09
Ninth	0.58	0.02	0.70	0.08	0.40	−0.10	0.35	0.00
Tenth	0.55	−0.10	0.68	0.10	0.38	−0.10	0.28	−0.22
Eleventh	0.53	−0.01	0.64	0.10	0.38	−0.04	0.24	−0.03
Twelfth	0.50	0.11	0.60	−0.21	0.38	0.03	0.20	−0.04
Standard deviation	1.32	0.27	2.95	0.95	1.38	0.44	2.53	0.84

Source: Barsky et al. (1988), p. 1142.
Note: The approximate standard errors for the autocorrelations (under the null that the series is white noise) are 0.08 for the 1957–1969 sample and 0.09 for the 1974–1984 sample.

demise of Bretton Woods mimics the increased persistence after 1914 and is thus more suggestive of the importance of the exchange rate regime than is the evidence from interest rates. It is worth noting that for both the 1957–1969 and 1974–1984 periods the autocorrelations in the wholesale price index inflation rate reported here are noticeably lower than those using the consumer price index inflation rate (Barsky 1987).

The second and perhaps more important piece of evidence on the relative role of the Fed and the exchange rate regime appears in tables 8.7 and 8.8, which show the correlations across countries in price levels, inflation rates, the level of interest rates, and changes in interest rates for the pre-1914 and the post-1914 sample periods. To a first approximation, these cross-country correlations change little across sample periods. If anything, inflation rates show more correlation across countries

Table 8.6
Autocorrelations of the one-month inflation rate

	United States		Britain	
	1957–1969	1974–1984	1957–1969	1974–1984
First	0.17	0.44	−0.15	0.58
Second	0.13	0.28	0.11	0.53
Third	−0.12	0.43	0.15	0.48
Fourth	0.08	0.13	0.02	0.40
Fifth	0.09	0.23	0.09	0.33
Sixth	0.19	0.24	0.01	0.39
Seventh	0.01	0.02	0.09	0.28
Eighth	0.07	0.12	0.02	0.32
Ninth	0.09	0.26	−0.02	0.36
Tenth	0.18	0.14	0.06	0.29
Eleventh	0.05	0.19	0.05	0.35
Twelfth	0.12	0.26	0.07	0.40
Standard deviation	3.76	8.35	4.62	7.35

Source: Barsky et al. (1988), p. 1142.
Note: The approximate standard errors for the autocorrelations (under the null that the series is white noise) are 0.08 for the 1957–1969 sample and 0.09 for the 1974–1984 sample.

Table 8.7
Correlations across countries in interest rates

	1890–1910	1920–1933
Level	0.627	0.790
One-month change	0.311	0.162
Three-month change	0.545	0.375
Six-month change	0.650	0.554

Source: Barsky et al. (1988), p. 1143.

Table 8.8
Correlations across countries in prices

	1890–1910	1920–1933
Price level	0.870	0.943
One-month inflation	0.347	0.447
Three-month inflation	0.539	0.626
Six-month inflation	0.540	0.687

Source: Barsky et al. (1988), p. 1143.

in the flexible rate period, contrary to the usual expectation based on purchasing power parity considerations.

If one asks what contribution the suspension of a gold standard could have made to interest rate stabilization, it appears that any answer must involve a freeing of domestic interest rates and price levels from the international constraints imposed by fixed exchange rates. Yet the breakdown of the gold standard in 1914 was not accompanied by an observed change in the international linkages of prices and interest rates. Of course, these cross-country correlations are properties of reduced-form relationships, and it is possible that two very different structures could have led to similar reduced-form observations. Nevertheless, nothing in the data suggests that the within-country changes in price and interest rates resulted from reductions in international linkages of interest rates and prices associated with the switch in the exchange rate regime.

Tables 8.9 and 8.10 present the correlations across countries for the Bretton Woods and recent flexible exchange rate periods. The evidence does not indicate that the change in exchange rate regime coincided with a change in the extent to which interest rates and prices move together, confirming the results in Mankiw (1986). This surprising finding warrants investigation in future work.

8.5   The Behavior of Real Interest Rates before and after 1914

Any discussion of interest rate stabilization would be incomplete without asking whether the stabilization of the nominal rate was accompanied by a change in the process followed by real rates. This section takes up that question. It focuses on the seasonal movements in real rates because seasonality is an identifiable source of predictable varia-

Table 8.9
Correlations across countries in interest rates

	1957–1969	1974–1984
Level	0.651	0.544
One-month change	0.018	0.071
Three-month change	0.075	0.152
Six-month change	0.041	0.176

Source: Barsky et al. (1988), p. 1144.

Table 8.10
Correlations across countries in prices

	1957–1969	1974–1984
Price level	0.911	0.986
One-month inflation	0.080	0.263
Three-month inflation	0.297	0.308
Six-month inflation	0.554	0.328

Source: Barsky et al. (1988), p. 1144.

tion in the nominal rate prior to 1914 that is clearly absent in the second sample period. As noted by Shiller (1980), the question thus becomes whether the disappearance of the seasonal in nominal rates was offset by a change in the inflation seasonal so that the seasonal pattern of the underlying expected real rate remained invariant.

The analysis follows the procedure of regressing ex post real rates on twelve dummies for the periods 1890–1910 and 1920–1933.[22] As Mishkin (1981) shows, this procedure provides consistent estimates of the seasonal in the ex ante real rate. Since unanticipated inflation adds noise, however, this seasonal pattern will be estimated less precisely than if it had used direct measures of the expected real rate.

The real rate is significantly seasonal at the 10 percent but not the 5 percent level for both countries in the earlier period. The later period shows no statistically significant evidence of a real rate seasonal in either country, suggesting a significant change in the seasonal in the real rate process might have occured. Tests of the hypothesis of no change, however, do not reject the null at any conventional significance level. The conclusion is the same as that of Shiller (1980), therefore: that the data do not allow any convincing inference about the change in the behavior of real rates.

The results do make the conclusion stated in Shiller (1980) more convincing. Shiller employs an interest rate series of questionable reliability (the four- to six-month commercial paper rate), and he merely examines plots of estimated seasonal patterns without carrying out hypothesis tests. In addition, the definition of seasonality that he employs (Census X-11) is inappropriate since the seasonal coefficients produced by this technique for any particular year are functions of the data for both sample periods. The analysis here uses a more accurate data series and a more appropriate statistical technique, in addition to computing results for an additional country. Thus, although the conclusion is identical to Shiller's, the evidence should help remove any residual doubt about the validity of his conclusion.

8.6   Conclusion

The analysis in this chapter has evaluated the role of two major institutional changes in contributing to observed changes in the seasonality and other behavior of interest rates and prices after 1914. The contribution lies in showing that the simultaneity of the changes in the processes for interest rates and prices in many countries does not, by itself, prove that the changes were due to the destruction of the gold standard rather than to the founding of the Fed. The model of policy coordination provides an example in which the introduction of the Fed leads to a stabilization of interest rates, even if the gold standard remains intact, and the empirical evidence suggests that the gold standard did not play a crucial role in precipitating the changes in interest rate behavior.

Thus, the conclusion of chapter 7—that seasonality played a crucial role in both the founding and the subsequent operations of the Federal Reserve—remains intact. This conclusion provides a dramatic example of how determining the causes and consequences of seasonal fluctuations can enhance understanding of the economy generally.

*The economy is experiencing an exogenous increase in the demand for goods and ser-
vices. How should the Fed respond?*

The previous two chapters argued that the original motivation for the
Fed's policy of smoothing interest rate seasonals was a desire to eliminate financial panics. Although this policy continued after the Great
Depression, the relative absence of financial panics since that period
probably reflects factors other than the accommodation of interest rate
seasonals, particularly the introduction of deposit insurance in 1934. In
addition, the elimination of financial panics need not be the only effect
of smoothing interest rate seasonals, even if this was the original motivation for the policy.

This chapter, which is based on Mankiw and Miron (1991), explains
that the effects of seasonal interest rate smoothing depend critically on
the extent of seasonal price rigidity in the economy. The analysis is
motivated by the question posed at the beginning of the chapter. One
possible answer, based on the standard Keynesian analysis of aggregate fluctuations, would assume that the question concerns an expan-
sionary shift in the IS curve and that the goal of monetary policy is
to stabilize output and employment. The answer, therefore, is that the
Fed should induce a contractionary shift in the LM curve. In response
to the increased demand for goods and services, the Fed should lean
against the wind by reducing the money supply and raising interest
rates.

Although this answer might seem natural to many economists, it is
precisely the opposite to the policy pursued by the Fed in one important instance: seasonal fluctuations in demand. Over the year, the demand for goods and services fluctuates substantially and predictably;

the most prominent example is the increase in the demand for consumer goods around Christmas. Yet the Fed does not follow the simple Keynesian prescription of leaning against the wind, nor does it follow Milton Friedman's (1982) recommendation that it keep the money supply growing smoothly over the seasons. Instead, the Fed pursues a policy of smoothing interest rates by expanding the money supply during times of the year when the demand for goods and services is high and contracting it when the demand is low.

This chapter appraises the seasonal monetary policy that the Fed has pursued since its founding in 1914. It does not advocate a particular alternative; rather, it raises a question that has received too little attention from monetary economists. The literature contains almost no discussion of how monetary policy should respond to seasonal fluctuations in demand. Yet seasonal fluctuations in output and employment are at least as large as business cycle fluctuations.

9.1   The Smoothing of Interest Rates in 1914

One of the most striking changes in the behavior of short-term interest rates occurred in 1914, the year the Fed began operations. A large part of this change was a substantial reduction in regular seasonal fluctuations.

Figure 9.1 presents the estimated seasonal pattern in the four- to six-month commercial paper rate during three different sample periods: the period before the founding of the Fed (1890:2–1914:11), the interwar period (1919:1–1940:12), and the period since World War II (1947:1–1988:12). The seasonal patterns were estimated by regressing the interest rate on twelve seasonal dummies and then subtracting the mean of the dummy coefficients.

The figure shows that the nominal interest rate was extremely seasonal during the pre-Fed period, displaying a pattern with amplitude greater than 100 basis points measured at an annual rate. During both the interwar and the postwar periods, however, the nominal rate has displayed much less seasonality. The amplitude of the cycle fell to 28 basis points during the interwar period and then rose again to 43 basis points during the postwar era.

Formal statistical tests confirm the visual impression in figure 9.1. These tests regressed the change in the interest rate on seasonal dummies and calculated the standard errors, allowing for serial correlation (Newey and West 1987). The tests show that the nominal rate is sea-

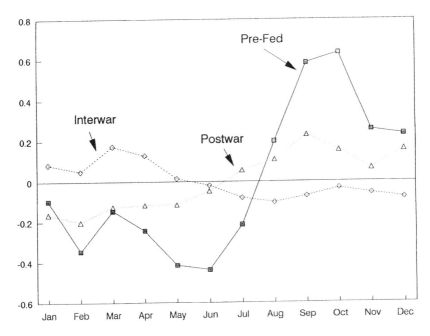

Figure 9.1
Seasonal pattern in nominal interest rate. Source: Mankiw and Miron (1991), p. 44.

sonal at a statistically significant level during all three periods. Moreover, the change in the pattern is strongly significant between the period before 1914 and either of the later periods. Yet one cannot reject
the hypothesis that the later two periods have the same seasonal pattern. The overall conclusion is that Fed policy has not completely eliminated seasonality in nominal interest rates; it has, however, reduced
its amplitude substantially.[1] The interpretation offered of this fact is
that the Fed began smoothing interest rate seasonals shortly after its
founding in 1914. Other interpretations are possible but appear less
likely.

9.2   The Cases for and against Smoothing Interest Rates

The normative question of whether the Fed should smooth interest
rates over the seasons is inexorably tied to the positive question of how
the economy behaves. This section discusses the normative question in
two steps. It first considers classical economies, in which real variables
such as output and employment are unaffected by monetary policy,

and then turns to Keynesian economies, in which price rigidities lead to monetary nonneutralities.

9.2.1   Classical Arguments

In a classical world, seasonal monetary policy—or indeed monetary policy of any sort—is not very important. The variables that matter most for economic welfare, such as real incomes, employment, and relative prices, are independent of monetary policy. Monetary policy influences only nominal variables, such as the price level and nominal interest rate.

Yet even in such a world, monetary policy can affect welfare by ensuring that individuals are not unnecessarily conserving on real money balances. Because the nominal interest rate is the opportunity cost of holding money, a high nominal interest rate reduces the quantity of real balances people hold and, thereby, their welfare. As Friedman (1969) emphasizes, this reasoning suggests that the money supply should grow—or, more likely, shrink—just enough to produce a zero nominal interest rate.

Phelps (1973) pointed out a possible exception to Friedman's optimal money rule. If seigniorage is an efficient way for government to raise revenue, then the optimal nominal interest rate is the tax on holding real money balances. Because lump-sum taxes are unavailable, a positive tax on real balances may be optimal.

If these public finance considerations are central to the conduct of monetary policy, then smoothing interest rates over the seasons is likely to be the appropriate policy. A tax rate on any economic activity that varied systematically over the seasons would induce people to move inefficiently some of that economic activity from high tax seasons to low tax seasons. In the specific case of monetary policy, if the nominal interest rate varied seasonally, the policy would fail to minimize the social cost of collecting seigniorage (Mankiw 1987).

The implication of this line of reasoning is that Friedman's (1982) suggestion that the money stock not fluctuate over the seasons is inconsistent with his optimal quantity of money arguments. With a constant money stock, a season of high output would also tend to be a season of high money demand, low prices, high expected inflation, and thus high nominal interest rates. If the nominal interest rate is to be kept smooth, the money stock must adjust to accommodate seasonal fluctuations in output.

9.2.2   Some Suggestive Calculations

To gauge the welfare gain from smoothing interest rates over the seasons, it is instructive to carry out a few calculations. The analysis here takes the standard approach of measuring the welfare costs of high nominal interest rates by the lost consumer surplus from money holding. That is, it measures social welfare by the area under the money demand curve (McCallum 1989, chap. 6). The calculations also assume that the Fed can control the money stock perfectly, that real output and the real interest rate are exogenous, that prices are completely flexible, and that uncertainty is absent. Thus, both output and the real interest rate are purely seasonal.

Under these conditions, the only effect of the Fed's choice of seasonal policy is whether the seasonality in output and the real interest rate is absorbed in the price level or the money stock. If the Fed chooses to keep the money stock nonseasonal, then the price level must move seasonally to clear the money market, and both the price level and the nominal interest rate will be seasonal. If instead the Fed makes the money stock seasonal in a way that makes the seasonal in the inflation rate equal to the negative of the seasonal in the real rate, then the money market clears without any seasonal in the nominal interest rate.

The Fed's seasonal actions thus affect the economy only through the inflation rate, and the welfare effects are limited to the distortion of agents' optimal pattern of money holdings. If the Fed eliminates seasonality from the money stock, welfare losses from insufficient money holding occur in those seasons when interest rates rise above their average level, and these are not fully offset in the seasons when interest rates fall below their average level. In this case, therefore, a policy of smoothing nominal interest rates raises welfare.

This conclusion is illustrated in figure 9.2, which compares a constant money supply rule to a constant nominal interest rate rule for an economy with only two seasons. When the Fed stabilizes the nominal money stock, the nominal interest rate fluctuates between i_{low} and i_{high}. (Note that because of seasonality in prices, the real money stock is not constant under this policy.) Alternatively, when the Fed stabilizes the nominal rate at i^*, the real money stock alternates between $(M/P)_{low}$ and $(M/P)_{high}$. The constant money policy involves welfare losses relative to the constant interest rate policy because, under constant money, the gain from having low interest rates in the low-demand season (the area ABCD) is less than the loss from having high interest rates in the high-demand season (the area AEFG).

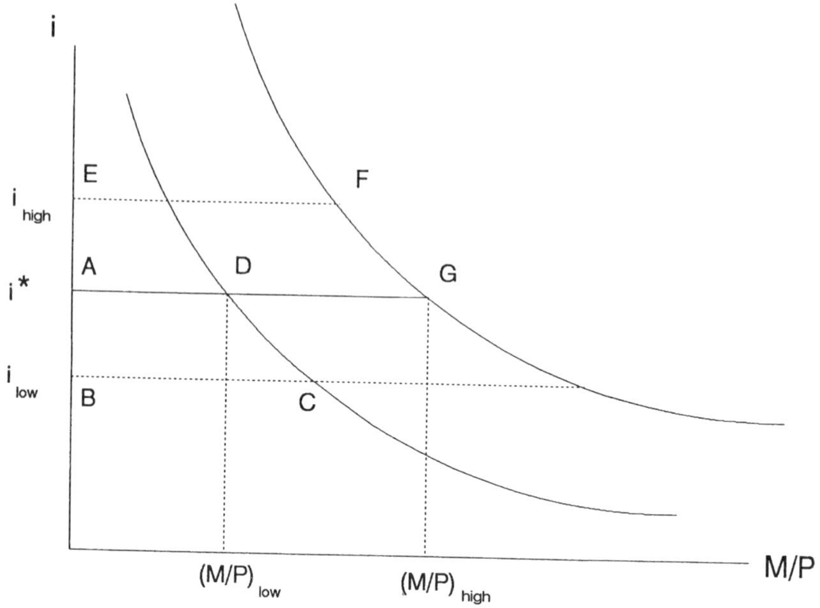

Figure 9.2
Welfare effects of stabilizing nominal interest rates. Source: Mankiw and Miron (1991), p. 49.

One can provide some approximate values for the welfare gain from stabilizing nominal rates in the U.S. economy. The conventional money demand function is

$$m_t - p_t = \theta_t - \beta(r_t + p_{t+1} - p_t),\tag{9.1}$$

where m_t and p_t are the logs of money and the price level, and r_t is the real interest rate. The term θ_t represents exogenous seasonal shifts in money demand, including those due to changes in output. The economy is fully classical, so r_t is exogenous with respect to prices. One can therefore calculate the effects of alternative monetary policies on prices from the money demand equation. The solution for p_t is

$$p_t = (1 + \beta)^{-1} \sum_{j=0}^{\infty} (\beta/1 + \beta)^j (m_{t+j} - \theta_{t+j} + \beta r_{t+j})\tag{9.2}$$

and the nominal interest rate is

$$i_t = r_t + p_{t+1} - p_t,\tag{9.3}$$

which implies

$$i_t = \beta^{-1}(\theta_t - m_t)$$

$$+ [\beta(1 + \beta)]^{-1} \sum_{j=0}^{\infty} (\beta/1 + \beta)^j (m_{t+j} - \theta_{t+j} + \beta r_{t+j}). \tag{9.4}$$

With these expressions for equilibrium prices and interest rates and estimates of the seasonals in money demand, one can compute the seasonal in nominal interest rates that would result from having the Fed make the nominal money stock nonseasonal and compute the welfare gain from stabilizing nominal interest rates.

The procedure for calculating the effects on nominal interest rates and welfare is as follows:

1. Because the nominal interest rate has been essentially nonseasonal, set the seasonal patterns in θ_t to equal the seasonal in real balances in the postwar data.

2. For a given i^* (set equal to the 1988 value of 6.7 percent per year), compute the pattern in the growth rate of money required to produce that i^*.

3. Compute the implied seasonality of interest rates for a constant money growth policy.

4. Calculate the seigniorage from each of these two policies.

5. Iterate to find the constant money growth rate that yields the same real seigniorage as the constant nominal interest rate policy.

6. For this rate of money growth, compute the welfare gain to interest rate stabilization (the increase in consumer surplus) as

$$\text{GAIN} = -\sum_{s=1}^{12} \int_{i_s}^{i^*} \exp(\theta_s - \beta i)di \tag{9.5}$$

To calibrate, choose the average value of θ so that the money demand equation "fits" when evaluated at the 1988 average values of m (ln Ml), p (ln CPI), and i (three-month Treasury bill rate). In addition, consistent with the results above, assume the real interest rate is nonseasonal; the calculations are invariant with respect to its value.

Table 9.1 shows the seasonal in nominal interest rates that would result from a nonseasonal money stock policy. The table also shows the welfare gain from stabilizing nominal rates compared to stabilizing the money stock. The table presents results for alternative values of the interest elasticity of money demand (which, evaluated at i^*, equals βi^*).

Table 9.1
The welfare gain from interest rate smoothing

β	9	18	45
Implied interest Elasticity at $i* = 6.7\%$	0.05	0.10	0.25
Nominal interest rate (annual rate)			
January	9.47	8.06	7.22
February	5.43	5.95	6.36
March	5.41	5.97	6.37
April	7.74	7.17	6.86
May	4.95	5.75	6.28
June	6.01	6.32	6.53
July	6.37	6.52	6.61
August	5.39	6.04	6.42
September	5.83	6.29	6.53
October	6.21	6.51	6.62
November	7.27	7.06	6.84
December	9.93	8.37	7.37
Welfare gain in 1988 dollars per person	0.32	0.16	0.07

Source: Mankiw and Miron (1991), p. 52.

Three results are apparent from these calculations. First, if the Fed adopted the policy of making the money stock nonseasonal, the nominal interest rate would be highly seasonal, perhaps with an amplitude as high as 500 basis points. Second, the welfare gain from stabilizing the interest rate is greatest when the interest elasticity of money demand is small because under a constant money stock policy, the smaller the interest elasticity is, the greater is the seasonality in the nominal interest rate. Third, for any reasonable interest elasticity, the benefit of stabilizing interest rates is extremely small. Even in the most extreme case, the benefit of eliminating the seasonal in nominal interest rates amounts to less than one dollar per person per year.

9.2.3   Keynesian Arguments

Economists in the Keynesian tradition emphasize that economic fluctuations often reflect inefficient failures of coordination and that monetary policy can potentially raise welfare by stabilizing these fluctuations. Many models of fluctuations fall within this tradition. Most of these models—including general disequilibrium models (Barro and Grossman 1971, Malinvaud 1977), labor contracting models (Fischer 1977, Gray 1976), and menu cost models (Ball, Mankiw, and Romer 1988; Blanchard and Kiyotaki 1987)—give a role to monetary policy because prices are not completely flexible in the short run.

In evaluating whether these models are useful for understanding seasonal monetary policy, the key question is whether prices are flexible in response to deterministic seasonal fluctuations. Certainly, some prices—the prices of vegetables and hotel rooms in the Caribbean, for example—do move over the seasons. At the same time, Stephen Cecchetti's (1986) study of magazine prices and Anil Kashyap's (1995) study of catalog prices show that many prices in the economy are fixed for years at a time. These findings suggest that some firms exhibit nominal price rigidity in response to seasonal fluctuations in demand.

Microeconomic evidence on price rigidity is hard to evaluate, in part because the implications for the overall economy are subtle. It may be sufficient that only some firms exhibit nominal rigidity to make the aggregate supply of goods and services highly elastic at a fixed nominal price. If other firms in the economy do not desire large changes in their relative prices—what Ball and Romer (1990) call real rigidity—then a small amount of nominal rigidity can make the overall price level sticky.

If the price level is sticky in response to seasonal fluctuations, then seasonal monetary policy will likely be able to influence output and employment. This assumption is implicit in, for example, Poole and Lieberman's (1972) discussion of seasonal monetary policy. It is hard to say whether a policy of stabilizing output would be desirable, however. Keynesian economists typically presume that the level of output should be kept close to the natural rate level. But not all models of price rigidity imply that fluctuations are undesirable, even if the fluctuations would not have occurred in an economy with flexible prices. In some Keynesian models, booms raise welfare and recessions lower it, so the net effect of fluctuations on welfare is ambiguous (Ball and Romer 1989). The question for seasonal policy is whether the Fed should give up the high employment in the fourth quarter in exchange for higher employment in the first quarter.

In evaluating whether the Fed should make this trade-off, the rate at which it can exchange output in high-demand seasons for output in low-demand seasons seems crucial. Many models adopt the natural rate hypothesis as a starting point, so monetary policy can influence only the second moment of output, not the first. Yet some economists question the natural rate hypothesis, asking whether monetary policy can raise output and employment during recessions without having an equal and opposite effect during booms (De Long and Summers 1988). If, for example, firms face capacity constraints that are binding during the season of high output, then stabilizing demand can potentially raise the average level of output. This line of reasoning led Simon Kuznets (1933) to conclude that seasonal fluctuations in the real economy are socially inefficient. This conclusion requires more assumptions than Kuznets stated—namely, that seasonal fluctuations interact with some preexisting distortion such as imperfect competition—but his "excess capacity" perspective nevertheless raises the possibility that stabilizing demand over the year might have welfare benefits.

9.3   A Model of Seasonal Monetary Policy

The previous section addressed the normative question of whether the Fed's policy of smoothing interest rates over the seasons is desirable. This section turns to the positive question of how a change in seasonal monetary policy would influence the behavior of the economy. In particular, it asks what would happen to incomes, prices, and interest rates if the Fed were to pursue an alternative seasonal monetary policy, such as Friedman's recommendation that the Fed remove seasonal fluctuations in the money supply.

Estimating how the economy would respond to a change in seasonal monetary policy requires a model of seasonal fluctuations. Yet just as no model of the business cycle commands a consensus among economists, no model of seasonal fluctuations receives universal approval. In some ways, the situation is even worse for seasonal fluctuations. Because the business cycle has received much attention from researchers over the years, many models—indeed, too many—are available for analyzing business cycle fluctuations. Seasonal fluctuations, on the other hand, have been largely ignored by researchers. Thus, relatively few models are available for addressing a question of seasonal monetary policy.

This section proposes a simple model of seasonal fluctuations, with three goals in mind. First, the model must incorporate, as special cases, classical and Keynesian perspectives on seasonal fluctuations. Second, the model should highlight some of the important questions that must arise in any attempt to explain seasonal fluctuations. Third, the model should be usable for simulating how a change in seasonal monetary policy would influence seasonal fluctuations.

9.3.1   Elements of the Model

The model is intended to describe deterministic seasonal fluctuations in incomes, prices, and interest rates. All variables are in logs (except for interest rates) and represent deviations from the annual mean. The model is composed of the following three equations:

$$m_t - p_t = \alpha y_t - \beta(r_t + p_{t+1} - p_t) + \epsilon_t^m \tag{9.6}$$

$$y_t = -\lambda r_t + \epsilon_t^d \tag{9.7}$$

$$y_t = \gamma p_t + \delta r_t + \epsilon_t^s, \tag{9.8}$$

where m is the money stock, p is the price level, y is real output, r is the real interest rate, and ϵ^m, ϵ^d, and ϵ^s are the exogenous seasonal shifts in the three equations.

This model is conventional in many ways. Equation 9.6 says that the supply of real money balances equals the demand and that money demand depends positively on output and negatively on the nominal interest rate. Equation 9.7 says that the demand for goods depends negatively on the real interest rate. Equation 9.8 says that the supply of goods depends positively on the price level and positively on the real interest rate.

If γ equals zero, then the model is a classical model similar to the one presented, for example, in Robert Barro's (1994) textbook. The supply of output depends positively on the interest rate because the interest rate influences intertemporal substitution in leisure: the higher the real interest rate, the higher the cost of leisure today relative to leisure in the future and thus the greater the supply of labor. Because equations 9.7 and 9.8 by themselves determine output and the real interest rate, the

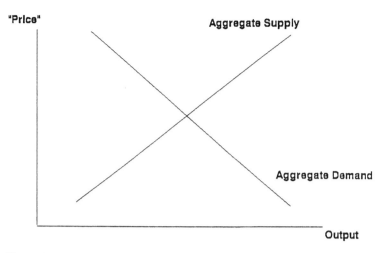

Figure 9.3
Aggregate supply and demand. Source: Mankiw and Miron (1991), p. 56.

money supply influences the price level and the nominal interest rate but not any real variable.

If δ equals zero, then the model resembles a textbook Keynesian model. Equation 9.6 describes the LM curve, and equation 9.7 describes the IS curve. Equation 9.8 describes the short-run aggregate supply curve. Because some wages or prices are sticky, increases in aggregate demand raise both prices and output. The slope of the aggregate supply curve (the parameter γ) determines how changes in aggregate demand are split between prices and output.

Both of these special cases can be represented on a familiar diagram of aggregate demand and aggregate supply, as in figure 9.3. The quantity of output is on the horizontal axis, and a "price" is on the vertical axis. The definition of "price," and the interpretation of this figure, depends on the case being assumed.

In the classical case, the "price" in figure 9.3 is the real interest rate. The aggregate demand curve represents goods demand (equation 9.7), and the aggregate supply curve represents goods supply (equation 9.8). When discussing the determination of output in the classical model, one can safely ignore the money market equilibrium condition (equation 9.6).

In the Keynesian case, the "price" in figure 9.3 is the price level. The aggregate demand curve represents the joint solution to the LM and IS curves (equations 9.6 and 9.7). The aggregate supply curve again repre-

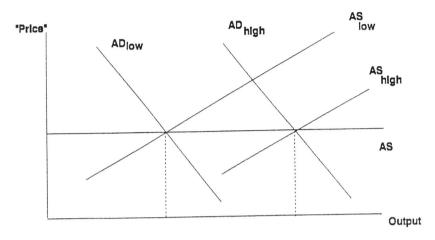

Figure 9.4
Alternative aggregate supply assumptions. Source: Mankiw and Miron (1991), p. 56.

sents goods supply (equation 9.8), but now goods supply depends on the price level rather than the real interest rate.

9.3.2   The Lesson from Christmas

With this model in mind, consider the impact of Christmas on the economy. Christmas causes an exogenous increase in the demand for goods and services—that is, a large value of ϵ^d. This exogenous increase in demand shifts out the aggregate demand curve, as shown in figure 9.4. What one should observe, therefore, is an increase in output and an increase in the "price."

What is actually observed, however, is puzzling from both classical and Keynesian perspectives. As the model predicts, the economy does experience an increase in output around Christmas: the seasonal pattern of real GNP reaches its peak in the fourth quarter, when it is 4.3 percent above the annual average. Yet no evidence indicates that "price" increases under any interpretation. As documented above, seasonality is absent from both market interest rates and aggregate price indexes.

The model can be reconciled with the facts in two ways. The first is to posit that the exogenous shift in aggregate demand just happens to coincide with exogenous shifts in aggregate supply. This explanation would be plausible if, for example, students' summer vacation from school occurred in the fourth quarter rather than the third, implying a large increase in labor supply. Yet it is hard to think of an important event that can explain such a large shift in aggregate supply in the fourth quarter.

The second and more plausible way to reconcile the model with the facts is to posit that the aggregate supply curve is extremely elastic. Many economists in the past have suggested that the aggregate supply is highly elastic over the business cycle (Hall 1986; Murphy, Shleifer, and Vishny 1989). This assumption is even more compelling for seasonal fluctuations, because these are more transitory than business cycle fluctuations.

An economist with a classical perspective could argue that aggregate supply is highly elastic because people are willing to substitute leisure intertemporally over short periods of time. Workers may be happy to reschedule vacations or overtime from one month of the year to another in response to small incentives. Real business cycle models often incorporate this sort of high intertemporal substitution over short periods with non–time separable utility functions (Kydland and Prescott 1982). For this simple model of seasonal fluctuations, these considerations argue that the supply parameter δ is very large.

An economist with a Keynesian perspective could argue that aggregate supply is highly elastic because firms do not alter their prices in response to temporary fluctuations in demand. This high elasticity arises if some firms have fixed prices (nominal rigidity) and if the remaining firms desire little change in their relative prices in response to temporary changes in output (real rigidity). In the model of seasonal fluctuations presented here, this stickiness in the price level corresponds to making the parameter γ very large.

Regardless of whether one accepts the classical or Keynesian interpretation of events, monetary policy has an important role in completing the story of seasonal fluctuations. In the classical case, a flat aggregate supply curve ensures that seasonal changes in demand do not alter the real interest rate. Monetary policy must be acting to prevent prices and nominal interest rates from fluctuating seasonally. In the Keynesian case, a flat aggregate supply curve ensures that seasonal changes in demand do not alter the price level. Monetary policy must be acting to prevent nominal and real interest rates from fluctuating seasonally. In both cases, the Fed's smoothing of nominal interest rates is crucial for explaining observed seasonal patterns.

9.3.3   Calibrating the Model

The results above suggest that aggregate supply is highly elastic over seasonal fluctuations. The calibration of the model therefore assumes infinitely elastic supply. In the classical simulations, δ is set to infinity; in Keynesian simulations, γ is set to infinity. In both cases, the values of the other supply parameter and the supply shock ϵ^s do not matter.

The next step is to choose values for the parameters α, β, and λ, based on reading of the relevant literature. For the money demand equation, the assumption is that of Faig (1989): the money demand function is nonseasonal ($\epsilon^m = 0$). Because the nominal interest rate is essentially nonseasonal, all fluctuations in real balances therefore come from changes in output. As Faig points out, this restriction allows one to estimate α, the elasticity of money demand with respect to output, using the seasonal variation in the data. Faig's estimate of α of 0.25 is also used in the simulations.

The value of the interest semielasticity of money demand, β, is chosen so that the interest elasticity of money demand, evaluated at the 1988 value of nominal rate, is .1. This value is on the low side of the range in the literature. But since the exercise analyzes only transitory fluctuations and since many estimated money demand equations imply slow adjustment, a low estimate seems reasonable.

The most difficult parameter to choose is the elasticity of demand with respect to the real interest rate. The simulations set λ equal to 12. This value implies that if the real interest rate (measured at an annual rate) rises by 100 basis points, the demand for goods and services falls by 1 percent.

This leaves ϵ^d, the seasonal shift in the demand for goods and services. Because the real interest rate is essentially nonseasonal, seasonal fluctuations in output must reflect seasonal fluctuations in ϵ^d. The simulations therefore set the seasonal in this error term equal to the current seasonal in output, which is proxied by real retail sales.

9.3.4   Simulation of Alternative Monetary Policies

The model can now be used to simulate the effects of two policies. The first adjusts the money stock to hold the nominal interest rate constant; this approximates current policy. The second holds the money stock constant, letting the nominal interest rate be whatever is required to

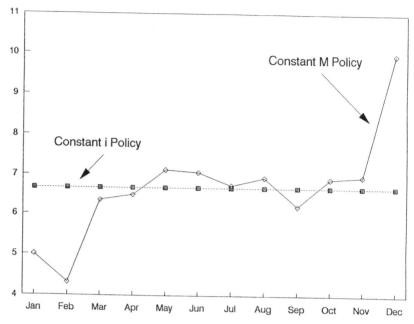

Figure 9.5
Seasonal in nominal interest rate, classical case. Source: Mankiw and Miron (1991), p. 59.

fit the model. Figure 9.5 shows the effects of these two policies on the nominal interest rate under the classical assumption that the real output and the real interest rate are determined independent of monetary behavior. Figures 9.6 and 9.7 show the effects of the two policies on the nominal interest rate and real output under the Keynesian assumption that the price level is predetermined.

Both sets of simulations show that if the Fed stopped stabilizing the seasonal in nominal rates, interest rates would be extremely seasonal. In both simulations, the implied amplitude of the seasonal cycle in nominal rates is about 500 basis points. Of course, the exact magnitude of the cycle depends on the parameters used to conduct the simulations. A decrease in the income elasticity of money demand, or an increase in the interest elasticity, for example, implies a cycle of smaller amplitude. It is noteworthy that the magnitude and timing of the cycle are extremely similar across the two extreme assumptions about the behavior of the economy.

Figure 9.7 shows that even under the extreme Keynesian assumption that the price level is predetermined, the policy of holding the

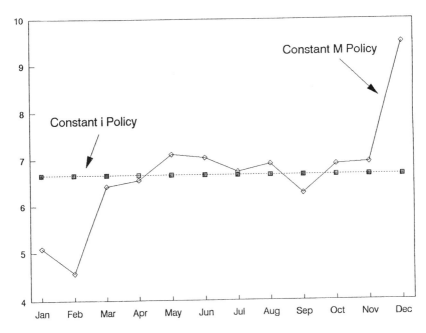

Figure 9.6
Seasonal in nominal interest rate, Keynesian case. Source: Mankiw and Miron (1991), p. 60.

money stock constant does not have a quantitatively large impact on real output. The explanation is that the choice of parameters here, and any choice consistent with the range of estimates in the literature, makes the interest elasticity of the demand for goods relatively small, implying that the IS curve is steep. A steep IS curve seems even more plausible for seasonal fluctuations than for business cycle fluctuations because many categories of demand would plausibly not respond to clearly transitory variation in the short-term interest rate. (Inventory investment is the most likely exception, because it is the most quickly reversible form of capital accumulation.) Therefore, the model implies that interest rate stabilization has a relatively small effect on output.

One might also ask, under the Keynesian parameterization, what monetary policy would stabilize output over the seasons. Additional simulations show that output stabilization would require the amplitude of the interest rate seasonal to be 3,000 basis points. Again, this conclusion arises because the current seasonal in output is large and

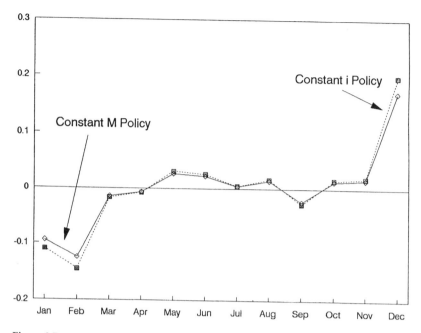

Figure 9.7
Seasonal in real output, Keynesian case. Source: Mankiw and Miron (1991), p. 61.

the response of demand to the short-term interest rate is small. Therefore, large changes in the interest rate are required to exert much influence on output.

9.4   What Can Be Learned from the Monetary Changes in 1914?

The model simulations suggest the kinds of effects that alternative policies toward seasonal fluctuations might have. Yet this exercise cannot settle the question of what effects alternative policies actually would have. This section presents evidence on the effects of the Fed's policy on the actual behavior of the economy. The founding of the Fed in 1914 provides a natural experiment for examining the effects of alternative policies. The nominal rate was strongly seasonal before 1914 and much less seasonal afterward. The question here is whether this change in the seasonality of the nominal rate was accompanied by a change in the seasonality of real variables.

The analysis considers the most important real variable: output. The output series examined is the monthly index of industrial production presented in Miron and Romer (1990). This series is a weighted average of the production of thirteen industrial products, such as pig iron, anthracite coal, textiles, and food products such as sugar, beef, and pork.

Although this output series is the best available for these purposes, it is not perfect. In many cases, the index uses data on shipments or purchases of raw materials to proxy the output of a particular commodity. It is therefore difficult to assign a precise interpretation to the timing of seasonal peaks and troughs in the index. For example, output of anthracite coal is proxied with shipments, so the peak in the index lags the true peak; similarly, output of coffee is proxied with imports of coffee beans, so the peak in the index leads the true peak. Under the null hypothesis that monetary policy is neutral, however, these timing relationships need not have changed with the introduction of the Federal Reserve. Therefore, the index should be useful for examining whether a significant change occurred in the real behavior of the economy in 1914.

Figure 9.8 shows the estimated seasonal in the log of real output for the periods 1890:2–1914:11 and 1919:1–1928:12. The seasonals in the level of output are computed by first estimating the seasonal pattern in the growth rate and then integrating seasonal coefficients for the growth rates to form an estimate of the seasonal in the level. The results are, however, robust to alternative ways of estimating the seasonal pattern.

The figure shows that the estimated seasonal is noticeably different in the two sample periods. The data can strongly reject the hypothesis that the seasonal pattern in the growth rates remains constant over the two samples. (This is true even allowing the mean growth rate in the two samples to differ.) Moreover, the seasonal in output is larger under the post-1914 policy of interest rate smoothing, as one would expect if money is nonneutral because of Keynesian price rigidities.

The size of the change in the seasonality of output is surprising. The simulations above suggest that interest rate smoothing should have only a small effect on output, even under the Keynesian assumption of predetermined prices. Yet figure 9.8 shows that the change was large. It is possible that the parameter measuring the response of goods demand to the interest rate (λ) is too small for the subset of goods in the Miron-Romer index. A larger value of this parameter would imply a greater effect of interest rate smoothing.

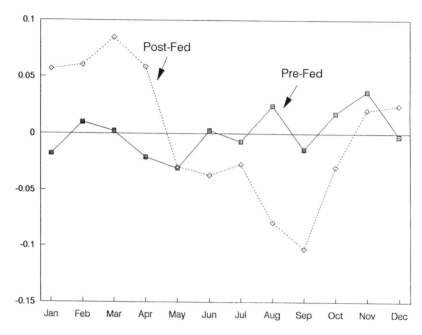

Figure 9.8
Seasonal in real output before and after 1914. Source: Mankiw and Miron (1991), p. 64.

Overall, the natural experiment of the founding of the Fed appears consistent with the view that seasonal monetary policy is nonneutral. In particular, the data show a significant increase in the seasonality of the real output after 1914. Undoubtedly, other possible explanations for this change exist, just as for the change in the behavior of interest rates in 1914. Yet this episode leaves open the possibility that alternative seasonal monetary policies can influence the seasonal business cycle.

9.5   Conclusion

Since the Federal Reserve began operations in 1914, its policy has been to smooth nominal interest rates over the year. Under this policy, neither the overall price level nor the real interest rate has exhibited a significant seasonal pattern, while real output and employment have exhibited substantial seasonal fluctuations. The goal in this chapter has been to discuss whether this policy is desirable and how the economy would be different if it were changed.

With economists' current understanding of fluctuations, and especially of seasonal fluctuations, any analysis of alternative seasonal monetary policies must be tentative. To evaluate the policy now in effect, or alternative ones that the Fed might consider, a crucial issue must be addressed before all others. Would introducing a seasonal pattern in the nominal interest rate cause a seasonal pattern to emerge in the real interest rate? Or would such a policy merely induce a seasonal pattern in inflation that would mirror the seasonal pattern in the nominal interest rate? In other words, does seasonal monetary policy have real effects?

According to the classical answer that seasonal monetary policy cannot influence real variables, the current policy of smoothing nominal interest rates is probably optimal. The nominal interest rate is the implicit tax on holding real money balances. Because it would be inefficient to make this tax rate vary over the year, the Fed should smooth the nominal interest rate, as it has done. The benefits to this policy, however, are probably very small. Compared to a policy of a nonseasonal money stock, a policy of a nonseasonal nominal interest rate raises welfare by less than one dollar per person per year.

A more Keynesian answer is that seasonal monetary policy can influence the real interest rate and, therefore, output and employment. Some evidence suggests that wage and price rigidities are important for understanding the business cycle in general and short-run effects of monetary policy in particular. If these rigidities are also important for understanding the seasonal cycle—and the evidence from 1914 suggests they might be—then the seasonal fluctuations in output and employment are neither unalterable nor necessarily optimal. Making welfare judgments about alternative monetary policies in the presence of seasonal price rigidities is an interesting task for future research.

10

Welfare Implications of Seasonal Cycles

One possible justification for the standard practice of studying business cycle fluctuations while ignoring the seasonal fluctuations is that the two kinds of fluctuations can be studied in isolation without significant loss of information about either. The evidence presented suggests this justification is not well founded. A second possible justification is that seasonal fluctuations have no interesting welfare consequences and are therefore associated with no interesting policy issues. This chapter demonstrates that seasonal fluctuations *do* raise welfare and policy questions and are therefore of interest per se, even if they are unrelated to business cycle fluctuations. The chapter also comments on existing government policies that affect seasonal fluctuations.

10.1 Efficient Models of Seasonality

Until recently, aggregate fluctuations were commonly viewed as involving significant welfare losses, and the desirability of reducing the amplitude of economic fluctuations was taken as given. This notion was challenged by the class of real business cycle models initiated by Kydland and Prescott (1982) and Long and Plosser (1983). In these models, fluctuations result from changes in the underlying technology, and since the economy has no sources of inefficiency, these fluctuations represent the economy's efficient response to changes in technological opportunities. In this world, stabilization reduces welfare. The real business cycle literature has shown that the magnitude of the fluctuations in output is approximately what one should expect based on the assumptions of competition, constant returns, and the properties of the estimated Solow residual.

This view of aggregate fluctuations has been extended to seasonal fluctuations by Braun and Evans (1994) and Chatterjee and Ravikumar (1992). These authors modify the standard real business cycle model by allowing seasonal shifts in tastes and technology (Braun and Evans also allow seasonal shifts in government purchases), and they compare the seasonal implications of their models to the observed seasonal movements in the data. They find that the models are in many respects consistent with observed seasonal fluctuations, although they fail to match the behavior of some key variables. The Braun and Evans (1994) specification does not capture the seasonals in fourth-quarter investment or labor hours; the Chatterjee and Ravikumar (1992) specification has difficulty with labor hours and the real wage.

These models illustrate how seasonal variation can be incorporated into models of aggregate fluctuations in a way that has no implications for welfare or policy. The seasonal shifts in preferences and technology imply seasonal changes in output and its composition, as well as in labor input, but this variation is the efficient response of the economy to changes in preferences or technological opportunities.[1] Policies that dampen seasonal fluctuations in such a world reduce welfare by preventing the economy from optimally shifting production into high-productivity or high-utility seasons. Of course, policies that increase the amplitude of seasonal fluctuations are costly as well.

10.2   Inefficient Models with Exogenous Seasonality

The first setting in which seasonality raises interesting welfare questions is one in which seasonality results from shifts in preferences and technology, as in the models already discussed, but the interaction of seasonal fluctuations with some distortion increases the effects of the distortion. Seasonal fluctuations are not special in this regard; any aspect of the economy may interact with a distortion, thereby affecting welfare. There is thus no presumption that policy should target seasonal fluctuations, and in many cases it is preferable to target the distortion directly. The point raised here is that in plausible cases the interactions between seasonal fluctuations in preferences or technology and distortions are quantitatively important, and thus stabilizing seasonal fluctuations might be an appropriate policy.

One model that may imply significant interactions between seasonal fluctuations and economic distortions is one in which firms make costly investments in capacity that are binding in the short to medium term. These investments need not be for physical capital. Any kind of commitment, such as a budget plan, can reduce flexibility in costly ways. In this setting, a crucial determinant of desired capacity is the amount of variation in demand. Under plausible assumptions, increased variation in demand, including fully predictable variation, causes firms rationally to hold capacity that is not fully utilized in the off-season. There are numerous examples of seasonally underutilized capacity: beach resorts during the winter, churches or football stadiums on days other than Sunday, and highways at night. The results in this book suggest that the same phenomenon occurs in the manufacturing sectors of OECD countries, since it is implausible that the capital stock changes much over the period from June to August while the rate of production changes dramatically in most countries and industries.

If there are no distortions in the economy, there is nothing suboptimal about unused capacity per se. If, however, firms operate in a noncompetitive environment, the quantity of capacity chosen can be excessive (Spence 1977, Dixit and Stiglitz 1977). More important for the purposes here, the extent of unused capacity increases with the variability of demand (Beaulieu, MacKie-Mason, and Miron 1992). By stabilizing the seasonal variation in demand, policy reduces firms' optimal choice of capacity. Since the degree to which firms' capacity choices are excessive depends on the determinants of those choices, it is possible that by reducing demand variability, policy reduces the extent to which the laissez-faire capacity choices deviate from the social planner's choices. Policy can therefore have a first-order effect on output and welfare.

The interactions between seasonal variation and economic distortion that arise in the class of models described above do not necessarily provide a motivation for stabilizing the seasonal fluctuations in demand. In this class of models, private capacity choices can be insufficient as well as excessive (Mankiw and Whinston 1986). In addition, if demand curves shift seasonally because consumers desire seasonal consumption (Miron 1986a, Osborn 1988, 1989), optimal policy will never smooth the seasonal variation entirely. The class of models already described nevertheless illustrates one possible interaction between seasonal fluctuations and economic distortions. It is also one possible rationalization for Kuznets's (1933) suggestion that policy dampen seasonal fluctuations in order to reduce the "waste" associated with seasonal excess capacity.

10.3   Inefficient Models with Endogenous Seasonality

The perspective adopted so far has been one in which the seasonal variation in economic activity is treated as exogenous; it results from shifts in preferences and technology. The discussion of the seasonal patterns in economic activity, however, shows that significant features of the seasonal patterns are not easily reconciled with such explanations. Instead, the data provide examples of endogenous seasonality, that is, changes in economic activity that arise because of increasing returns or synergies across agents that make it desirable to concentrate activity in particular seasons, even when these seasons are not substantially different from the ones in which less activity takes place.[2]

The best example of such an endogenous cycle is weekends. As discussed in Hall (1991), much agglomeration of economic activity appears excessive relative to the observable exogenous factors that might explain the agglomeration; examples include cities, business cycles, holidays, seasonal cycles, days versus nights, and weekends. For most of these examples, it is plausible that some of the agglomeration reflects changes in tastes and technology, but in the case of weekends, no such ambiguity arises. The preferences and technology of the economy do not know whether it is Tuesday or Sunday. The fact that activity has a seven-day cycle is therefore a result of agents' endogenously choosing to bunch activity rather than the result of agents' adjusting to exogenous changes in the economic environment.

The literature on business cycles has recently focused considerable attention on models with endogenous fluctuations (Grandmont 1985; Shleifer 1986; Murphy, Shleifer, and Vishny 1989; Diamond and Fudenberg 1989; Boldrin and Woodford 1990; Woodford 1990). In these models, two main mechanisms give rise to endogenous cycles. In some models, any given agent's level of activity increases the attractiveness of similar activity for other economic agents. This implies that agents coordinate on particular periods in which to produce, although the preferences and technology are no different than in adjacent periods. The other main factor contributing to producing bunching is increasing returns, which make it desirable to bunch the production of goods so long as they are storable.

In general, the models cited display two features of interest here. First, they have multiple equilibria, and at least some of these equilibria are periodic. In this sense the models are better candidates as models of seasonal cycles than of business cycles. Second, the laissez-faire outcomes are not necessarily optimal. In many cases the equilibria can be Pareto ranked, but nothing guarantees that the best equilibrium occurs. Thus, these models as applied to the seasons suggest that the bunching of activity over the year may be inefficient. They do not indicate whether the private degree of bunching is too great or too small.

One potentially important difference between the application of these models to seasonal cycles as opposed to business cycles is that for seasonal cycles, observable factors help pin down the equilibrium that occurs, even though such factors do not by themselves produce substantial bunching. Thus, the slowdowns in industrial production that take place in either July or August appear too great to be due solely to the difference in the weather between the month of the slowdown and adjacent months, but the fact that the weather is better during the summer than during other times of the year does determine why the lack of activity coordinates on some month during the summer. It is interesting to note in this regard that for weekends, where technological factors do not pin down a particular day of the week as the low-productivity period, different cultures choose different Sabbaths (Friday for Muslims, Saturdays for Jews, Sundays for Christians), although all choose a seven-day week.

With these models as background, it is useful to reconsider the summer slowdown periods documented above.[3] On the production side, any individual firm has an incentive to shut down in July given that all other firms do the same. The individual firm may not capture the total benefits of coordinating its activity level with that of other firms, however, suggesting that from this perspective, the private degree of bunching may be insufficient. Alternatively, in choosing to concentrate production in a particular period, each firm likely ignores any congestion effects that its activities might have with respect to scarce general capacity (e.g., electric power generation), so some forces make the private degree of bunching excessive. On the consumer side, every individual may prefer July relative to June or August as a vacation month. In making that choice, however, the individual does not take into account the crowding effect on others of his presence on the beach. Under plausible conditions, too many individuals choose to take their vacations in the "best" month. Thus, the seasonal cycles that arise endogenously as the result of synergies across agents are not necessarily optimal, but they can be either too large or too small.

10.4   Existing Government Policies toward Seasonality

The suggestions made above about the possible welfare effects of seasonal fluctuations need to be developed more fully in order to isolate the direction and magnitude of the welfare effects. The point here is to dispute the presumption that seasonal variation is uninteresting from a welfare or policy perspective and to suggest there may be a case for stabilizing seasonal fluctuations. One can object that designing a policy optimally to shift a fraction of vacations from July to August, or to reduce the concentration of work on weekdays relative to weekends, requires too much detailed information about the structure of the economy, even if shown desirable on theoretical grounds. Nevertheless, since it is easier to smooth seasonal cycles than business cycles (long and variable lags are not a problem), such policies deserve some consideration. Alternatively, even if one accepts the exogenous, efficient view of seasonality, it is important to determine that policies do not distort the economy's seasonal fluctuations from their laissez-faire values. This section therefore turns to discussing existing government policies that may have significant effects on seasonal variation.

A potentially important example of a policy that affects seasonal fluctuations is the provision of imperfectly experienced rated unemployment insurance (UI). As discussed in Feldstein (1976, 1978) and Topel (1984), imperfectly experience-rated UI subsidizes temporary layoffs, and one important category of such layoffs is seasonal layoffs. By subsidizing seasonal layoffs, UI tends to make seasonal fluctuations in some industries larger than they otherwise would be, and it transfers resources, ceteris paribus, from nonseasonal industries to seasonal ones (Topel and Welch 1980, Card and Levine 1992).

An important example of an explicitly seasonal policy is the practice of most central banks of smoothing nominal interest rates over the seasons. The impact and desirability of this policy depends crucially on the degree of price stickiness in the economy. In a fully classical world, where all prices are fully flexible with respect to changes in the nominal money stock, alternative seasonal monetary policies affect only the seasonality of the nominal interest rate and real balances. It is therefore generally optimal for the monetary authority to hold the nominal rate constant over the seasons (i.e., accommodate seasonal shifts in asset demands) because this policy minimizes the intertemporal tax distortion associated with the collection of seignorage (see also Chatterjee 1988).

If prices are not fully flexible in response to seasonal changes in money, then alternative seasonal monetary policies have real effects that may make the policy of smoothing nominal interest rates less desirable. If prices are sticky over the seasons, firms are likely to hold excess capacity, and the extent of such excess capacity increases with the amount of seasonal variation in demand. The Fed's policy of accommodating seasonal aggregate demand shifts, therefore, may significantly increase the amount of excess capacity that firms hold, thereby affecting welfare.

The other important government policy that tends to produce seasonal cycles is legally mandated holidays. By shutting down on certain days of the year, the government encourages the concentration of leisure time in certain seasons. Such policies may or may not be welfare improving. If there are fixed costs of going to work as well as synergies from having everyone work at the same time, it may be desirable for the government to help private agents coordinate on a particular equilibrium in which bunching occurs (e.g., daylight savings time). In considering such policies, however, the congestion effects must be balanced against the synergies. The question of the optimum number of holidays is thus a nontrivial problem for economic analysis.

Notes

Chapter 2

1. He does, however, find some evidence of seasonal duration dependence of cycles.

Chapter 3

1. Because of the nature of data collection, employment may be overstated in the third quarter in particular. This is because the establishment survey counts as employed anyone who is reported by firms as receiving compensation, including those on vacation. (Employees on strike or taking sick leave are also reported as employed.)

2. See table 5.6, p. 66, of the July 1984 *Survey of Current Business* for a list of the components of investment purchases of producers' durables, which demonstrates the plausibility of this hypothesis.

3. This hypothesis is called into question to some degree by the marked absence of any movement in real wages in July, although if firms smooth wages over the year (Hall and Lilien 1979), the shadow cost of labor might be seasonal even though measured wages are smooth.

4. Cooper and Haltiwanger (1993b) discuss a different example of a seasonal synergy. Before the National Industrial Recovery Act (NIRA) of 1935, automakers retooled their plants for the new model year during the winter demand slowdown, just before the important winter auto shows. This timing created large seasonals in employment and cash flows in several areas dominated by automobile production. While automakers thought individually about moving the timing of retooling, they were dissuaded because of the practices of others. With the NIRA, which attempted to mandate smooth employment over the seasons, the retooling period was moved to the late summer–early fall months, a practice that persists to this day, even though the Supreme Court voided the NIRA in 1934. Not only did this move change the seasonal pattern of production, employment, and productivity in the automobile industry, but it also affected the seasonal pattern in important supplier industries such as iron and steel. This identifiable experiment suggests that the seasonal pattern in production does not depend only on simple seasonal fundamentals such as weather, vacation preferences, and the like.

5. The dramatic December increase in retail sales in Japan corresponds to a gift-giving holiday that is often referred to as Christmas. The significant increase in January sales in Spain corresponds to the widespread celebration of Twelfth Night on January 6.

Chapter 4

1. See especially Burns and Mitchell (1946) Friedman and Schwartz (1963a, 1982), and Zarnowitz (1985).

2. West (1988) presents evidence against the production-smoothing model in seven OECD countries. Fair (1989) suggests that much of the evidence against production-smoothing results from inappropriate use of data on deflated nominal values. Using physical units data, he finds less evidence against production smoothing. Krane and Braun (1991) make a similar point. Kahn (1990), however, finds significant evidence against production smoothing using the physical units data analyzed by Fair, as well as the physical units data from Blanchard (1983).

3. Analogous graphs for the United States using index of industrial production (IP) data show strong similarities in the timing of the seasonals in production and shipments, but in many cases the amplitude of the seasonal in production is dampened relative to that in shipments. As a rule, however, this dampening occurs in exactly those industries for which IP data are estimated on the basis of labor input. Since the Fed assumes no seasonality in the relation between labor input and output, these data do not suggest any qualification to the conclusions offered above. Kayshap and Wilcox (1993), Krane (1993), and Kahn (1990) show that the seasonals in production and shipments are similar in many cases using physical units data.

4. See also Fair (1969), Sims (1974a), Fay and Medoff (1985), and Bernanke and Parkinson (1991), as well as the extensive literature review in Fay (1980).

5. One can also compute the elasticity of output with respect to labor input using three alternative measures of labor input: total employment times average hours of production workers, production worker employment, and total employment. The results are similar to those reported below, although the elasticities with respect to each of these measures are generally higher than the elasticity with respect to total production worker hours.

6. As discussed in Miron and Zeldes (1989), industrial production series are often constructed using data on labor input. Therefore, estimates of labor productivity based on these data should be interpreted with caution.

7. Fama (1982) notes that both nominal money and real output are highly seasonal. He does not, however, examine the seasonal patterns or note the correlation between the two seasonals.

8. This coefficient and standard error are from an instrumental variables (IV) regression of real output growth on nominal money growth, with seasonal dummies as the only instruments.

9. Barsky and Miron (1989) show that the fourth quarter increase in money in the United States is due to increases in both high-powered money and the money multiplier.

Chapter 5

1. The formulas for the standard deviations include a degrees-of-freedom correction to account for the fact that $x_t^{i,s}$ and $x_t^{i,n}$ are estimated:

$$\hat{\sigma}_i^s(x) = (\tfrac{T-1}{T-12}\operatorname{var}(\hat{x}_t^{i,s}))^{\frac{1}{2}}, \qquad \hat{\sigma}_i^n(x) = (\tfrac{T-1}{T-12}\operatorname{var}(\hat{x}_t^{i,n}))^{\frac{1}{2}}.$$

2. In the cross-sectional regressions for countries, the number of time-series observations on a given variable often differs across countries. This difference produces heteroskedasticity in the cross-sectional errors. To correct for this heteroskedasticity, the regressions weight $\hat{\sigma}_i^n$ and $\hat{\sigma}_i^s$ by $(T_i - 1)^{\frac{1}{4}}$, where T_i is the number of time-series observations for a specific series in country i. The same procedure is applied to the price regression for manufacturing industries. For the remaining series, the estimation is by OLS.

3. The OLS standard error of $\hat{\beta}_2$, does not necessarily converge to the true, asymptotic standard error as the number of sectors grows large. Even if v_i is homoskedastic, the measurement error in $\hat{\sigma}_i^n$ surely varies across sectors (i) when the number of time-series observations is held constant. Thus, the observed residuals in the cross-sectional regression, which include both v_i and measurement error, are heteroskedastic. To account for this heteroskedasticity, the estimation uses White's (1980) method to estimate the covariance matrix. This method is consistent as the number of countries or industries grows large.

4. All variables are measured as log growth rates except where noted in section 3.2 and except for real rates, which are measured as levels of the nominal rate minus the log growth rate of prices over the time horizon of the nominal rate.

5. The results for industrial production use total industrial production. Beaulieu, MacKie-Mason, and Miron (1992) also compute the regressions reported in this section with manufacturing industrial production, with results virtually identical to those presented here.

6. These include the share of output in agriculture, the share of output in manufacturing, the percentage of the industry that is unionized, the ratio of nonproduction workers to total employment, the four-firm concentration ratio, a dummy variable for whether an industry produces to stock (Belsley 1969), and a dummy variable for whether the industry is classified as producing durables or nondurables.

7. These derivations assume that x_1^n and x_2^n are stationary and ergodic. If the assumption is violated, then one can take $\bar{x}_1$ and $\bar{x}_2$ to be the initial values of x_1 and x_2, respectively. In this case, a Taylor approximation will likely be poor for t much larger than its initial value. Furthermore, this approximation is likely to be poor if $\tilde{x}_i^s$ or $\tilde{x}_i^n$ is large. Including further terms to provide a better approximation does not affect the subsequent analysis.

8. The analysis also assumes that the higher moments of x_2^n are independent of the season.

9. Ghysels (1988), Braun and Evans (1994), and Chatterjee and Ravikumar (1992), among others, also present models that are potentially consistent with the facts documented here. With the exception of Chatterjee and Ravikumar (1992), however, none of these papers discusses the cross-sectional correlations discussed here, and even Chatterjee and Ravikumar do not show that their model necessarily implies the facts presented here.

10. The main points made in this section can be shown most simply in a model with linear marginal cost (MC) curves, with firms able to purchase ex ante the slope of the curve. The flatter the curve is, the greater is the output response to a demand shock. The simple linear MC model, however, is not particularly interesting since almost all firms appear to operate sometimes in a region where MC turns up sharply. Moreover, linear marginal cost curves predict homoskedasticity in the growth rates of output across seasons, whereas this model predicts heteroskedasticity.

11. Beaulieu, MacKie-Mason, and Miron (1992) also construct a model in which the firm fixes a single price at the beginning of the year and charges that price regardless of season or realization of the nonseasonal shock. Such behavior may be explained by high "menu costs" of changing prices or by customer loyalty considerations. Thus, prices are not seasonal. They use the same marginal cost and demand curves as above and assume that the firm sells either the quantity demanded at its preannounced price or the quantity at which marginal cost is equal to price (whichever is smaller, and thus optimal, for the firm). This model generates the same result as above: a positive cross-sectional correlation between the standard deviations of seasonal and nonseasonal output as the seasonal demand shift changes. The other results discussed below also hold in the fixed-price model.

12. Beaulieu, MacKie-Mason, and Miron (1992) also calculate the Pearson correlation coefficients between the variance of the production growth rates and the level of production. The results are similar to those reported above.

13. Under the null of independent observations, the probability of observing only two positive correlations out of twenty is .000. Under the null that there are only ten independent observations, the probability of observing one positive correlation is .011.

Chapter 6

1. This includes studies by Blinder (1986), Eichenbaum (1984), and Maccini and Rossana (1984). Blanchard (1983) and Reagan and Sheehan (1985) begin with the seasonally unadjusted data and then adjust the data with seasonal dummies. Few studies examine whether the seasonal fluctuations themselves are consistent with the model of inventories. Exceptions are Ward (1978), who finds evidence that firms alter production rates differently in response to seasonal versus nonseasonal variations in demand; West (1986), who includes a version of his variance bounds test based on both the seasonal and nonseasonal variations in the data; and Ghali (1987), who uses data from the Portland cement industry and finds that seasonal adjustment of the data is an important factor in the rejection of the production-smoothing model. Irvine (1981) uses seasonally unadjusted data, with no seasonal dummies, to examine retail inventory behavior and the cost of capital.

2. For example, Census X-11 can be well approximated by such filters (Cleveland and Tiao 1976, Wallis 1974).

3. If storage costs come in the form of depreciating inventories, then the accounting identity definition of output would be $y_t = x_t + (n_t - n_{t+1}(1 - s'_{t-1}))$. The analysis here constructs output in the standard way, $y_t = x_t + (n_t - n_{t-1})$. If, rather than coming in the form of depreciated stocks, storage costs are paid out and these costs are proportional to the replacement cost of the goods, then the model and this constructed output measure are mutually consistent. In either case, the equations are correct for the IP measure of output. If the costs are paid out in dollars, in an amount related to the goods stored, the equation is approximately correct.

4. If average storage costs (s'_t) equal $s_1 + (s_2/2)n_t$, marginal storage costs (s_t) equal $s_1 + s_2 n_t$.

5. This model imposes the constraint that inventories are nonnegative, and the Euler equation is valid in a given period only if the nonnegativity constraint is not binding

in that period. This is potentially problematic. Consider a certainty version of the model without the nonnegativity constraint imposed. Assuming that s_1 and s_2 are nonnegative, equation 6.3 implies that when inventories are positive, firms want the level of marginal costs to rise over time. If the marginal cost function is constant or falling (due to growth in the capital stock), this implies that output rises over time—that is, that firms push production toward the future and run down inventory stocks today. In fact, only if inventories are negative could steady state exist with constant marginal costs. Thus, in a model in which the nonnegativity condition is imposed, it will at times bind, and therefore the Euler equation will not be satisfied in some periods. With s_1 sufficiently negative, a steady state exists in the certainty version of the model that has a positive level of inventories. This still does not imply that inventories never hit the constraint. For a further discussion of this issue, see Schutte (1983).

6. This smoothing that arises from a convex cost function is different from the smoothing induced by introducing costs of adjusting output (as in, for example, Eichenbaum 1984). For further discussion, see Blanchard (1983).

7. This assumes that period t output decisions are made contingent on period t economic variables. An alternative assumption is that production decisions are made before demand for the month is known. This creates a stock-out motive for holding inventories (Kahn 1987). The results below address this issue by using alternative instrument lists.

8. Most of the estimation was also carried out defining inventories as the sum of finished-goods inventories and work in progress. The results are almost identical to those reported in the text.

9. These results use Blinder's procedure to obtain detrended levels of the data. The log of each series is regressed on a constant, time, and a dummy variable that is one beginning in October 1973. The coefficients are estimated by generalized least squares (GLS), assuming a second-order autoregressive process for the error term. The antilogs of the fitted values of this regression are then subtracted from the levels of the raw data to define the detrended data. IP is converted from an index into a constant-dollar figure by multiplying it by the ratio of average Y4 to average IP (i.e., by setting the average of the two series equal to each other). This detrending procedure is applied to IP, Y4, and shipments, and the detrended series are then regressed on a constant and eleven seasonal dummies. The seasonal and nonseasonal variances are estimated using the fitted and residual values of this regression, respectively.

In the last section of his paper, West (1986) describes a variance bounds test that includes the deterministic seasonal variation in the data. He finds that the variance bounds are rejected for each of the three industries examined.

10. The seasonal coefficient plotted for each month is the average percentage difference in that month from a logarithmic time trend.

11. The series is, of course, the estimated rather than the true seasonal in sales growth.

12. Since there is essentially no seasonality in energy prices, raw materials prices, or interest rates, the regressions omit these variables.

The precise procedure is to estimate equation 6.17, with sales growth included, using seasonal dummies as the only instruments. The coefficient estimates are numerically identical to those produced by the procedure described in the text, but this instrumental variables procedure produces correct standard errors. The resulting t-statistic on sales growth is reported in table 6.4.

Chapter 7

1. In the pre-Fed period, demand and time deposits were much closer substitutes than they are today. Demand deposits sometimes paid interest, and time deposits could be transferred by check. The data do not distinguish between demand and time deposits (Friedman and Schwartz 1963a, p. 4). The assumption here is that all deposits are demand deposits that do not pay interest.

2. Friedman and Schwartz (1963a), pp. 89–90.

3. E. W. Kemmerer (1910, pp. 223–224) mentions increased rail and barge activity during warm weather and holiday seasons as additional reasons for seasonal activity in the financial markets. A. Piatt Andrew (1906) discusses the influence of agriculture on economic activity during the pre-Fed period, and J. Laurence Laughlin (1912, pp. 309–342) discusses the seasonal cycle in general economic activity. See also O. M. W. Sprague (1910), C. A. E. Goodhart (1969), and John James (1978, pp. 127–137) for discussions of the seasonal flows within the country that accompanied the seasonal changes in interest rates and reserve positions of banks.

4. See Andrew (190, p. 559) and Timberlake (1978, p. 181). See Andrew (1907) also for an interesting analysis of Shaw's other activities and Timberlake (1963) for a critique of Andrew's analysis.

5. Sprague (1910, pp. 33, 108–114, 124–152, 167, 246–256); Kemmerer (1910, pp. 222–223).

6. See Friedman and Schwartz (1963a, pp. 305, 308, 313, 324).

7. Friedman and Schwartz (1963a, p. 235) and Cagan (1965, p. 225) also note the absence of financial panics during this recession.

8. The text presents results for the 1890–1908 period because that is the period for which Kemmerer and Sprague identified the dates of financial panics. Data for the entire 1890–1914 period confirm the results presented here.

9. Weekly data are available only starting in 1922. Monthly data, which begin in August 1917, confirm the results discussed here.

10. See Friedman and Schwartz (1963a, pp. 305, 308, 313, 324).

11. See Trescott (1982) for a more detailed examination of this aspect of Fed policy.

12. Friedman and Schwartz (1963a, pp. 411–419, 692–693) discuss in detail the effects of Strong's death on the power structure of the Fed.

Chapter 8

1. A variety of institutions, including the U.S. Treasury and the New York Clearing House, performed limited central banking functions at times during the national banking period. On the role of the Treasury, see Andrew (1907) and Timberlake (1963, 1978). On the New York Clearing House, see Timberlake (1984).

2. Bloomfield (1959) counts central banks or quasi–central banks in an additional sixteen countries as of 1880, as well as three more by 1907.

3. See Bordo and Schwartz (1984), Eichengreen (1985), and the references in those works for discussion of this point.

4. See also the papers in Bordo and Schwartz (1984) for detailed discussions of the features of a gold standard.

5. China, El Salvador, and Honduras maintained silver standards during this period (Eichengreen 1985, p. 6).

6. See, for example, the *First Interim Report* of the Cunliffe Committee (1918) in Britain. Keynes (1923) was an outspoken opponent of the return to gold.

7. Data for other countries confirm the main results presented below. See especially Clark (1986) and Morgenstern (1959). Clark shows that interest rate seasonality diminished substantially after 1914 in France and Germany, as well as in the United States and Britain. Morgenstern notes that the seasonality of financial variables diminished significantly in all four countries.

8. The results are essentially unchanged omitting the years 1929–1933 from the second sample period.

9. The series is described more fully in Mankiw, Miron, and Weil (1987, 1990).

10. This is the open market rate on bankers' bills, not the Bank of England's discount rate, known as the bank rate.

11. See the *Economic Journal* (1886, pp. 592, 648) for details on the construction of the index.

12. The hypothesis tests were carried out on the seasonal dummy coefficients in the change in the short rate because the level is probably nonstationary in the second sample period. The tests were performed on the OLS estimates of seasonal dummy coefficients, with the standard errors corrected using the Newey and West (1987) procedure.

13. These were calculated by regressing the inflation rates on seasonal dummies whose coefficients were constrained to follow a fifth-order polynomial.

14. The test statistics refer to OLS estimates of the seasonal dummy coefficients, with standard errors computed using the Newey and West (1987) procedure.

15. A similar model is presented in Eichengreen (1984). That model does not focus on interest rate stabilization, however.

16. See Shiller and Seigel (1977) on the Bank of England.

17. The bank dislikes gold outflows because they threaten its ability to maintain convertibility. It dislikes gold inflows (probably to a lesser degree) because of the resource cost of holding an excessive quantity of reserves and because the accumulation of gold by the home central bank implies a greater likelihood of a convertibility crisis in some other country. See Mankiw (1987) for an optimal tax justification of the bank's nominal interest rate target.

18. With an arbitrary nominal interest peg, $\bar{i}_t$, the implied inflation rate may not be compatible with the long-run maintenance of the gold standard. The time subscript indicates that the central bank periodically revises its interest rate target with this consideration in mind. Although the bank cannot set the long-run nominal rate arbitrarily, it can still offset seasonal and other transitory disturbances.

19. As far as distinguishing between these two possibilities, however, the results of such dating are inconclusive.

20. The data series used for these calculations are monthly observations on the three-month U.S. and British Treasury bill rates (both taken from the first week of each month) and monthly observations on the United States and British wholesale price indexes. The early sample period begins in 1957 because that is when wholesale price index data for Britain are first available.

21. The volatility of interest rates increases, in contrast to the results for 1914.

22. Again, the standard errors are computed using the Newey-West procedure.

Chapter 9

1. The results in figure 9.1 are robust to alternative data on short-term interest rates; see Mankiw and Miron (1986) and Mankiw, Miron, and Weil (1987).

Chapter 10

1. Output is not storable in these models, so it is efficient to produce in the seasons when consumers prefer consumption.

2. The discussion in this section borrows heavily from Hall (1991).

3. See Cooper and Haltiwanger (1992, 1993a) for a discussion of the issues considered here in the context of business cycle fluctuations.

References

Andrew, A. Piatt. 1906. "The Influence of Crops upon Business in America." *Quarterly Journal of Economics* 20 (May): 323–353.

Andrew, A. Piatt. 1907. "The Treasury and the Banks under Secretary Shaw." *Quarterly Journal of Economics* **21**(3) (August): 529–568.

Bagehot, Walter. 1873. *Lombard Street.* New York: Scribner.

Ball, L., and D. Romer. 1989. "Are Prices Too Sticky?" *Quarterly Journal of Economics* 104:507–524.

Ball, Laurence, and David Romer. 1990. "Real Rigidities and the Non-Neutrality of Money." *Review of Economic Studies* **57**:183–203.

Ball, L., N. G. Mankiw, and D. Romer. 1988. "The New Keynesian Economics and the Output-Inflation Tradeoff." *Brookings Papers on Economic Activity* 1:1–82.

Barro, Robert J. 1994. *Macroeconomics.* New York: Wiley.

Barro, R. J., and H. I. Grossman. 1971. "A General Disequilibrium Model of Income and Employment." *American Economic Review* 32:1123–1147.

Barsky, Robert B. 1987. "The Fisher Hypothesis and the Forecastability and Persistence of Inflation." *Journal of Monetary Economics* 19, no. 1 (January): 3–24.

Barsky, Robert B., N. Gregory Mankiw, Jeffrey A. Miron, and David N. Weil. 1988. "The Worldwide Change in the Behavior of Interest Rates and Prices in 1914." *European Economic Review* 32:1123–1154.

Barksy, Robert B., and Jeffrey A. Miron. 1989. "The Seasonal Cycle and the Business Cycle." *Journal of Political Economy* 97, no. 3 (June): 503–535.

Beason, Dick. 1993. "Tests of Production Smoothing in Selected Japanese Industries." *Journal of Monetary Economics* 31:381–394.

Beaulieu, J. Joseph, Jeffrey K. MacKie-Mason, and Jeffrey A. Miron. 1991. "Why Do Countries and Industries with Large Seasonal Cycles Also Have Large Business Cycles?" Working paper 3635. National Bureau of Economic Research.

Beaulieu, J. Joseph, Jeffrey K. MacKie-Mason, and Jeffrey A. Miron. 1992. "Why Do Countries and Industries with Large Seasonal Cycles Also Have Large Business Cycles?" *Quarterly Journal of Economics* 107, no. 2 (May): 621–656.

Beaulieu, J. Joseph, and Jeffrey A. Miron. 1990a. "Seasonality in U.S. Manufacturing." Working paper 3450. National Bureau of Economic Research.

Beaulieu, J. Joseph, and Jeffrey A. Miron. 1990b. "A Cross Country Comparison of Seasonal Cycles and Business Cycles." Working paper 3459. National Bureau of Economic Research.

Beaulieu, J. Joseph, and Jeffrey A. Miron. 1991. "The Seasonal Cycle in United States Manufacturing." *Economic Letters* 37 (October): 115–118.

Beaulieu, J. Joseph, and Jeffrey A. Miron. 1992. "A Cross Country Comparison of Seasonal Cycles and Business Cycles." *Economic Journal* **102** (July): 772–788.

Beaulieu, J. Joseph, and Jeffrey A. Miron. 1993. "Seasonal Unit Roots and Deterministic Seasonals in Aggregate U.S. Data." *Journal of Econometrics* **55** (March): 305–328.

Belsley, David A. 1969. *Industrial Production Behavior: The Order-Stock Distinction*. Amsterdam: North-Holland.

Bernanke, B. S., and M. L. Parkinson. 1989. "Procyclical Labor Productivity and Competing Theories of the Business Cycle: Some Evidence from Interwar U.S. Manufacturing Industries." *Journal of Political Economy* 99:439–459.

Bils, Mark. 1987. "Cyclical Pricing of Durable Luxuries." Manuscript. University of Rochester.

Blanchard, Olivier J. 1983. "The Production and Inventory Behavior of the American Automobile Industry." *Journal of Political Economy* 91:365–400.

Blanchard, O. J., and N. Kiyotaki. 1987. "Monopolistic Competition and the Effects of Aggregate Demand." *American Economic Review* 77:647–666.

Blinder, Alan. 1986. "Can the Production Smoothing Model of Inventory Behavior Be Saved?" *Quarterly Journal of Economics* 101:431–454.

Blinder, A., and S. Fischer. 1981. "Inventories, Rational Expectations, and the Business Cycle." *Journal of Monetary Economics* 8:277–304.

Bloomfield, Arthur I. 1959. "Monetary Policy under the International Gold Standard: 1880–1914." New York: Federal Reserve Bank of New York.

Boldrin, M., and M. Woodford. 1990. "Equilibrium Models Displaying Endogenous Fluctuations and Chaos: A Survey." *Journal of Monetary Economics* 25:189–222.

Bordo, Michael D., and Anna Schwartz, eds. 1984. *A Retrospective on the Classical Gold Standard*. Chicago: Chicago University Press.

Braun, R. A., and C. L. Evans. 1991. "Seasonal Solow Residuals and Christmas: A Case for Labor Hoarding and Increasing Returns." Working paper 91-20. Federal Reserve Bank of Chicago.

Braun, R. A., and C. L. Evans. 1994. "Seasonality and Equilibrium Business Cycle Theories." *Journal of Economic Dynamics and Control* 19:503–531.

Brown, William Adams, Jr. 1940. *The International Gold Standard Reinterpreted*. New York: National Bureau of Economic Research.

Burns, Arthur F., and Wesley C. Mitchell. 1946. *Measuring Business Cycles.* New York: National Bureau of Economic Research.

Bursk, J. Parker. 1931. *Seasonal Variations in Employment in Manufacturing Industries.* Philadelphia: University of Pennsylvania Press.

Cagan, Phillip. 1965. *Determinants and Effects of Changes in the Stock of Money, 1875–1960.* New York: Columbia University Press.

Card, D., and P. B. Levine. 1992. "Unemployment Insurance Taxes and the Cyclical and Seasonal Properties of Unemployment." Working paper 4030. National Bureau of Economic Research.

Cecchetti, S. G. 1986. "The Frequency of Price Adjustment: A Study of the Newsstand Prices of Magazines." *Journal of Econometrics* 31:255–274.

Cecchetti, S. G., A. K. Kashyap, and D. W. Wilcox. 1995. "Do Firms Smooth the Seasonal in Production in a Boom? Theory and Evidence." Working paper 5011. National Bureau of Economic Research.

Cecchetti, Stephen G., and Anil K. Kashyap. 1995. "International Cycles." Ohio State University. Mimeographed.

Chandler, Lester. 1958. *Benjamin Strong, Central Banker.* Washington, D.C.: Brookings Institution.

Chatterjee, S. 1988. "Money in a Model of Seasonal Fluctuations." Working paper 88-2. Department of Economics, University of Iowa.

Chatterjee, S., and B. Ravikumar. 1992. "A Stochastic Growth Model with Seasonal Perturbations." *Journal of Monetary Economics* 29:59–86.

Clark, Truman. 1986. "Interest Rate Seasonals and the Federal Reserve." *Journal of Political Economy* 94, no. 1 (February): 76–125.

Cleveland, W., and G. Tiao. 1976. "Decomposition of Seasonal Time Series: A Model for the Census X-11 Program." *Journal of the American Statistical Association* 71:581–587.

Cooper, Russell, and John Haltiwanger. 1992. "Macroeconomic Implications of Production Bunching: Factor Demand Linkages." *Journal of Monetary Economics* 30:107–127.

Cooper, Russell, and John Haltiwanger. 1993a. "Macroeconomic Implications of Machine Replacement: Theory and Evidence." *American Economic Review* 83:360–382.

Cooper, Russell, and John Haltiwanger. 1993b. "Automobiles and the NIRA: Evidence on Macroeconomic Complementarities." *Quarterly Journal of Economics* 108:1043–1072.

Cunliffe Committee. 1918. *First Interim Report.* London: The committee.

De Long, J. Bradford, and Lawrence H. Summers. 1988. "How Does Macroeconomic Policy Affect Output?" *Brooking Papers on Economic Activity* 2:433–480.

Diamond, P., and D. Fudenberg. 1989. "Rational Expectations Business Cycle in Search Equilibrium." *Journal of Political Economy* 97:606–619.

Dixit, A., and J. Stiglitz. 1977. "Monopolistic Competition and Optimum Product Diversity." *American Economic Review* 67:297–308.

Dornbusch, Rudiger, and Stanley Fischer. 1987. *Macroeconomics*. New York: McGraw-Hill.

Eichenbaum, M. 1984. "Rational Expectations and the Smoothing Properties of Inventories of Finished Goods." *Journal of Monetary Economics* 14:71–96.

Eichenbaum, Martin. 1989. "Some Empirical Evidence on the Production Level and Production Cost Smoothing Models of Inventory Investment." *American Economic Review* 79, no. 4 (September): 853–864.

Eichengreen, Barry. 1984. "International Policy Coordination in Historical Perspectives." Discussion paper 1081. Cambridge: Harvard University.

Eichengreen, Barry. 1985. Introduction to Barry Eichengreen, ed., *The Gold Standard in Theory and History*. New York: Methuen.

Engle, Robert F., Clive W. J. Granger, Svend Hylleberg, and H. S. Lee. 1993. "Seasonal Cointegration: The Japanese Consumption Function, 1961.1–1987.4." *Journal of Econometrics* 55.

Faig, M. 1989. "Seasonal Fluctuations and the Demand for Money." *Quarterly Journal of Economics* 104:847–862.

Fair, Ray C. 1969. *The Short-Run Demand for Workers and Hours*. Amsterdam: North-Holland.

Fair, Ray C. 1989. "The Production Smoothing Model Is Alive and Well." *Journal of Monetary Economics* 24:353–370.

Fama, Eugene F. 1982. "Inflation, Output, and Money." *Journal of Business* 55, no. 2: 201–231.

Fay, Jon A. 1980. "The Response of Production Labor to Cyclical Changes in Product Demand." Senior thesis, Harvard University.

Fay, Jon A., and James L. Medoff. 1985. "Labor and Output over the Business Cycle: Some Direct Evidence." *American Economic Review* 75, no. 4 (September): 638–655.

Feldstein, M. 1976. "Temporary Layoffs in the Theory of Unemployment." *Journal of Political Economy* 84:937–958.

Feldstein, M. 1978. "The Effect of Unemployment Insurance on Temporary Layoff Unemployment." *American Economic Review* 68:834–846.

Fischer, Stanley. 1977. "Long-Term Contracts, Rational Expectations, and the Optimal Money Supply Rule." *Journal of Political Economy* 85, no. 1 (February).

Fisher, Irving. 1920. *Stabilizing the Dollar*. New York: Macmillan.

Fisher, Irving. 1930. *The Theory of Interest*. New York: Macmillan.

Friedman, Milton. 1959. *A Program for Monetary Stability*. New York: Fordham University Press.

Friedman, Milton. 1969. *The Optimum Quantity of Money and Other Essays*. Chicago: Aldine.

Friedman, Milton. 1982. "Monetary Policy: Theory and Practice." *Journal of Money, Credit and Banking* 14:98–118.

Friedman, Milton, and Anna J. Schwartz. 1963a. *A Monetary History of the United States, 1967–1960.* Princeton: Princeton University Press.

Friedman, Milton, and Anna J. Schwartz. 1963b. "Money and Business Cycles." *Review of Economics and Statistics* 45, no. 1:32–64.

Friedman, Milton, and Anna J. Schwartz. 1982. *Monetary Trends in the United States and the United Kingdom.* New York: National Bureau of Economic Research.

Garber, P., and R. King. 1984. "Deep Structural Excavation? A Critique of Euler Equation Methods." Technical working paper 83-14. National Bureau of Economic Research.

Gendreau, Brian C. 1979. "Bankers' Balances Demand Deposit Interest, and Agricultural Credit before the Banking Act of 1933." *Journal of Money, Credit, and Banking* 11, no. 4 (November): 506–514.

Gendreau, Brian C. 1983. "The Implicit Return on Bankers' Balances." *Journal of Money, Credit, and Banking* 15, no. 4 (November): 411–424.

Ghali, M. 1987. "Seasonality, Aggregation, and Testing of the Production Smoothing Hypothesis." *American Economic Review* 77:464–469.

Ghysels, Eric. 1988. "A Study toward a Dynamic Theory of Seasonality for Economic Time Series." *Journal of the American Statistical Association*, 83(401): 168–172.

Ghysels, E. 1991. "On Seasonal Asymmetries and Their Implications for Stochastic and Deterministic Models of Seasonality." University of Montreal. Mimeographed.

Glass, Carter. 1927. *An Adventure in Constructive Finance.* New York: Doubleday, Page and Co.

Goodhart, C. A. E. 1969. *The New York Money Market and the Finance of Trade, 1900–1913.* Cambridge: Harvard University Press.

Grandmont, J. M. 1985. "On Endogenous Competitive Business Cycles." *Econometrica* 53:995–1046.

Gray, J. 1976. "Wage Indexation: A Macroeconomic Approach." *Journal of Monetary Economics* 2:221–235.

Hall, R. 1978. "Stochastic Implications of the Life Cycle–Permanent Income Hypothesis: Theory and Evidence." *Journal of Political Economy* 86:971–987.

Hall, R. 1986. "Market Structure and Macroeconomic Fluctuations." *Brooking Papers on Economic Activity* 2:285–338.

Hall, Robert E. 1988. "The Relation between Price and Marginal Cost in U.S. Industry." *Journal of Political Economy* 96, no. 5 (October): 921–947.

Hall, Robert E. 1991. *Booms and Recessions in a Noisy Economy.* New Haven: Yale University Press.

Hall, Robert E., and David M. Lilien. 1979. "Efficient Wage Bargains under Uncertain Supply and Demand." *American Economic Review* 69, no. 5 (December): 868–879.

Hodrick, Robert J., and Edward C. Prescott. 1980. "Post-War U.S. Business Cycles: An Empirical Investigation." Working paper. Carnegie-Mellon University.

Hubbard, R. Glenn. 1986. "Comment." *Brookings Papers on Economic Activity* 2:328–336.

Hylleberg, Svend. 1986. *Seasonality in Regression.* New York: Academic Press.

Hylleberg, S., R. Engle, C. W. J. Granger, and B. S. Yoo. 1990. "Seasonal Integration and Co-Integration." *Journal of Econometrics* 44.

Irvine, F. O., Jr. 1981. "Retail Inventory Investment and the Cost of Capital." *American Economic Review* 71:633–648.

James, John A. 1978. *Money and Capital in Postbellum America.* Princeton: Princeton University Press.

Jevons, William Stanley. 1884. "On the Frequent Autumnal Pressure in the Money Market, and the Action of the Bank of England." In William Stanley Jevons, *Investigations in Currency and Finance.* London: Macmillan.

Kahn, J. A. 1987. "Inventories and Volatility of Production." *American Economic Review* 77:667–679.

Kahn, James A. 1990. "The Seasonal and Cyclical Behavior of Inventories." Working paper 223. Rochester Center for Economic Research.

Kashyap, A. 1995. "Sticky Prices: New Evidence from Retail Catalogs." *Quarterly Journal of Economics* 110:245–274.

Kashyap, Anil K., and David W. Wilcox. 1993. "Production Smoothing at the General Motors Corporation during the 1920s and 1930s." *American Economic Review* 83, no. 3 (June): 383–401.

Kemmerer, Edwin W. 1910. *Seasonal Variations in the Relative Demand for Money and Capital in the United States.* National Monetary Commission. Senate doc. 588. 61st Cong., 2d sess.

Keynes, John M. 1923. *A Tract on Monetary Reform.* London: Macmillan.

King, Robert G., and Charles I. Plosser. 1984. "Money, Credit, and Prices in a Real Business Cycle." *American Economic Review* 74:363–380.

Krane, Spencer D. 1993. "Induced Seasonality and Production-Smoothing Models of Inventory Behavior." *Journal of Econometrics* 55, no. 1/2:135–168.

Krane, S., and S. Braun. 1991. "Production Smoothing Evidence from Physical-Product Data." *Journal of Political Economy* 99:558–581.

Kuznets, Simon. 1933. *Seasonal Variations in Industry and Trade.* New York: National Bureau of Economic Research.

Kydland, Finn E., and Edward C. Prescott. 1982. "Time to Build and Aggregate Fluctuations." *Econometrica* 50, no. 6 (November): 1345–1370.

Laughlin, J. Laurence. 1912. *Banking Reform.* Chicago: National Citizens League for the Promotion of a Sound Banking System.

Long, John, and Charles Plosser. 1983. "Real Business Cycles." *Journal of Political Economy* 91 (February): 39–69.

Long, John, and Charles I. Plosser. 1987. "Sectoral vs. Aggregate Shocks in the Business Cycle." *American Economic Review* 77, no. 2 (May): 333–336.

Lucas, Robert E., Jr. 1970. "Capacity, Overtime, and Empirical Production Functions." *American Economic Review* 60, no. 2 (May): 23–27.

Lucas, Robert E., Jr. 1972. "Expectations and the Neutrality of Money." *Journal of Economic Theory* 4:103–124.

Lucas, Robert E., Jr. 1973. "Some International Evidence on the Output-Inflation Trade-offs." *American Economic Review* 63, no. 3 (June): 326–334.

Lucas, Robert E., Jr. 1976. "Econometric Policy Evaluation: A Critique." In Karl Brunner and Alan Meltzer, eds., *The Phillips Curve and Labor Markets*, 1:19–46. Carnegie-Rochester Conference on Public Policy. Amsterdam: North-Holland.

Lucas, Robert E., Jr. 1977. "Understanding Business Cycles." Carnegie-Rochester Conference Series, vol. 5.

Macaulay, Frederick R. 1938. *Some Theoretical Problems Suggested by Movements of Interest Rates, Bond Yields and Stock Prices in the United States since 1856.* New York: National Bureau of Economic Research.

Maccini, L. J., and R. J. Rossana. 1984. "Joint Production, Quasi-Fixed Factors of Production, and Investment in Finished Goods Inventories." *Journal of Money, Credit, and Banking* 16:218–236.

Malinvaud, E. 1977. *The Theory of Unemployment Reconsidered.* Oxford: Blackwell.

Mankiw, N. Gregory. 1986. "The Term Structure of Interest Rates Revisited." *Brooking Papers on Economic Activity* 1:61–96.

Mankiw, N. Gregory. 1987. "The Optimal Collection of Seignorage: Theory and Evidence." *Journal of Monetary Economics* (September): 327–341.

Mankiw, N. Gregory, and Jeffrey Miron. 1986. "The Changing Behavior of the Term Structure of Interest Rates." *Quarterly Journal of Economics* 101, no. 2 (May): 211–228.

Mankiw, N. Gregory, and Jeffrey A. Miron. "Should the Fed Smooth Interest Rates? The Case of Seasonal Monetary Policy." *Carnegie Rochester Conference Series* 34:41–70.

Mankiw, N. Gregory, Jeffrey A. Miron, and David N. Weil. 1987. "The Adjustment of Expectations to a Change in Regime: A Study of the Founding of the Federal Reserve." *American Economic Review* (June): 358–374.

Mankiw, N. W., J. A. Miron, and D. N. Weil. 1990. "The Adjustment of Expectations to a Change in Regime: Reply." *American Economic Review* 80:977–979.

Mankiw, N. Gregory, and Lawrence H. Summers. 1986. "Money Demand and the Effects of Fiscal Policies." *Journal of Money, Credit and Banking* 18, no. 4 (November): 415–429.

Mankiw, N. G., and M. D. Whinston. 1986. "Free Entry and Social Inefficiency." *RAND Journal* 17:48–58.

McCallum, B. T. 1989. *Monetary Economics: Theory and Policy.* New York: Macmillan.

Miron, Jeffrey A. 1984. "The Economic of Seasonal Time Series." Ph.D. dissertation, MIT.

Miron, Jeffrey A. 1986a. "Financial Panics, the Seasonality of the Nominal Interest Rate, and the Founding of the Fed." *American Economic Review* 76, no. 1 (March): 125–140.

Miron, Jeffrey A. 1986b. "Seasonal Fluctuations and the Life Cycle–Permanent Income Model of Consumption." *Journal of Political Economy* 94, no. 6 (December): 1258–1279.

Miron, Jeffrey A. 1994. "The Economics of Seasonal Cycles." In *Advances in Econometrics: The Sixth World Congress of the Econometric Society* 1:213–251. Cambridge: Cambridge University Press.

Miron, Jeffrey A. 1996. "Seasonal Fluctuations and Financial Crises." In David Glaesner, ed., *Encyclopedia of Business Cycles, Panics, Crises and Depressions*. Washington, D.C.: Garland Publishing.

Miron, J. A., and C. Romer. 1990. "A New Index of Industrial Production." *Journal of Economic History* 50:321–337.

Miron, Jeffrey A., and Stephen P. Zeldes. 1988. "Seasonality, Cost Shocks, and the Production Smoothing Model of Inventories." *Econometrica* 56:877–908.

Miron, Jeffrey A., and Stephen P. Zeldes. 1989. "Production, Sales, and the Change in Inventories: An Identity That Doesn't Add Up." *Journal of Monetary Economics* 24:31–51.

Mishkin, Frederic S. 1981. *The Real Rate: An Empirical Investigation*. Carnegie-Rochester Conference Series on Public Policy, vol. 12. Amsterdam: North-Holland.

Mitchell, W. C. 1927. *The Business Cycle: The Problem and Its Setting*. New York: National Bureau of Economic Research.

Morgenstern, Oskar. 1959. *International Financial Transactions and Business Cycles*. Princeton, N.J.: Princeton University Press.

Murphy, Kevin M., Andrei Shleifer, and Robert W. Vishny. 1989. "Building Blocks of Market Clearing Business Cycle Models." In *NBER Macro Annual*. Cambridge: MIT Press.

Newey, Whitney, and Kenneth West. 1987. "A Simple, Positive Definite, Heteroskedasticity and Autocorrelation Consistent Covariance Matrix." *Econometrica* 55:703–708.

Osborn, D. R. 1988. "Seasonality and Habit Persistence in a Life-Cycle Model of Consumption." *Journal of Applied Econometrics* 3:255–266.

Osborn, D. R. 1989. "The Performance of Periodic Autoregressive Models in Forecasting Seasonal U.K. Consumption." *Journal of Business and Economic Statistics* 7:117–127.

Osborn, Denise R. 1990. "A Survey of Seasonality in U.K. Macroeconomic Variables." Manuscript, University of Manchester.

Phelps, E. S. 1973. "Inflation in the Theory of Public Finance." *Swedish Journal of Economics* 75:67–82.

Pierce, David A. 1978. "Seasonal Adjustment When Both Deterministic and Stochastic Seasonality Are Present." In Arnold Zellner, ed., *Seasonal Adjustment of Economic Time Series*. Washington, D.C.: Bureau of the Census.

Poole, W., and C. Lieberman. 1972. "Improving Monetary Control." *Brookings Papers on Economic Activity* 2:293–335.

Prescott, Edward C. 1986. *Theory Ahead of Business Cycle Measurement*. Carnegie-Rochester Conference Series, vol. 25. Amsterdam: North-Holland.

Ramey, Garey, and Valerie Ramey. 1991. "Technology Commitment and the Cost of Economic Fluctuations." Manuscript, University of California, San Diego.

Rasche, Robert. 1972. "A Review of Empirical Studies of the Money Supply Mechanism." *Federal Reserve Bank of St. Louis Review* 54:11–19.

Reagan, Patricia, and Denis P. Sheehan. 1985. "The Stylized Facts about the Behavior of Manufacturers' Inventories and Backorders over the Business Cycle, 1959–1980." *Journal of Monetary Economics* 15:217–246.

Roll, Richard. 1972. "Interest Rates on Monetary Assets and Commodity Price Index Changes." *Journal of Finance* 27 (May): 251–277.

Rotemberg, Julio J., and Lawrence H. Summers. 1988. "Labor Hoarding, Inflexible Prices and Procyclical Productivity." Manuscript, MIT.

Rotemberg, Julio J., and Garth Saloner. 1989. "The Cyclical Behavior of Strategic Inventories." *Quarterly Journal of Economics* 104:73–98.

Sargent, Thomas J. 1978. "Rational Expectations, Econometric Exogeneity, and Consumption." *Journal of Political Economy* 86, no. 4 (August): 673–700.

Sargent, Thomas J. 1986. *Rational Expectations and Inflation.* New York: Harper & Row.

Sayers, Richard S. 1936. *Bank of England Operations, 1890–1914.* London: P. S. King.

Schutte, D. P. 1983. "Inventories and Stickey Prices: Note." *American Economic Review* 73:815–816.

Shiller, Robert J. 1980. "Can the Fed Control Real Interest Rates?" In Stanley Fischer, ed., *Rational Expectations and Economic Policy.* Chicago: University of Chicago Press.

Shiller, Robert J., and Pierre Perron. 1985. "Testing the Random Walk Hypothesis: Power versus Frequency of Observation." *Economic Letters* 13:381–386.

Shiller, Robert J., and Jeremy Seigel. 1977. "The Gibson Paradox and Historical Movements in Real Interest Rates." *Journal of Political Economy* 85:891–907.

Shliefer, A. 1986. "Implementation Cycles." *Journal of Political Economy* 94:1163–1190.

Sims, Christopher A. 1974a. "Output and Labor Input in Manufacturing." *Brooking Papers on Economic Activity* 3:695–735.

Sims, Christopher A. 1974b. "Seasonality in Regression." *Journal of the American Statistical Association* 69:618–626.

Spence, A. Michael. 1977. "Entry, Capacity, Investment, and Oligopolistic Pricing." *Bell Journal of Economics* 8:534–544.

Sprague, O. M. W. 1910. *History of Crises under the National Banking System.* National Monetary Commission. Sen. Doc. 538. 61st Cong., 2d sess.

Stephenson, James A., and Helen T. Farr. 1972. "Seasonal Adjustment of Economic Data by Application of the General Linear Model." *Journal of the American Statistical Association* 67:37–45.

Stiglitz, Joseph. 1984. "Price Rigidities and Market Structure." *American Economic Review* 74, no. 2 (May): 350–355.

Summers, L. 1981. "Comment on 'Retail Inventory Behavior and Business Fluctuations,' by Alan Blinder." *Brookings Papers on Economic Activity* 2:513–517.

Summers, Lawrence H., and Sushil B. Wadhwani. 1987. "Some International Evidence on Labor Cost Flexibility and Output Variability." Discussion paper 1353. Harvard Institute for Economic Research.

Summers, Robert, and Alan Heston. 1988. "A New Set of International Comparisons of Real Product and Prices for 130 Countries, 1950–1985." *Review of Income and Wealth* 34, no. 1 (March).

Timberlake, Richard H. 1963. "Mr. Shaw and His Critics: Monetary Policy in the Golden Era Review." *Quarterly Journal of Economics* 77, no. 1 (February): 41–54.

Timberlake, Richard H. 1978. *The Origins of Central Banking in the United States.* Cambridge: Harvard University Press.

Timberlake, Richard H. 1984. "The Central Banking Role of Clearing House Associations." *Journal of Money, Credit and Banking* 15, no. 1 (February): 1–15.

Tobin, James. 1970. "Money and Income: Post Hoc Ergo Propter Hoc." *Quarterly Journal of Economics* 84:301–317.

Topel, R. H. 1984. "Experience Rating of Unemployment Insurance and the Incidence of Unemployment." *Journal of Law and Economics* 27:61–90.

Topel, R. H., and F. Welch. 1980. "Unemployment Insurance: Survey and Extensions." *Economica* 47:351–379.

Trescott, Paul B. 1982. "Federal Reserve Policy in the Great Contraction: A Counterfactual Assessment." *Explorations in Economic History* 19:211–220.

Wallis, K. F. 1974. "Seasonal Adjustment and the Relation between Variables." *Journal of the American Statistical Association* 69:13–32.

Warburg, Paul M. 1930. *The Federal Reserve System: Its Origins and Growth.* Vol. 2. New York: Macmillan.

Ward, M. P. 1978. "Optimal Production and Inventory Decisions: An Analysis of Firm and Industry Behavior." Ph.D. dissertation, University of Chicago.

West, Kenneth. 1986. "A Variance Bounds Test of the Linear Quadratic Inventory Model." *Journal of Political Economy* 94, no. 2 (April): 374–401.

West, Kenneth D. 1988. "Evidence from Seven Countries on Whether Inventories Smooth Aggregate Output." Working paper 2664. National Bureau of Economic Research.

White, Eugene N. 1983. *The Regulation and Reform of the American Banking System, 1900–1929.* Princeton, N.J.: Princeton University Press.

White, Halbert. 1980. "A Heteroskedasticity-Consistent Covariance Matrix Estimator and a Direct Test for Heteroskedasticity." *Econometrica* 50:483–499.

Willis, H. Parker. 1915. *The Federal Reserve: A Study of the Banking System of the United States.* New York: Doubleday, Page and Co.

Woodford, M. 1990. "Equilibrium Models of Endogenous Fluctuations: An Introduction." Working paper 3360. National Bureau of Economic Research.

Working, Holbrook. 1960. "A Note of the Correlation of First Differences of Averages in a Random Chain." *Econometrica* 28:916–918.

Woytinsky, W. S. 1939. *Seasonal Variations in Employment in the United States.* Washington, D.C.: Social Science Research Council.

Zarnowitz, Victor. 1985. "Recent Work on Business Cycles in Historical Perspectives." *Journal of Economic Literature* 23, no. 2 (June): 523–580.

Index